# China's
# Imperial Way

# China's
# Imperial Way

### Retracing an Historical Trade
### and
### Communications Route
### from
### Beijing to Hong Kong

**KEVIN BISHOP**
*with additional text by* **ANNABEL ROBERTS**

An Odyssey Book.
© 1997 The Guidebook Company Limited,
2 Lower Kai Yuen Lane, North Point, Hong Kong.
Tel: (852) 2856 3896  Fax: (852) 2565 8624
e-mail: odyssey@asiaonline.net
ISBN: Hardback edition 962-217-511-2
        Softback edition  962-217-520-1

China Books & Periodicals, Inc.
2929 24th Street, San Francisco, CA 94110
Tel: (415) 282 2994   Fax: (415) 282 0994
e-mail: cb@chinabooks.com
URL: http://www.chinabooks.com
ISBN: Softback edition  0-8315-2599-8

Text and photographs © Kevin Bishop 1997
e-mail: kbish@iohk.com

Grateful acknowledgement is made to the following:
Royal Geographical Society, 1 Kensington Gore, London, for the reproduction of
William Alexander's sketches that appear in plates 1–13;
Wattis Fine Art, 20 Hollywood Road, Hong Kong, for the reproduction of Auguste
Borget's sketch in plate 14.

Editor: Evelyn Peplow
Designer: Aubrey Tse

Production by:
Twin Age Limited 4/F, 20 Hollywood Road, Hong Kong.
Printed in China.

# HITACHI

## Main Sponsor of
## CHINA'S IMPERIAL WAY

Dear Reader

For more than 700 years the Imperial Way linked Beijing with the Pearl River delta region. The Imperial Way was a conduit for important messages to and from the emperor, and a vital route for China's trade. Near the mouth of the Pearl River, at the southernmost end of the route, lay the territory which was later to become known as Hong Kong.

Towards the end of the nineteenth century the Imperial Way fell into disuse and, superseded by modern forms of transport, this once bustling artery was forgotten. Meanwhile Hong Kong, partitioned from the mainland through a succession of treaties, began its rise to world prominence.

Early in 1995 Kevin Bishop approached Hitachi Asia (Hong Kong) Ltd. with his ambitious project to retrace the Imperial Way, and to subsequently publish a book on the subject. To do so at a time when Hong Kong was preparing for its reunion with China, thereby once again linking the two ends of this ancient trade route, I found intriguing and irresistible.

Furthermore, Kevin Bishop and his publisher generously agreed to donate the proceeds of their book to ORBIS, to assist with this charity's commendable work in China restoring the sight of the blind.

Hitachi Asia (Hong Kong) Ltd. are pleased to have had this opportunity of participating as main sponsors of 'China's Imperial Way,' and we welcome the involvement of the supporting sponsors. Hitachi congratulates all involved in the publication of this book.

Kiyoshi Urakami
*Managing Director*
*Hitachi Asia (Hong Kong) Ltd.*

**Supporting Sponsors**
**of**
# CHINA'S IMPERIAL WAY

 Swire Group

 富士胶卷

 KCRC
九 廣 鐵 路 公 司

 National Mutual
國 衛 集 團

 ERNST & YOUNG

 DIAMONDBACK

 DRAGONAIR
港龍航空

BYRNE & HICKMAN & PARTNERS

奥比斯
**ORBIS**

There is a proverb that says 'A journey of a thousand miles begins with one step'. Kevin Bishop and Annabel Roberts embarked on a journey that followed in the historical footsteps of the Imperial Way. ORBIS is also on a journey: a journey that started in 1982 by one doctor who had a vision to share his knowledge and the knowledge of nations for the benefit of those in need—those who suffer from blindness.

ORBIS is a non-profit organization dedicated to fighting blindness worldwide and to promoting peaceful cooperation among nations.

Known for its unique flying eye hospital housed in a converted DC–10 jet, ORBIS provides teaching and training for doctors and nurses in all areas of ophthalmology through ORBIS DC–10 medical missions and through 'off plane' programmes in surgery, nursing, education and community health. To date, ORBIS has treated over 19,000 blind people, trained over 32,000 doctors and nurses and has carried out over 300 medical programmes in 72 countries throughout the world.

Since its first steps ORBIS has grown, and ties with China and Hong Kong have blossomed. ORBIS works tirelessly to combat blindness. In China alone, there are seven million blind people—with our help two-thirds of those could see again. ORBIS is committed to China, planning future DC–10 medical missions and related projects. ORBIS will continue to support the ORBIS Taiyuan Training Centre in Shanxi Province—our first land-based joint venture—which will provide ophthalmic training for Shanxi Province and eventually the region.

On behalf of ORBIS, I would like to thank Kevin Bishop for donating the proceeds of this book to ORBIS programmes in China. Each book sold represents a step towards helping people to see again.

YVONNE GAUTIER
*Director, ORBIS Hong Kong*
*Hong Kong 1997*

# Contents

# Individual Topics

# Maps

# Historical Plates

# Preface

by Alain Peyrefitte

China's Imperial Way, along which this fine book will take the reader, runs from Beijing to Hong Kong. Although far more than just the Grand Canal, it is this watercourse that forms the backbone of the Imperial Way—linking the north and the south of China.

Ibn Batuta said of the Grand Canal, around 1330, that it was 'the richest region on Earth'. Why such wealth? The Armenian, Hethum, had arrived at an answer twenty-five years earlier: 'Cathay people are the most learned and skilled of all men in their material undertakings.' To their credit, among other wonders, is the Yunhe.

Yunhe actually means 'transport river'. But the word yun, whose character strangely resembles a sailing junk, also means 'fate', 'good or bad fortune'. So that, by one of those ambiguities the Chinese like so much, Yunhe can also be understood as 'the course of fate'.

Indeed, the construction of the Yunhe has changed the fate of China, where huge distances have always been, and still are, a great problem. The Grand Canal impressed some travellers I had the pleasure to meet again in these pages: the ambassador Lord Macartney and his companions. 'We have entered a canal built at the expense of endless troubles and great costs,' writes one of them, the soldier Else. After meeting the emperor, they crossed his empire, escorted on the Yunhe, in the autumn of 1793.

Yun also means 'to turn, to move round'—just as the great artery does. 'The canal is meandering around here, and its banks plunge into the water,' Else observes. Indeed, the waterway follows contour lines, natural courses, flows round hills, and stretches across lakes and marshes. 'The banks of the canal are usually steep, so that from the windows of our boats we cannot see the scenery,' notices Thomas Staunton, pageboy of the ambassador. Macartney himself is enthusiastic: 'The canal is now supplied by an extensive lake stretching to our left. The view at sunrise was most delightful.' He later adds, 'The canal is now conducted over a great morass, which appears without limits on each side, and above which it is raised and embanked by immense mounds of earth very high and very thick. It is a most stupendous work.'

The Grand Canal is as famous as the Great Wall, and their historical fates bear some resemblance. It has been said that, given the colossal scale of the rehabilitation of the Wall at the end of the sixth century, the task cost the Sui dynasty the Mandate of Heaven—only thirty years into its reign. We are also indebted to them for the construction of the original Grand Canal. It was then forty metres wide and flanked by a road with intermittent post houses. The Yuan, at the end of the thirteenth century, restored the canal, which had silted up due to the neglect of the Song, following their withdrawal to Hangzhou in 1126. They also gave it its modern-day course: it crosses the Yellow River much further downstream than the Sui canal. The short section linking Tianjin to Beijing was also their work.

The Ming restored the Wall, naturally neglected by the Yuan who were Mongols. They also regulated the course of the Yunhe, creating a set of fifteen locks in the hills of Shandong. And how proud they were! 'Nothing of the kind has ever been made before,' states one of their reports. 'The Yuan tried, but without real success. Under the current dynasty, the structure has been renovated and widened. The Yuan used it for the shipment of only a few hundreds of thousands of grain measures. We transport four millions. Ten times more.' The Yunhe is also called Yunlianghe, 'the river carrying the grain'. In this huge centralized empire, the tax, originally paid in grain, had to be collected. In a country with fifty dialects and numerous regions, the canal allowed the centralization of the markets—an issue in the past, and still an issue today.

Macartney and his fellow travellers journeyed along the Imperial Way to Guangzhou. Kevin Bishop followed the same route, via Poyang Lake in Jiangxi Province, and the Meiling Pass. It is remarkable to see how the accounts of travellers from past centuries interpret what he sees himself. He even went as far as to recognize drawings by Alexander in the scenery he encountered! This juxtapostion of the past and the present is nowhere better experienced than in China: no other civilization seems to have, like China, cultivated a self-centered belief, reproducing itself from century to century. This Confucian fidelity to the past always increases the weight of time, and is what makes the Chinese civilization so remarkable.

Bishop's witnesses come not only from recent centuries, but also from earlier times: Matteo Ricci who came to China at the end of the sixteenth century, Marco Polo in the thirteenth century, Odoric of Pordenone who, disembarking in Guangzhou around 1320, visited Hangzhou, Yangzhou, and reached Khanbaliq (Beijing's Mongolian name at the time). For several days he followed 'the large river going up to the East, from the Yellow River' which was the new Mongolian course of the Yunhe.

This book invites us to a wonderful journey in time and space. A pleasant odyssey where even the dimension of the future is not forgotten. Indeed, Kevin Bishop is right to state it: China awakening and developing will also have to expand its waterways—and reopen the Yunhe.

Only in China could the course of destiny, in the twenty-first century, be dependent on the revitalization of a work created around the time of King Arthur. A quirk of history? No, the benefit of age for the oldest civilization alive...

# Author's Foreword

It was a cold, blustery January night in 1993. I was on my way home to one of Hong Kong's outlying islands. As I sat huddled on the ferry, reading a book about Hong Kong walks (I am a keen explorer of the New Territories), a passing mention of the old Imperial Way caught my attention. I read how messengers carrying dispatches from a garrison outpost on the south coast of China would traverse the country on foot, bound for the capital in the far north.

This fired my imagination. What was it like to travel through China hundreds of years ago? What did the landscape look like and how did it differ from that to be seen today? What did the messengers encounter on their journey? I had an overwhelming desire to explore the route.

——··•◉◉●··——

In front of me, there were three heavy volumes. The thick leather binding crackled as I opened the largest—it was almost 200 years old. On the thick rough-edged folio parchment were printed exquisite engravings portraying scenes in China from the Qing dynasty: palaces, temples, pagodas, cities, lakes and canals, together with large maps and charts of the regions.

These were the journals of Sir George Leonard Staunton, then secretary to Lord Macartney, Ambassador to the Imperial Court in 1793. The embassy's mission was to counteract the influence of the Dutch and Portuguese, as well as the Jesuit missionaries in Beijing, and to gain trading concessions at the port of Guangzhou.

They failed in their aim and subsequently travelled back from Beijing to Guangzhou overland, but Staunton's account of their journey, and of the people and sights they encountered along the route, fascinated me. I was captivated by the sketches and drawings executed in intricate detail by William Alexander, the brilliant young artist who accompanied the embassy. Staunton described in painstaking detail the experiences of the expedition's members and their reactions to the people and sights they encountered along the way. Over a distance of 3,500 kilometres, along canals and rivers, across mountain passes and fertile lowlands, they followed a route that for centuries had been used extensively by soldiers, missionaries, merchants and messengers, travellers, traders, tributaries and diplomats. This was China's Imperial Way.

For several weeks I pored over Staunton's journals at the University of Hong Kong library, enthralled by his party's journey through China. Gradually the seed of an idea grew. Apart from being an interesting and challenging route to retrace, I thought it would make excellent material for a book. Obviously things would have changed, many beyond recognition. But surely there would be some aspects of life that were much as Staunton had seen them two centuries earlier? As a photographer I was further inspired by Alexander's engravings and excited at what might be found in this vast country today.

I made detailed notes and plotted the route on maps. I gathered more information about others who had journeyed along this or similar routes hundreds of years before Staunton arrived in China.

About eighteen months after the original idea, I travelled to China to see if my plan to walk the route was practicable. Being a keen walker and someone not known for taking the easy option, I had given very little consideration to travelling any other way! However, I very quickly realized that if I wanted to carry sufficient film and camera equipment along with a modest change of clothes, then walking was out of the question. The exertion of carrying a backpack in thirty-eight degrees of heat very quickly sapped my enthusiasm for photography, not to mention walking. The lack of a clear walking route was another major problem. The towpaths that had once run alongside the canals, and which I had planned to use, had long since disappeared.

Most travellers in China are forced to take uncomfortably overcrowded public transport, scenery flashing past the window, unable to stop en route should they see something interesting. After hiring bicycles in a few cities to explore the surrounding countryside, I realized it was possible to escape the restrictions imposed by a transport system geared to herding people en masse from one town to the next. A bicycle was the answer.

Kevin Bishop
*Lamma Island, Hong Kong*
*March 1997*

# Acknowledgements

The research, writing and production of this book took four and a half years to complete. During this time, a large number of people were more than generous with their assistance and advice and, above all, at times when it most mattered, their encouragement. I am greatly indebted to them all.

In Hong Kong, I would particularly like to thank Dr. Joseph Ting of the Hong Kong Museum of History and Nigel Cameron who offered guidance; the staff of the University of Hong Kong Library, where I did most of my initial research, in particular Mr Y C Wan of the Special Collections; Josephine Kwan 關敏儀 for introducing me to the world of computers; Ghene and Susanna Snellen and Rudolph Kan at Scientific Communications International Ltd; Linda Au 區慧明 for her translation work; Mr Chiu Siu-tsan 招紹瓚 at the Antiquities and Monuments Office; Professor K C Lok at Macau University and David Melville of the World Wide Fund for Nature.

Friends Dave Marchant and Rob and Christine Walker, together with Mr Lee and Ted Remédios at Flying Ball Bicycle Co, who put me on the right track as far as bikes were concerned; Paul Marriage for convincing me I could write the thing myself; Jan Lund, Miles and Lucy Spink, Jósef Fung, Chang Yan 唱燕 , Almond Chu 朱德華 and Ann Mak 麥惠儀 for their valuable support and Gwenaëlle Ansieau for translating Mr Peyrefitte's preface.

James Melon for his very generous personal donation to the expedition funds.

In Beijing, Xia Hongtu 夏宏圖 , for her research and translation work; Michael Crook and Professor Hou Ren-zhi 侯仁之 , for taking time to share their historical knowledge of Beijing; Tan Xu Ming 譚徐明 of the China Institute of Water Resources & Hydropower Research; Ren Xiu Xia 任秀俠 of the Beijing Liao-Jin City Wall Museum; Stephen Hallett; Chen Yang 陳泱 ; Paul and Eileen Mooney; William and Qi Lindesay; Ed Radcliffe; Jamie Heywood; Julia Capp in Hong Kong and Kate Whight in Shanghai for taking good care of my films.

A special thanks to my publisher, Magnus Bartlett, who had confidence in me and offered encouragement and advice throughout; to my editor, Evelyn Peplow; Aubrey Tse who worked so hard on the layout of the book at the same time as organizing her wedding; Li Suk Woon and her staff at Twin Age; Jane Finden-Crofts at the Guidebook Company; Professor Bai for his meticulous cartography and to Hilary Binks for restoring my confidence.

I am particularly indebted to Alain Peyrefitte for his inspiration and for kindly agreeing to write a preface to this book.

I would also like to express my sincere gratitude to the various companies that sponsored the project. Most especially to Hitachi Asia (Hong Kong) Ltd for their extremely generous and considerable financial support and encouragement—in particular to Yuji Miyamoto, Kiyoshi Urakami, Masao Kamimura, Daniel Chu and Benjamin Wong; at John Swire & Sons, Nick Rhodes and Charlie Stewart-Cox and the staff of Group Public Affairs; Rowena Li of Fuji Photo Products in Hong Kong and Stella Zhang in Shanghai; Rowena Ho, Michelle Leung and Yvonne Kwok of Kowloon–Canton Railway Corporation; John Snelgrove and Dominic Lam at National Mutual Insurance; Sophia Zilo, Philip Norman at Ernst & Young; Benjamin Favin and Megan Tjia at Diamond Back International; Jacqui Donaldson at

Dragonair; Ken-ichi Takahashi, Dexter Fu at Nikon Hong Kong; Peter Cho of Peter Cho's Color Workshop and Janice Morton and the physiotherapy staff at Byrne & Hickman & Partners.

And a final and very special thank you, for his inspiration, inexhaustible advice and tireless encouragement, to my great friend and mentor Edward Stokes, without whom this book would have remained just a good idea.

# Introduction

*Every ten li a station swirling with dust,*
*Every five li a post to urge couriers on;*
*Men die like flies, their corpses line the road,*
*So that lychees and longans may be delivered to court.*
*Carriages race over hills, boats sweep through the seas,*
*With new plucked fruit on fresh boughs, the leaves still dewy,*
*All to win a smile from the beauty in the palace,*
*Though it cost bloodshed and strife, and its effect remains for ever.*

Extract from 'A Lament for Lychees' by
Song dynasty poet Su Shi 蘇軾 (Su Dongpo) (1037–1101).

China's imperial rulers were not renowned for their generosity or compassion towards their subjects. Once ensconced in their opulent new capitals, the emperors would stop at nothing to ensure the royal household was kept in unimaginable luxury. Only the best was set on the imperial banquet table—delicious fruit like the longan or the unique striped lychee grown only in Guangdong Province far to the south, or special rice from Sha Tin in what is now the New Territories of Hong Kong. Such things had to be transported, in this case over thousands of kilometres, to the capital. Sometimes, as in Su Shi's poem, speed was demanded, regardless of the pain and misery this caused.

To achieve this, it was vital to have a good transport and communications system. Over the centuries the Chinese have put together an extensive network of roads, rivers and canals. The Yangtze River with its numerous tributaries formed an immense network of waterways linking ten provinces, while the Yellow River flowed across a large part of northern China. Water transport played a crucial role, initially to transport soldiers and labourers, and subsequently to supply grain to the capital, vital to its survival when it was situated in the north. However, with the five major rivers all running in an east-west direction, canals had to be dug to provide north-south communication.

All this may seem rather strange to Europeans, who may judge from maps that one could take a shorter and a less expensive route to [Beijing] by sea. This may be true enough, but the fear of the sea and the pirates who infest the seacoast has so penetrated the Chinese mind, that they believe the sea route would be far more hazardous for conveying provisions to the royal court. *(Matteo Ricci)*

Thus the inland waterways became indispensable. The barges that sailed on them could not rely on wind alone and frequently had to resort to manpower in the form of trackers. These were often local peasants press-ganged into service by the military. They would trudge along in teams, yoked like animals to the heavy barges, beside rivers and canals. Therefore waterways were flanked by towpaths, if not paved roads on which imperial messengers on horseback, runners on foot, or even lychees by the cart-load, could move swiftly from place to place.

The attraction and challenge in retracing this route lies in the way it weaves together stretches of country that are far from the modern tourist trail, and little known outside China today, with some well-trodden areas and popular cities. It is a route that was once widely travelled but has now largely fallen into disuse, and in some parts obscurity.

This book divides the Imperial Way into sections according to provinces which are often quite different in many ways, and presents each in a separate chapter. With a background of history, and supported by narratives and anecdotes from a variety of characters who travelled in China during five centuries, it aims to paint a picture of what life used to be like in the various regions and the important part the Imperial Way played in the lives of the people and the development of towns and cities. This is contrasted with a broad-brush present-day description, juxtaposed to short vignettes on a more personal level about experiences we had and people we met during our journey.

The historical characters from whose accounts I have quoted are introduced in an appendix at the end of the book. The spelling and punctuation of the original text has been used wherever possible to preserve the writers' sometimes quaint and idiosyncratic style. Chinese towns and cities had an annoying habit of changing their names over the course of time, and furthermore, each traveller seemed to use a different spelling. Therefore, in order not to assault the reader with a confusing array of place names I have taken the liberty of replacing them with the present-day name in the historical extracts. They are printed in square brackets. Throughout the book most Chinese personal and place names are spelled according to the widely accepted Pinyin phonetic system. The exceptions are familiar names, for example, Yangtze, Sun Yat-sen, etc. that have well-established English spellings, and some names in the section on Hong Kong in Chapter Seven, which are spelled according to the local Cantonese dialect. Given the rather vague nature of Pinyin and for the reader with a knowledge of Chinese, I have also endeavoured, where they are known to me, to include the Chinese characters in their traditional form after the initial occurrence of such a word.

Where amounts of money are mentioned, the equivalent value in US dollars is also shown. This has been converted at the exchange rate at the time of writing: 1 yuan = US$ 0.1212

--------•◉●•------

While researching this book, I turned up some fascinating historical information and was often intrigued at what must have gone on behind the scenes. The hard work of the peasant farmers is seldom recorded by history. However, it was these ordinary people who quite literally shaped China. Throughout history they dug the canals, built the walls, constructed the palaces and produced the food. Without them the rulers, many of them cruel and ruthless tyrants, would have achieved little.

The lasting impressions from my exploratory trip along a section of the Grand Canal in August 1994, were of the people that I met. My Chinese was sufficient to get me through everyday situations and simple conversations, but not to talk in depth—to find out more about their lives; where they lived; how they lived; what work they did; what memories they had; their hopes and aspirations for the future. Although today the Imperial Way would mean little or nothing to most of them, it helped to shape the land they live in and influence its development. I wondered what role, if any, it still played in China today. I decided I would need to return with someone fluent in Chinese if I were to answer any of these questions.

That someone would also have to be fit and able to ride a bicycle for at least 3,500 kilometres—for that was the distance involved if one were to trace the route all the way from Beijing to Hong Kong. In fact, with all the exploratory detours I estimated this could stretch to something like 5,000 kilometres—a figure which was to prove uncannily accurate. The search for such a person would surely not be easy but the obvious place to start was in the gym I used in Hong Kong, where I had been training in preparation for the trip. I put up a notice and that same evening it was answered. This is how I came to be accompanied on the journey by Annabel Roberts.

Annabel had studied Chinese at university, but as anyone with even a rudimentary knowledge of the language will know, China has countless local dialects, sometimes varying even from town to town. When one is listening to these tongues tackling Putonghua (the lingua franca, more commonly known as Mandarin) one inevitably encounters a baffling array of accents, especially amongst the rural population. This is evident even to an untrained ear such as mine. During our trip, after a long day on the bike, all I wanted was to relax quietly and eat my dinner in peace. Instead we were frequently surrounded by a cluster of people, pressing ever closer, eager to find out what we were up to. Annabel's patience and capacity to understand and converse with these people, who would often bombard her with the same old questions wherever we stopped, was certainly impressive.

I had always planned to incorporate some short pieces about the characters I met on the journey, and because it was Annabel who was usually in direct communication with them, I invited her to write a series of vignettes on a more personal level about some of the many memorable experiences we had in China. These occur throughout the book in the form of boxed texts to separate them from the main body of the book. They can be read as part of the main text or individually.

Most of the photographs in this book were taken during the bicycle journey from Beijing to Hong Kong, from September to December 1995. However, the research spanned a significantly longer period than the four months spent retracing the route. Some of the photographs in the chapters on Jiangsu and Zhejiang provinces were taken during an earlier reconnaissance trip in August 1994. A few others were taken on subsequent visits to Zhejiang, Jiangxi and Beijing in 1996.

All the photographs were taken on Fuji Velvia or Provia film using the following camera equipment: Nikon F90 and F2 camera bodies, with 20–35mm, 28–70mm and 80–200mm zoom lenses, and SB-25 Speedlight. Polarizing and warming filters were occasionally used.

# Chapter 1

# The Origins
# of the
# Imperial Way

The history of the Imperial Way, and to a large extent China itself, is intertwined with that of the Grand Canal. To begin, we must go back to the fifth century BC—to the Spring and Autumn period of the Zhou dynasty. At that time, China had a well-developed east-west transport network along the middle and lower reaches of the Yellow River. This region, one of several cradles of Chinese civilisation, was already densely populated. There existed a prosperous economy with an established culture. The problem was a lack of north-south communication. All the major rivers flowed from west to east. An illustration of this can be seen during the Shang and Zhou dynasties (from the eleventh to the ninth centuries BC): the Yellow River valley had already entered the Bronze Age, while the vast regions to the north and south were still foundering in the Neolithic Age.

## HONG GOU CANAL 鴻溝

The first breakthrough came with the digging of China's earliest man-made canal—the Hong Gou Canal, linking the Yangtze River (Chang Jiang 長江) with the Huai River 淮江. It was built some time during the Spring and Autumn period (770–476 BC) on the orders of King Fuchai of the state of Wu. Irrigation canals were already widespread by this time. In fact the very earliest projects are thought to date from before the eighth century BC. The Hong Gou Canal ('Wild Geese Canal') was different. This was built for military purposes; to transport the king's troops and keep them supplied with food during their campaign.

There were originally some sixteen independent states grouped mainly over China's northern plains. After two centuries of mayhem this number was whittled down; seven remained in contention. One of the most ambitious was the state of Wu. It was also one of the most innovative, making use of rivers to launch attacks on unsuspecting neighbours. In 506 BC they stole up the Yangtze River to the very gates of Ying, the capital of the state of Chu (which approximates to the modern province of Hubei).

However, when the king wished to wreak havoc on the two small states of Song and Lu to the north, he found there was no convenient river he could use. Undeterred, he ordered a canal to be dug to connect the Yangtze with the Huai River. Now, to excavate a canal more than 150 kilometres long is not something that can be stealthily accomplished overnight, even using modern technology. You would think that the kingdoms of Song and Lu would have seen them coming. Apparently not, because in 486 BC these hapless states were gobbled up by the warriors of Wu.

The routine chaos of the Spring and Autumn period carried over into the Warring States (475 BC–221 BC), an apt name for what seems to have been a period of total anarchy, and constant battles between rival warlords vying with each other for control over the region. It was an age of monstrous brutality, of summary executions where men were put to death by being boiled alive in a cauldron, or strung between two chariots heading in opposite directions, or merely hacked in two.

The warmongers finally got their comeuppance. In 473 BC, the state of Wu, which had its capital at Gusu (Suzhou 蘇州 ), was overwhelmed by the state of Yue, its eastern neighbour in the lower Yangtze valley. They in turn were vanquished in 333 BC by a resurgent state of Chu. This whole messy business of the Warring States was sorted out once and for all when Chu itself was conquered by the western state of Qin in 223 BC.

## LING QU CANAL 靈渠

The state of Qin plays an important role in the next phase of our story, and indeed the history of China itself. The king of Qin restyled himself Qin Shihuangdi 秦始皇帝 , which, roughly translated, means the First Emperor of the Qin dynasty. Best known for his 'Terracotta Army' which is still being excavated near the city of Xi'an 西安 , his ancient capital, Qin Shihuangdi is sometimes called the Napoleon of China. It was he who first unified the country, both physically and culturally. He was responsible for the standardization of writing, currency, weights and measures, and even the wheelbase of handcarts. He had some 6,500 kilometres of highways built, as many as the Roman Empire. But most importantly, as far as we are concerned, in 219 BC he ordered the digging of a canal which was to join the great water systems of central and southern China for the first time. He had obviously learned a thing or two from the king of Wu, because he had the canal built so he could invade the areas to the south which, until then, had remained out of the main picture. Named the 'Magic Transport' canal, or Ling Qu 靈渠 Canal, it was cut across mountains to the north-east of what is today the city of Guilin 桂林 thus linking the Xiang River 湘江 , a southern tributary of the Yangtze, to the headwaters of a northern tributary of the West River 西江 which flows all the way to Guangzhou 廣州 . This made possible the uninterrupted transport by boat of troops, grain and other supplies to sustain his military campaign. Because these southern territories were richly fertile and well-watered it meant that Qin Shihuangdi's conquests were of great social and economic importance to the country as a whole.

Records show that weirs and dams had been constructed on some waterways during the period between the Han dynasty (206 BC–AD 220) and the Northern and Southern dynasties (AD 420–581). Boats were towed over them using manpower or animal haulage. It was also around this time that winches were developed. These were the earliest known ship-lifting devices and would have been the forerunners of the mechanisms encountered by Macartney and his party during their voyage along the canal some 1,500 years later.

## SUI DYNASTY GRAND CANAL

The next major step in the overall construction of the Grand Canal came about during the Sui dynasty (AD 581–618), when the emperor Yangdi came to power. Often portrayed as a vain, ambitious and reckless megalomaniac, he commissioned the building of a new capital at Luoyang 洛陽 . Constructed in AD 605, it involved hundreds of thousands of workmen. With a new capital in place, Yangdi then had to ensure adequate communication with other parts of his empire. So his next, and biggest project was the digging of a canal to join permanently the northern and southern provinces together.

It was a gigantic undertaking. Although it linked many smaller, existing but derelict canals, which had to be dredged, it nonetheless involved the construction of huge sections of new waterways. The emperor achieved this by press-ganging five-and-a-half million peasants into virtual slave labour. In some areas all males between the ages of fifteen and fifty were forced to work, watched over by armed guards. For anyone that dared to slack there awaited an array of punishments, ranging from decapitation or flogging, to the wearing of weights hung around the neck, or the confiscation of property. Every fifth family was made to contribute one member of the household to assist in the supply and preparation of food for the workers and guards.

The result was a 2,500-kilometre canal, rising at one point to forty-two metres above sea level, covering ten degrees of latitude. Stretching all the way from Beijing 北京 to Hangzhou 杭州 with Luoyang at its centre, it connected China's five main rivers and linked the north to the fertile Yangtze river basin for the first time. It had taken just six years. During this time some two million workers were classified as *zhe* 折, a rather vague term meaning lost or missing.

This new canal meant that barges could transport food and commodities virtually the whole length of the country—in particular, grain from the lower Yangtze basin to the northern regions, to feed the emperor's troops who were pursuing the latest of Yangdi's despotic schemes: the invasion and conquest of Korea. However, it proved to be his 'bridge too far' and he suffered a defeat that contributed to his downfall and that of his dynasty—a brief but turbulent twenty-nine years. Often accused of sheer extravagance in building the Grand Canal so that he could travel in luxury from his capital Luoyang, to his holiday city of Hangzhou, he is seldom credited for the real economic benefit that it brought to China.

## YUAN DYNASTY GRAND CANAL

It is not until the thirteenth century that we see any further significant addition to the Grand Canal. By this time the Mongols, swooping down from the steppes, had invaded the north of China and put an end to the Jin dynasty.

Kublai Khan, the grandson of Genghis Khan, ruled the Mongol world from 1260–1294 and became Emperor of China in 1271. Calling his dynasty Yuan 元 or 'origin', he built his new capital on part of the site occupied by present-day Beijing. Most of the previous emperors had built their capitals further south, to make it easier to defend themselves from the Mongols and to be closer to sources of food supply. However, Kublai Khan, with an empire extending well into Central Asia, decided to build his new city closer to his tribal homelands on the northern steppes and nearer to his palace at Shangtu (the Xanadu of Coleridge's famous poem).

Khanbaliq, as the new capital was called, was totally dependent on the Grand Canal for its survival. The emperor of the new Yuan dynasty was aware that he needed to improve its efficiency and therefore set about transforming it. By cutting a new section between the Yangtze and the Yellow rivers, he shortened its length from 2,500 to 1,780 kilometres, significantly improving delivery time for grain and the transportation of other supplies from the southern provinces.

A land road also exists, for the earth dug from those channels has been thrown up so as to form an embanked road on either side. (*Marco Polo*)

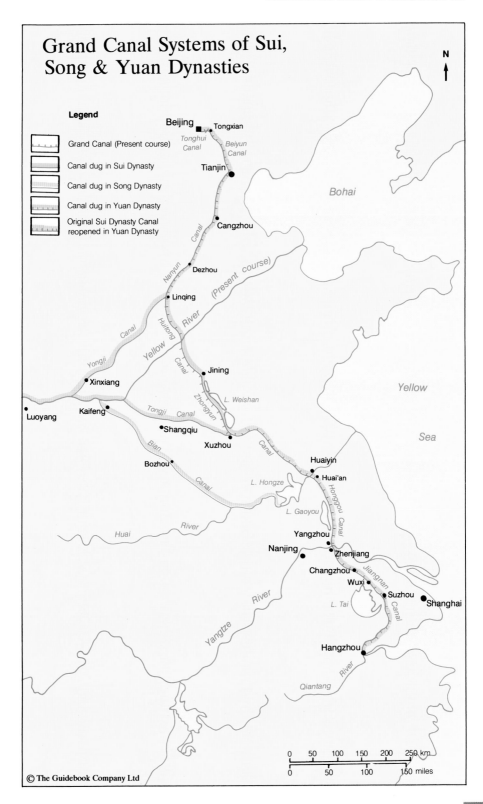

# Grand Canal Systems of Sui, Song & Yuan Dynasties

N

**Legend**

Grand Canal (Present course)

Canal dug in Sui Dynasty

Canal dug in Song Dynasty

Canal dug in Yuan Dynasty

Original Sui Dynasty Canal reopened in Yuan Dynasty

Beijing
Tongxian
Tonghui Canal
Beiyun Canal
Tianjin
Bohai
Canal
Cangzhou
Nanyun
Dezhou
(Present course)
Linqing
Huitong
Yellow
Canal
River
Yongji
Canal
Jining
Xinxiang
Zhongyun
L. Weishan
Yellow
Luoyang
Kaifeng
Tongji Canal
Shangqiu
Bian
Xuzhou
Canal
Sea
Bozhou
Huaiyin
Canal
Huai'an
L. Hongze
Honggou Canal
L. Gaoyou
Huai
River
Yangzhou
Nanjing
Zhenjiang
Changzhou
Jiangnan
Wuxi
River
Suzhou
L. Tai
Shanghai
Yangtze
Hangzhou
Qiantang
River

0    50    100   150   200   250 km
0        50        100       150 miles

© The Guidebook Company Ltd

Kublai caused the sides of the embankments to be revetted with stone in order to prevent the earth giving way. Along the side of the canal runs the high road to [the southern provinces] ... and this has been paved throughout, so that travellers and their animals may get along during the rainy season without sticking in the mud. The two sides of the road are planted with willows and other shady trees, and no one is allowed, whether soldier or otherwise, to break branches off those trees or let cattle feed on the leaves. Shops, taverns, and villages line the road on both sides, so that dwelling succeeds dwelling without intermission... *(Rashiduddin)*

## GRAIN TRIBUTE

During the earlier dynasties, like the Qin and Han, the imperial court had brought in grain from the region around the middle and lower reaches of the Yellow River. Following the Sui dynasty, however, demand had grown to such an extent that it was necessary to draw on the regions south of the Yangtze. Wheat and rice were levied as tax on the peasants and sent to the capital by the provinces as tribute to the emperor. By the tenth century something like 300,000 tonnes of grain annually were being shipped north on the canal. Marco Polo writes of the city of Guazhou 瓜洲 that was once at the junction of the Grand Canal with the Yangtze River:

At this place are collected great quantities of corn and rice to be transported to the great city of Khanbaliq for the use of the Khan's court; for the grain for the Court all comes from this part of the country. *(Polo)*

None of the cost of running such a vital artery was contributed by the government. It was maintained by the labour of local peasants who also worked as trackers. When the wind failed or the barge was travelling against the flow of water, teams of men would be pressed into service. One rope would be fastened to the mast and another to the barge's bow, and the men would be harnessed by means of a length of flat wood attached to the ropes, which was placed across their chests. For their labours the trackers would be paid a mere pittance, if anything at all. Because of this, and knowing that they would have to find their own way home again afterwards, many of them would desert under cover of darkness.

...when they are all ready, the leader of them gives the signal: they then begin a particular kind of march, the regularity of whose step is essential to the draft of the vessel, and can only be maintained by a sort of chime which they chant on the occasion. These words are sung in a regular tune; and so universal is this custom among the class of labouring Chinese, that they cannot perform the most ordinary work, where numbers are employed together, without the aid of this vocal accompaniment; which I was disposed to think had some agreeable notes in it. *(Aeneas Anderson)*

By the middle of the fifteenth century there were 11,775 grain boats handled by 121,500 officers and troops operating on the canal. Even these soldiers were not properly paid, having to rely on carrying private cargo in their barges to make a living.

## SOUTHERN ROUTES

But the Grand Canal is only half the story. To examine the Imperial Way, we must look at the overall picture of transportation and communication covering China from north to south. The principal communication was limited to three main options. The main route—provided by the Grand Canal—was through the northern provinces, from Beijing to Hangzhou. About three-quarters of the way towards its southern end it crossed the Yangtze, China's longest river, near the city of Yangzhou 揚州 .

Travelling from Beijing to the southern port of Guangzhou (or Canton as it used to be known by Europeans), the most direct route was to turn off the Grand Canal at this point and head up river as far as Poyang Lake 鄱陽湖 . Turning south, boats would then follow the Gan River 贛江 almost to its source, high in the mountains that form the boundary between Jiangxi and Guangdong Provinces.

Here nature defeated the ingenious Chinese water engineers. The steep topography, over 1,000 metres above sea level, prevented the digging of a canal linking two rivers. So, for a short distance of about thirty kilometres travellers and cargo alike had to proceed overland, through the famous Meiling Pass 梅嶺關 , before picking up headwaters which led into the North River 北江 and all the way to Guangzhou and the South China Sea.

A second, but less direct, alternative was to follow the Yangtze further upriver, through Dongting Lake 洞庭湖 and into the Xiang River, following this towards its source close to the modern city of Guilin. There, using the Ling Qu canal constructed by the emperor Qin Shihuangdi, it was possible to pass into the West River which, similarly, flowed into the sea beyond Guangzhou. Although an uninterrupted waterway, this route had the disadvantage of involving an additional 1,000 kilometres. For an average journey by water this would involve almost a month's travel. For this reason it had little use as a direct route to connect the south with the Grand Canal.

Both these routes cut out the major cities of Suzhou and Hangzhou, which lay at the southern end of the Grand Canal, south of the Yangtze River. The third alternative was used to link these important cities with the north and south. To reach them from the north it was simply a matter of crossing the Yangtze and continuing along the Grand Canal.

The shortest route connecting Hangzhou and the Grand Canal with southern China can best be seen by looking at the incense cultivated exclusively in and around the area that is now Hong Kong 香港 . This incense was one of several products from the region that was much coveted in the southern provinces. It was sent in large sailing vessels up the Pearl River 珠江 to Guangzhou. From there it was distributed all over southern and eastern China. That which was destined for the cities of Hangzhou and Suzhou travelled the usual route north by boat to as far as Poyang Lake, crossing the Meiling Pass on the way. But instead of sailing through the lake to the Yangtze, it was possible to branch east onto the Xin River 信江 . Following this all the way to its headwaters, and across another short overland section at the border between Jiangxi and Zhejiang provinces, it was possible to join the Qu River 衢江 which flows into the Qiantang River 錢塘江 to Hangzhou and the Grand Canal. During the wet summer season, when water levels were high, this would have been a far more direct route between Guangzhou and the southern canal cities and would cut by half the distance that had to be travelled via the Yangtze River.

It is this route of the Imperial Way that we concentrate on here, for two reasons. Firstly, the Yangtze River has been well-travelled and already documented in many publications. Secondly, this was the route taken by Lord Macartney and recorded so faithfully in the journals of his secretary, Sir George Staunton, and other members of the embassy.

...the great route from [Beijing] to [Guangzhou] is by way of [Nanjing] and through the Poyang lake but as we left [Nanjing] on our right hand in order to come to [Hangzhou] we deviated from the

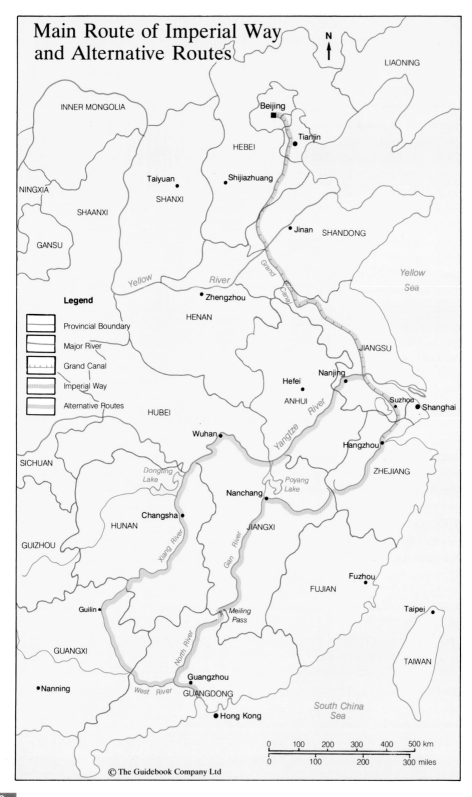

# Main Route of Imperial Way and Alternative Routes

N

LIAONING

INNER MONGOLIA

Beijing

Tianjin

HEBEI

Taiyuan

Shijiazhuang

NINGXIA

SHANXI

SHAANXI

Jinan

SHANDONG

GANSU

Yellow

River

Yellow
Sea

Grand Canal

**Legend**

Provincial Boundary

Major River

Grand Canal

Imperial Way

Alternative Routes

Zhengzhou

HENAN

JIANGSU

Nanjing

Hefei

ANHUI

Suzhou

Shanghai

HUBEI

Wuhan

Hangzhou

SICHUAN

Dongting
Lake

Poyang
Lake

ZHEJIANG

Nanchang

Yangtze River

Changsha

HUNAN

JIANGXI

GUIZHOU

Xiang River

Gan River

Fuzhou

FUJIAN

Guilin

Meiling
Pass

Taipei

GUANGXI

North River

TAIWAN

Nanning

Guangzhou

West River

GUANGDONG

Hong Kong

South China
Sea

| 0 | 100 | 200 | 300 | 400 | 500 km |

| 0 | 100 | 200 | 300 miles |

© The Guidebook Company Ltd

26

common track by which means we have had an opportunity of seeing a part of China which probably no European ever visited before. *(Lord Macartney)*

The imperial courts came to rely on the vast region to the south of the Yangtze for the supply of such things as textiles, tea, sugar, salt, fruits, game, fish, meat, cooking oil, medicinal herbs; paper, writing brushes and inkstones; porcelain, lacquerware, pearls, hawksbill turtles, jadeite and flowers; timber, bamboo, reed, bricks and stone; mineral ores—especially copper and lead for casting coins. Some of these were carried from as far afield as Guangzhou, and for the delivery of many goods it was speed that was of the essence.

Each year the southern provinces provide the king with everything needed or wanted to live well in the unfertile province of [Beijing]... all of which must arrive on a fixed day, otherwise those who are paid to transport them are subject to a heavy fine.

The boats called cavaliers are commanded by palace eunuchs, and they always travel rapidly, in fleets of eight or ten. The canal is navigable only during the summer season, when the water is high, perhaps due to the melting of the snow in the mountains where the river takes its rise.

During the hot summer season much of the food stuffs... would spoil before reaching [Beijing]; so they are kept in ice, to preserve them. The ice gradually melts, and so great stores of it are kept at certain stops, and the boats are liberally supplied with enough of it to keep their cargoes fresh until arrival. *(Ricci)*

Not just food but also messages from the far corners of the empire, such as news of a rebellious warlord or a peasant revolt, had to be delivered with all possible haste—sometimes on horseback, sometimes on foot, along the towpaths or roads beside the waterways. (*see* Qing Dynasty Postal System in Chapter Three.)

For centuries water transport formed the backbone of trade and transport within the Middle Kingdom. The Chinese developed an array of different craft to suit the volume of cargo or the depth of water. During Macartney's voyage south they and their baggage were transferred several times to barges of differing beams and draughts depending on the size of the river or canal and the amount of water flowing during that season.

## DECLINE OF THE GRAND CANAL

At the beginning of the nineteenth century the Grand Canal went into decline. Following the abdication of the emperor Qianlong 乾隆 in 1796, and his death three years later, the Qing dynasty began to weaken. Corruption became rife amongst officials in charge of water management. Maintenance was neglected and sections of the canal became silted up, seriously hampering navigation and delaying shipments and transport. This was especially true after the great flood of the Yellow River in 1855 when large amounts of silt blocked the canal for more than a decade. Canal transportation was further interrupted by the Taiping Rebellion in the mid-nineteenth century. Later attempts by the Qing rulers to restore the canal were half-hearted. An increasingly larger volume of the all-important grain was taken instead by sea. This marked a gradual rejuvenation of sea transport, until finally in 1902 the emperor simply dismissed all officials in charge of canal management, and with the commutation of the ancient grain tribute to a cash payment in 1900 the Grand Canal became all but obsolete. All this signalled the sharp decline of industry and commerce in many of the trading towns and cities along the route and the loss of livelihood for thousands of bargemen, carters, innkeepers and businessmen.

A further death knell for canal transport was the coming of the railway in the early twentieth century. The first line was built between Tianjin 天津 and Pukou 浦口 on the north bank of the Yangtze opposite Nanjing, and from Tianjin to Beijing. The railways began to supersede all other traditional forms of transport and the Grand Canal was never to recover.

The year 1949 saw large-scale renovation along sections of the canal in Jiangsu Province. New sluices were constructed and old ones rebuilt. Where the canal crosses the Yellow River new dykes and flood control sluices were built in an effort to prevent the river's silt from flowing into the canal. In 1958 the construction of a major pumping station for irrigation and drainage meant that Hongze Lake 洪澤湖 was able to regulate the level of the Grand Canal and drain off excess flood water directly into the sea.

Schemes to rejuvenate the Grand Canal in the north of the country were instigated in the early 1980s and for a time water flowed northwards once more. But due to the age-old problem of water shortages in this arid part of the country they were not a long-term success and, as we shall see on our journey, the canal in the north is very much redundant as far as transportation is concerned.

In the southern provinces, beyond the Grand Canal, the rivers always were affected by seasonal variations in water levels, and with the advent of the railways along with improved road transportation, they too largely fell into disuse. Because this is a mountainous region many of them have now been dammed to provide much needed hydroelectric power, thus preventing any further long-distance navigation.

# Chapter Two

# Beijing, Tianjin & Hebei Province
# 北京、天津、河北省

## BEIJING 北京

Aaa-HAAAH! The cry echoes around the trees. The air is warm and still. Aaaa-HAAY! comes a response, drifting from the other side of the park. A weak sun is rising behind a smog-tinged haze. Young autumn sunlight filters through the trees and bathes the pavilion in a soft early morning glow. Beneath its eaves of turquoise and yellow glazed tiles, an old man with a wispy beard sits playing a bamboo flute. Before long a crossfire of assorted shouts and cries is floating back and forth across the hillside.

It is dawn in Jing Shan Park 景山公園 (Prospect Hill) in the centre of Beijing, overlooking the Forbidden City—the Imperial Palace. The city's old folk are gathering for their early morning constitutional. Some climb the paths that wind up to the five pavilions sitting symmetrically atop the wooded hill. As the old men hang their caged birds in the trees the occupants begin their early morning chorus. Meanwhile their frail and wrinkled human counterparts perform their own chorus of hearty, lung-clearing shouts that reverberate around the park at the start of each day. Inside the main gate, beside an exhibition of prize blooms and bonsai trees, exercise groups are already going through their paces. In unison they are performing the slow, flowing movements of tai chi 太極. Some are following the more upbeat rhythms of modern dance.

The man-made hill is said to have been built using the earth taken from excavations of the palace moat and dredging of the neighbouring lakes. It commands an impressive view over the serried ranks of orange-tiled roofs of the Imperial Palace, the layout of which has changed little since it was first built in the Ming dynasty by the emperor Yongle 永樂.

Those roofs, uninterrupted by chimneys, and indented in the sides and ridges into gentle curves... were adorned with a variety of figures... the whole shining like gold under a brilliant sun, immediately caught the eye with an appearance of grandeur *(Sir George Staunton)*

Not far from the north-west corner of the old Yuan dynasty city wall stands a marble stele bearing an inscription written by the Qing dynasty emperor Qianlong referring to the ancient city of Ji 薊. Historians believe this to be the earliest known settlement on the site of modern Beijing, dating back to around the eleventh century BC, although the true site is now known to have been much further south, corresponding to the present-day area of Guang'anmen 廣安門. Later it became the capital of the northern Kingdom of Yan 燕, but this was destroyed by Qin Shihuangdi in 221 BC.

Later during the Tang dynasty it became a provincial capital known as Youzhou 幽州 . But the city's turbulent history continued. The Qidan 契丹 were the first of the Mongolian tribes to invade northern China founding the Liao dynasty (916–1125). They built a secondary capital on the site in AD 938, changing its name to Nanjing 南京 . Following their defeat at the hands of the Nuzhen 女真 (Jurchen), tartars of northern Manchuria, it was expanded and in 1153 became the capital of the Jin dynasty. It was later abandoned in favour of Kaifeng in 1214. Genghis Khan and his Mongol armies swept into northern China and overcame the Nuzhen in 1234, bringing to a close the Jin dynasty. Initially however, the Mongol leader chose to make his capital far to the north-east at Karakoram.

When Kublai Khan, the grandson of the Great Khan, became the first emperor of the Yuan dynasty in 1271, he established his capital on the site of present-day Beijing. At first, he lived on the island in what is now Bei Hai Lake 北海 (the site of the old Jin dynasty Summer Palace). Later he commissioned the building of a new imperial palace which was completed around 1290. It was constructed next to Bei Hai Lake in the south of the new capital city which he named Khanbaliq (meaning City of the Great Khan). The Chinese called it Dadu, 大都 (meaning Great Capital). The layout of the new city had been designed by Liu Bing Zhong 劉秉忠 , a particularly learned scholar and close friend of the Khan. Unfortunately Liu died before the construction could be completed. It had been he who suggested the name Yuan for the new dynasty.

The city was situated at the northern extremity of the great North China Plain, a vast region of fertile soil laid down over millennia by the wandering Yellow River, stretching as far south as modern Jiangsu Province. The site not only lacked the capability to support and feed a large population, but was plagued by inherent water supply problems—the ground on which the city stood is slightly higher than the surrounding land.

During the Jin dynasty (1115–1234) the city, then called Zhongdu 中都 (Middle Capital), was centred on an area in the south-west of today's city now known as Xuan Wu Qu 宣武區 . An attempt was made to cut a canal through to the nearby city of Tongzhou 通州 (nowadays called Tongxian 通縣 ) at the northern end of the Grand Canal, to facilitate the transportation of the grain tax to the capital. The canal, named Jin Kou He 金口河 , channelled water from the Lu Gou River 盧溝河 , a large river running to the west of the city. However, because of its steep gradient the flow of water was impossible to control and it flooded disastrously. The engineer responsible was executed. A satisfactory canal system was never built and transportation between the two cities continued largely by road.

When Kublai came to power, however, he realized that an efficient grain supply to his new capital was of the utmost importance. He had the Grand Canal modified by building a new section of waterway between Zhenjiang 鎮江 in Jiangsu Province and Linqing 臨清 in Shandong Province (*see* page 22).

By the year 1291 the Jinghang Canal 京杭河 as it became known, stretched from Hangzhou in the south to Tongzhou in the north. But there was still that problematic stretch of about eighteen kilometres from Tongzhou to Dadu itself. Guo Shou-jing 郭守敬 , an eminent astronomer

*Guo Shou-jing (1231–1316), astronomer, scientist and engineer, created the Baifu and Tonghui canals.*

*Although it follows the route of Guo Shou-jing's original thirteenth-century canal,*
*today the Baifu Canal carries water to Beijing from the Huairou and Miyun reservoirs.*
*The capital has an insatiable appetite for water,*
*for domestic needs as well as for industry and farming. Due to its excessive use of*
*underground water, Beijing has subsided more than sixty centimetres in the past forty years.*

and scientist, and a student of the trusted Liu Bing Zhong, received orders from Kublai to oversee the digging of a canal to cover this distance.

He initially looked at ways of reopening the old, defunct Jin dynasty canals, but found their gradients to be unsuitable and his first two attempts failed. In the spring of 1292, after extensive field surveys of the topography and hydrology of the area around Dadu, Guo Shou-jing drew up a scheme and personally supervised its construction. He had located a spring to the north of the capital at Baifu village 白浮 in Changping county 昌平縣 . A thirty-kilometre-long canal, known as the Baifu Canal 白浮堰 , was dug from there, looping around the foot of the western mountains to maintain its gradient, all the way to Dadu. It also acted as a catchment, collecting additional water from other springs and rivers along the way. Guo Shou-jing's idea was to channel this water through a system of lakes and canals in and around Dadu, and then to Tongzhou to connect with the Grand Canal.

Water from the Baifu Canal was collected in an enlarged natural lake, Weng Shan Po 瓮山泊 , to the north-west of the city. It still exists today as Kunming Lake 昆明湖 at the Summer Palace. This acted as a regulating reservoir. The Changhe Canal 長河 (Long River) led from the lake, through what is the present-day site of Beijing Zoo, to Gaoliang Bridge 高梁橋 . Passing through the city walls the water then flowed into Jishuitan lagoon ( 積水潭 literally, store-water-pool), effectively the port of the Yuan dynasty capital.

From the southern end of Jishuitan the canal then continued around the eastern wall of the Imperial Palace, along what is now Beiheyan 北河沿大街 and Nanheyan 南河沿大街 streets, joining the moat outside the southern city wall. It then flowed east, more or less

*One of perhaps only two original locks built by Guo Shou-jing that still survive today.*
*This lock at Gao Bei Dian, about eight kilometres east of Beijing on the Tonghui Canal,*
*has one remaining crane arm. There were two pairs of these inclined arms set opposite one another.*
*They held windlasses or pulleys used for raising and lowering a set of wooden baulks that*
*slid in a groove in the stone piers on each side. Built in 1293,*
*it demonstrates a technique that had already been in use in China for more than 200 years.*

*A technique used for locking together stone blocks
that dates back to before the tenth century.
Iron dovetails called yinding 銀錠 were set in
corresponding slots in the stone. The earliest yinding
were made of wood or brick.*

along the line of the present-day Chang'an Avenue
長安街 , to Tongzhou (later, in the Ming dynasty,
it flowed along what is now Zhengyi Road 正義路
before heading east following the line of Qianmen
Street 前門大街 ; the Ming city wall having been sited further south). Because of the
topography of the area, Guo Shou-jing had to construct a total of twenty-four sluice gates at
eleven different sites along the canal in order to control the water level and regulate its
supply.

The new canal was completed in the autumn of 1293. When Kublai Khan returned
from a hunting trip in the north, he was so delighted to find his capital bustling with grain
barges from the Grand Canal that he named the new canal Tonghui He 通惠河 ('The
Channel of Communicating Grace').

The water supply for the Imperial Palace came from a separate source. The water
filling the lakes within the palace walls came from Jade Spring Mountain 玉泉山 , just to the
west of Weng Shan Po. This had almost certainly been part of Liu Bing Zhong's original plan
for the city. Records in the Qing dynasty show it being also transported by carriage direct to
the palace for drinking water.

From the northern end of Jishuitan, a further canal, acting as an overflow, led due
west and drained into the Wenyu River 溫榆河 . This, along with other rivers, fed directly
into, and in effect became, the Grand Canal at Tongzhou. It is quite possible that in the Yuan
dynasty grain barges would have entered Dadu via this more direct northern route, thereby
avoiding the lock gates on the Tonghui He.

The junction of the Tonghui Canal and the Grand Canal was sited just to the north of
the town of Tongzhou and enabled barges to sail directly into the Tonghui Canal to the
capital. Upon arrival at Dadu the boats, heralded by much banging of gongs and drums,
would sail into the city and enter Jishuitan, where they would unload their valuable cargo.
Staunton writes about seeing 'immense magazines of rice' near the gate of the Imperial
Palace. Many of the grain barges were articulated. The hull was constructed in two parts so
that the bow and stern sections could be turned separately in narrow rivers or canals.

Guo Shou-jing's innovative scheme to divert water through the city not only solved the
capital's water supply problem and created direct access for barges from the Grand Canal,
but also provided additional, much-needed water for irrigation of the surrounding farm land.
Primarily an important route for the supply of food, it was also widely used to transport
construction materials. Bricks, for example, came from Wuqing 武清 near Tianjin and from
Linqing (*see* Chapter Three). And as a result of the water catchment system from Baifu,
timber from the western mountains could be floated downstream to the capital.

At the beginning of the Ming dynasty, however, the capital was shifted south to Nanjing
南京 . During this period the Tonghui He and Baifu Canal fell into disuse and silted up—it
was no longer needed to transport the essential grain tribute. Beijing was renamed Beiping
北平 (Northern Peace). When in 1420 the capital once more reverted to Beijing, the original
Yuan dynasty canal system could no longer be used in its entirety. Although the Tonghui
Canal was still in existence, the northern section of the Grand Canal (known as the Beiyun

Canal 北運河 ) had changed its course and a stone dam was constructed between the two canals to preserve the water level. Therefore grain had to be transferred by hand to barges waiting in the Tonghui Canal and a port was established in Tongzhou itself. Once at Beijing the boats were no longer able to enter the city itself. They instead unloaded in the moat outside the eastern wall, and the grain was carted through the gates and stored in large purpose built warehouses.

To alleviate growing problems of water shortage at this time, some of the original sluices were discarded; only five sluices and two dams were retained. During the grain transportation season the gates were not opened and grain had to be transferred over each gate to barges waiting on the other side. In spite of the difficulties large-scale transportation of supplies from the south resumed.

When the emperor Yongle moved the Ming capital from Nanjing to Beijing, he completely rebuilt the city, the fundamental layout of which has remained more or less the same up to the present day. He was also responsible for the building of Jing Shan, the Temple of Heaven, the Summer Palace and the Ming Tombs. All the timber, bricks, and paint needed for the construction of his new city came via the Grand Canal.

It was in the year 1600 that the Jesuit priest, Matteo Ricci, finally reached Beijing from Nanjing by means of the Grand Canal. He comments on the enormous amount of barge traffic on the canal—not just those bringing grain from the southern provinces, but a great many more besides, including those belonging to magistrates and officials and those engaged in private trade.

*Xiu Yi Bridge 繡漪橋 , known locally as the 'hunchback bridge', stands at the southern end of Kunming Lake. Here water is funnelled into the Changhe canal on its way to Beijing. Built in the Qing dynasty, the bridge was passed by the imperial court on their way to the Summer Palace—a journey that inspired the emperor Qianlong to write several poems.*

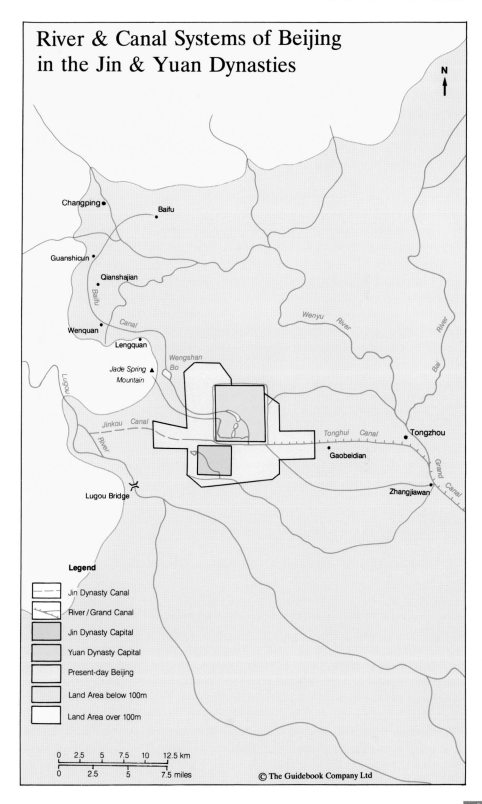

# River & Canal Systems of Beijing in the Jin & Yuan Dynasties

N

Changping●
Baifu

Guanshicun ●

Qianshajian

Baifu

Canal

Wenyu River

River

Wenquan ●
Lengquan

Wengshan Bo

Jade Spring ▲
Mountain

Lugou

Jinkou Canal

River

Tonghui Canal

Tongzhou

Gaobeidian

Bai

Lugou Bridge

Zhangjiawan

Grand Canal

**Legend**

Jin Dynasty Canal

River / Grand Canal

Jin Dynasty Capital

Yuan Dynasty Capital

Present-day Beijing

Land Area below 100m

Land Area over 100m

| 0 | 2.5 | 5 | 7.5 | 10 | 12.5 km |

| 0 | 2.5 | 5 | | 7.5 miles |

© The Guidebook Company Ltd

Entrance to the city of [Beijing] from the river, and also an exit from it are made by means of canals, constructed for boats bringing cargoes into the city. They say there are ten thousand boats engaged in this commerce...

Private merchants coming in from the [Yangtze] River are not permitted to enter these canals... they disembarked... on the river bank about a day's journey from the city walls. There was a canal running from there into the city, but... only those conveying cargoes to the royal court were permitted to use it. This law was passed in order to prevent the multitude of boats from clogging the traffic, and cargoes destined for the royal city from being spoiled. All other consignments were carried into the city by wagons or pack-horses or porters. *(Ricci)*

With the building of the Summer Palace beside Kunming Lake to the north-west of Beijing, the Changhe Canal took on an additional significance. During the Ming and Qing dynasties the imperial family spent a great deal of time at this private retreat. Boarding their imperial barges at Gaoliang Bridge 高梁橋, just outside Xizhimen gate 西直門, the emperors used the Changhe to travel to and from the Summer Palace. Midway along the canal, its banks then, as now, draped with willows, stood the Wanshou Si 萬壽寺 (Longevity Temple). Originally built in 1577 as a Buddhist temple and library, it also served as a stopping-off point on the way to the Summer Palace. Extended over the years into a complex of halls in a series of courtyards, it has been likened to a miniature Forbidden City, and was used not only as a place of worship by the imperial family but also for special celebrations. On one notable occasion, attended by 1,000 monks, the Qing emperor Qianlong threw a grand party for his mother's seventieth birthday. He was often inspired to put pen to paper during these trips to the Summer Palace, and an interesting extract from one of his poems mentions changing barges at the Guangyuan Zha lock gate 廣源閘 not far from Wanshou Temple.

> *Guangyuan lock sits on the banks of the Long River,*
> *Dividing the waters between high and low;*
> *Crossing the lock, one walks but a few paces,*
> *To change boats for the upstream journey west.*
>
> *Wanshou Temple is barely two li distant,*
> *high over its walls embroidered banners flutter.*
> *Vermilion robed monks kneel before the temple gates...*[1]

Built in 1292, the Guangyuan Zha was one of Guo Shou-jing's original locks. A large part of the stone work has been preserved and can still be seen a short distance east of the Wanshou Temple.

The original Baifu Spring, its low grey granite wall carved with nine dragon's heads, out of which the water used to spurt, also still exists today. It has been preserved beneath a pavilion behind a small hill, a short distance east of the modern Changping expressway. A stone tablet explains its significance. Although the spring has long since run dry, it is possible, with the aid of modern plumbing and the flick of a switch, to see the water flow from the dragon's heads once more. The water in the nearby canal, however, flows permanently. It now originates from the Huairou 懷柔 and Miyun 密雲 reservoirs far to the north-west of Beijing, but from Baifu it still traces Guo Shou-jing's original route, skirting the western mountains all the way to Kunming Lake. And, as in the Yuan dynasty, it once again supplies the capital with water.

[1] Taken from Rixia Jiuwen Kao 日下舊聞考 (Old Hearsay of the Capital) published in Qianlong 39. Translated by Michael Crook.

The road between Tongxian and the capital is now a six-lane expressway, but Anderson and Staunton give us a pretty good idea of what this road must have been like in the Qing Dynasty.

The road along which we travelled, is not only broad but elegant... The middle of this road consists of a pavement of broad flag stones about twenty feet wide, and on each side of it there is sufficient space to admit of six carriages to run abreast. The lateral parts are laid with gravel stones, and kept in continual repair by troops of labourers, who are stationed on different parts of the road for that purpose. *(Anderson)*

This road forms a magnificent avenue to [Beijing], for persons and commodities bound for that capital from the east and... was bordered in many places with trees, particularly willows of a very uncommon girth. *(Staunton)*

With the establishment of the People's Republic of China in 1949, the Tonghui Canal was no longer required for transportation and instead became a popular place for boating. The canals within the city walls have since been filled in and roads laid in their place, although some in the south-east of the city were still in existence until the 1960s.

Nowadays the recently renovated canal between Beijing and Tongxian is used as a stormwater and drainage channel from the capital and is heavily polluted with sewage and factory waste. What remains of the Jishuitan lagoon can still be seen today as a chain of three lakes, just inside the inner ring road of Beijing. At their northern end, beside the highway at Jishuitan intersection, on a low hill, stands a small museum commemorating the accomplishments of Guo Shou-jing.

--·--··●●◗●●●··--·--

[Beijing] exhibited, on the entrance into it, an appearance contrary to that of European cities, in which the streets are often so narrow, and the houses so lofty... Here few of the houses were higher than one story; none more than two; while the width of the street which divided them was considerably above one hundred feet. It was airy, gay, and lightsome. *(Staunton)*

Perhaps one of the first things that strikes a visitor to modern Beijing is the overwhelming feeling of spaciousness. Chang'an Avenue, a vast ten-lane boulevard, two lanes of which are reserved for the city's multitude of bicycles, extends to bisect the city from east to west (with various changes in its name). In the centre of the city it passes the vermilion walls of the magnificent Tian'anmen 天安門 , the Gate of Heavenly Peace, the entrance to the Imperial Palace. In existence since the Ming dynasty, this is the same route by which, nearly 400 years later, Lord Macartney and his embassy passed through the city.

Opposite Tian'anmen lies the expanse of Tian'anmen Square where, during the heady days of Mao Zedong 毛澤東 , huge crowds of up to one million people gathered. Even such imposing buildings as the Great Hall of the People, which stands along the western side of the square, seem dwarfed by the effect of so much open space.

On days when the air pollution is particularly bad it can be difficult to see from one end of the square to the other. But with luck, especially after heavy rain when the air has been washed clean, one can stand on Chang'an Avenue opposite Tian'anmen, and the sky

VIEW of one of the WESERN GATES of the

will clear and reveal the western mountains along the horizon.

Today, wandering along the streets and hutongs that follow the course of the old canal, one can still see signs of history preserved in the names of the roads themselves. The very word hutong 胡同, meaning alley or lane, dates back to the Yuan dynasty and is derived from a Mongol word. Evidence of the trades that used to take place in these small streets, or goods that were stored there, suggests their importance in days gone by.

The names of several alleys around the Imperial Palace end with the character *ku* 庫,

PEKIN.

**Plate No. 1**

*"The city walls were about forty feet in height. The thickness of the walls was at the base about twenty feet... Several horsemen were able to ride abreast upon the ramparts, ascending to them upon slopes of earth raised on the inside."* (Staunton)

*"There is a grand gate in the centre of each angle, and... lesser ones at each corner of the wall: they are strongly arched, and fortified by a square building, or tower, of seven stories, that springs from the top of the gateway. The windows of this building are of wood, and painted to imitate the muzzle of a great gun, which is so exactly represented, that the deception is not discoverable but on a very near approach."* (Anderson)

*These great city walls were sadly torn down in the late 1950s and early 1960s to make way for a much needed ring road. A few crumbling sections of this old grey brick wall can still be seen just south of the Railway Station near Dongbianmen.*

meaning warehouse, such as Miliang ku 米糧庫 granary; Ciqi ku 磁器庫 porcelain warehouse; Duan ku 緞庫 satin; La ku 腊庫 dried meat; Huoyao 火葯 gunpowder and, in the next alley, Huoyaotou 火葯頭 fuse.

In the east of the city within the line of the old city wall are several other examples where the hutongs carry the ending *cang* 倉 , also meaning warehouse—Lumi cang 祿米 倉 meaning salary grain warehouse; Haiyun cang 海運倉 sea cargo, as well as Gongjiangying hutong 弓匠營胡同 bow-makers factory lane. Both Nanmencang 南門倉 and Dongmencang 東門倉 hutongs are on the site of a large number of Yuan dynasty granaries. At the northern end of Dongmencang hutong is a compound of about a dozen warehouses dating from the Ming dynasty. Squat, with thick inward-sloping walls of grey brick (the manufacturers stamp clearly visible on a few), they look almost fortress-like; their grey-tiled roofs are supported on heavy wooden beams and each distinguished by a short ventilation tower on top. They still serve as warehouses, only nowadays they store general merchandise instead of grain.

# Life In Old Beijing—Literary excerpts

## POPULATION

According to the best information given to the Embassy, [the population] was about three millions. The low houses of Pekin seem scarcely sufficient for so vast a population; but very little room is occupied by a Chinese family... (*Staunton*)

Though the houses at [Beijing] are low and mean, when considered with respect to size and domestic accommodation, their exterior appearance is very handsome and elegant, as the Chinese take a great pride in beautifying the fronts of their shops and dwellings; the upper part of the former is ornamented with a profusion of golden characters; and on the roofs of the latter are frequent galleries, rich in painting and other decoration; where numerous parties of women are seen to amuse themselves according to the fashion of the country. (*Anderson*)

## PROBLEM OF DUST

I observed, as we passed along, a great number of men who were sprinkling the streets with water, in order to lay the dust, which, in dry weather, would not only be troublesome to passengers, but very obnoxious also to the shops. (*Anderson*)

Very few of the streets in [Beijing] are paved with brick or stone, and it is difficult to say which season of the year is more objectionable for walking. The mud in the winter and the dust in the summer are equally obnoxious and fatiguing. As it seldom rains in this province, the surface earth dissolves into a coating of dust, which even a slight wind raises, blowing it into the houses, where it covers and soils nearly everything. In order to overcome this dust nuisance, they have introduced a custom which is probably unknown anywhere else. During the dust season here, nobody of any class would think of going out, either on foot or in conveyance, without wearing a long veil, falling in front from the hat, and thus sheltering the face. (*Ricci*)

## TRANSPORT

There are no carriages standing in the streets for the convenience of the inhabitants, like our hackney coaches in London: the higher classes of people keep palanquins, and others of less distinction have covered carts drawn by an horse or mule. (*Anderson*)

## TRADES

Besides the variety of trades which are stationary in this great city, there are many thousands of its inhabitants who cry their goods about, as we see in our own metropolis. They generally have a bamboo placed across their shoulders, and a basket at each end of it, in which they carry fish, vegetables, eggs, and other similar articles.

Barbers also are seen running about the streets in great plenty, with every instrument known in this country for shaving the head and cleansing the ears: they carry with them for this purpose a portable chair, a portable stove, and a small vessel of water, and whoever wishes to undergo either of these operations, sits down in the street... That this trade in China is a very profitable one may be pronounced, because every man must be shaved on a part of the head where it is impossible to shave himself. (*Anderson*)

## APPEARANCE & DRESS

The best dressed men wore a sort of velvet cap on their heads; a short jacket, buttoned close round the neck, and folded across the breast, the sleeves remarkably wide; the materials cotton cloth, black, blue, or brown silk; they wore quilted petticoats, and black satin boots. The common people were dressed in large straw hats, blue or black cotton frocks, wide cotton trowsers, and thick clumsy shoes, sometimes made of straw. Some had coarse stockings of cotton cloth; the legs of others were naked. A single pair of drawers constituted indeed the whole clothing of a great portion of the crowd. *(John Barrow)*

The women we saw on our passage through [Beijing] possessed, in general, great delicacy of feature, and fair skins by nature, with which, however, they are not content, and therefore whiten them with cosmetics; they likewise employ vermilion, but in a manner wholly different from the application of rouge among our European ladies, for they mark the middle if their lips with it by a stripe of its deepest colour, which... certainly heightened the effect of their features. Their eyes are very small, but powerfully brilliant, and their arms extremely long and slender. The women of [Beijing] ... wear a sharp peak of black velvet or silk, which is ornamented with stones, and descends from the forehead almost between their eyes; and that their feet, free from the bandages... were suffered to attain their natural growth. *(Anderson)*

Moreover 'tis the mark of gentility in that country to have the nails long; and some let their thumb-nails grow to such an extent that they grow right round the hand. And with the women the great beauty is to have little feet; and for this reason mothers are accustomed, as soon as girls are born to them, to swathe their feet tightly so that they can never grow in the least. *(Odoric of Pordenone)*

*A train crosses a bridge over the Tonghui Canal beside Dongbianmen watchtower.*
*Water still passes through Beijing, but nowadays is channelled underground—*
*many of the original canals having been filled in to make way for roads.*
*A culvert can be seen on the left of the picture*
*where water from Jishuitan and Beihai Lake exits the city and feeds into the Tonghui He.*

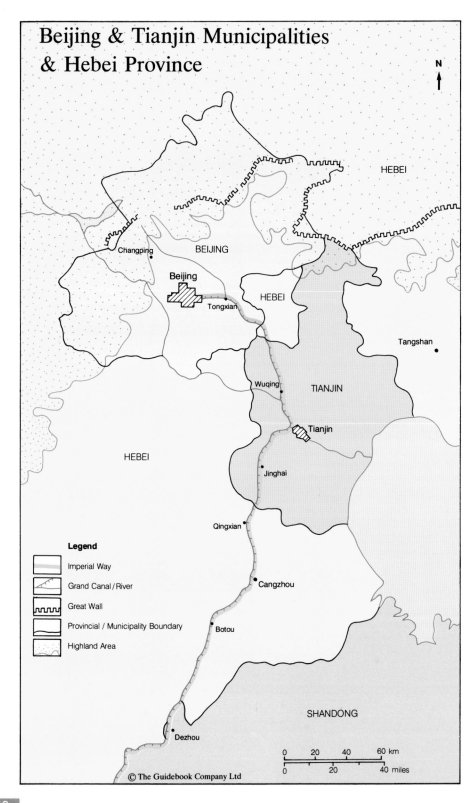

# Beijing & Tianjin Municipalities & Hebei Province

N

HEBEI

Changping

BEIJING

Beijing

Tongxian

HEBEI

Tangshan

Wuqing

TIANJIN

Tianjin

HEBEI

Jinghai

Qingxian

Cangzhou

**Legend**

Imperial Way

Grand Canal / River

Great Wall

Provincial / Municipality Boundary

Highland Area

Botou

SHANDONG

Dezhou

| 0 | 20 | 40 | 60 km |

| 0 | 20 | 40 miles |

© The Guidebook Company Ltd

It is a heavily overcast morning at the end of August. A light drizzle is falling. A diesel locomotive growls slowly over a bridge across the Tonghui Canal as it hauls its long line of carriages slowly past the grey and imposing Dongbian Gate and into Beijing Railway Station. The coaches are packed with travellers, many having come from Shanghai, almost 1,500 kilometres away. Below them water, black and soupy with effluent, drifts out of a culvert into the canal—all that remains of the bustling waterway that once connected Beijing to the Grand Canal.

A paved promenade runs alongside the recently renovated canal—a first step in an attempt to clean up its fetid waters—and a handful of people, undeterred by the weather, are taking their early morning exercise. On the other side, a main road leading into the city is packed with cyclists bedecked in colourful rain capes, on their way to work. A young man, one of many at this hour, pedals his tricycle cart piled high with a huge load of vegetables destined for the morning market. Standing out of the saddle and grimacing, he strains every muscle on a slight incline, finally having to get off and push.

# Tongxian 通縣

## TONGXIAN PAGODA

Sunday, 3 September 1995. The day of our departure was wet. I pulled rain covers over my bags and, swathed in a voluminous purple cagoule, hoisted myself into the saddle. On swishing tyres we rolled through the leafy quiet of Beijing's embassy compound and out onto the sludgy streets of the capital. The grey drizzle neutralized any colour in the city. Mud from the roads flicked up on to our gleaming bicycles and before long they too had lost all sparkle. 'A journey of one thousand miles starts with one step' is a hackneyed Chinese proverb. Our 'first step' was ordinary, without fanfare. There was no great rush of excitement or apprehension: we were just eager to get going.

We headed for Tongxian, now an unremarkable suburb of Beijing, which sits at the northernmost point of the Grand Canal. There is a pagoda, dating from the middle of the sixth century, that served as a landmark for traders and travellers. This was where they had to turn westwards for the capital along the smaller Tonghui Canal. From the opposite bank we could see the thirteen-storey tower rising above low buildings, but the entrance was elusive. The pagoda was buried in a maze of alleys and surrounded on all sides by a high wall. After cycling around the labyrinth for half an hour we finally reached a park gate where we had to abandon our heavily laden bikes. The rain clouds had dispersed and the park was full of children decked out in frilly red dresses and checked trousers, running helter-skelter between doting parents. We picked our way through the Sunday strollers, past lily ponds and weeping willows, to a narrow footbridge spanning a quiet lane and so to the pagoda. The gracious building stands in a neat courtyard. More than 2,000 wind bells hang from its eaves. Planted beside it is a low tree that once grew on the roof. It was removed ten years ago with great ceremony and even greater difficulty, according to a notice-board detailing the exercise. Seeded by roosting birds it had flourished on its lofty perch until the authorities decided it was dangerous. An arch leads out of the courtyard to a small Buddhist shrine, honouring one Ran Deng. I imagined that thousands of travellers had knelt before him over the years in the hope of procuring a safe passage and I eagerly presented my credentials. It was strangely comforting to feel that I was merely one of a very long line of ghosts who had wandered the length of China.

[The pagoda] has very much the appearance of antiquity, [and] stands in a remote corner of [Tongxian]. It is built of brick, and in its exterior form resembles what are called in Europe Chinese pagodas, and supposed to be places of religious worship. But the present building cannot have had such a destination, being, tho of considerable diameter, perfectly solid in the first and second story. There is not even the appearance of a door or window in either. There are no remains of steps, or other means of ascent to the third story, in which there is a door; the several stories, eleven in number, distinguished by a belt of brick on the outside, continue to be entire, tho weeds and shrubs are growing out of many parts of them. It is thought most probable that this building was erected prior to the existence of [Tongxian], and perhaps of the great Chinese wall... *(Staunton)*

We left Tongxian not long before dark. The road we followed towards Tianjin ran directly beside the canal (as would so many of our roads over the coming months). The sun was sinking; a glorious blaze of red light bounced off the water. We had no place fixed to spend the night and cycled on as dusk turned to darkness. Hordes of insects were slamming into my eyes and mouth, interfering with both seeing and breathing. In desperation I donned my orange fog-glasses (a donation from sponsors that I had not imagined being useful) and immediately dissolved into a world so surreal and spacey that I forgot to worry about accommodation. Darkness was transformed to a blistering orange by the headlamps of a passing lorry; it was a psychedelic riot. So engrossed was I that I cycled past a hostel for long distance lorry drivers. Fortunately Kevin noticed it.

Later, replete after a wholesome meal of cabbage, aubergines and rice, I reflected on a day of promise. Tongxian pagoda had magically brought us face to face with the purpose of our journey. Here was a building that had been remarked on by people who had travelled our route in the past. That we could establish this link on our first day was perfect. This trip was clearly going to be rich in rewards.

A.R.

# TONGXIAN TO TIANJIN　通縣 – 天津

*When orioles have stopped warbling, grey dawn is on the horizon;*
*The drooping willows on the banks cast shadows upon the green grass;*
*Tender flowers cannot be seen hidden under luxuriant leaves;*
*I feel a warm breeze blowing into our sails.*

Leaving Zhangjiawan 張家灣 at Dawn, by Ming dynasty poet Xu Tianxi.

Zhangjiawan located a few kilometres to the south-east of Tongxian, was an important transit

*Tongxian pagoda was originally built by Buddhist monks in the Northern Zhou period (AD 557–581). The top of the solid stone base has been shaped to form a ring of lotus leaves, above which, suspended from the eaves of its thirteen roofs, are 2,248 wind bells. Staunton describes seeing an eleven-storey tower which suggests that a further two floors were added during a later restoration.*

*This section of the Grand Canal, called the Beiyun Canal, runs between Beijing and Tianjin. The area around the nearby town of Wuqing was once an important source of bricks. The canal here, now succumbed to the age-old problem of silting, coupled with a shortage of water, is shallow and stagnant. Its only apparent use is to grow duckweed, collected by commercial fish farmers as fish food.*

station for passengers leaving or arriving in Beijing by canal. It was also a major clearing house for grain and other goods during the Yuan and Ming dynasties. Probably towards the end of the Ming and during the early Qing dynasty the Beiyun Canal re-routed itself due to silting. This left the town high and dry and inevitably brought about its decline. Nowadays it lies some five kilometres west of the canal but one can still see evidence of its past. The Tongyun Bridge 通運橋, a triple-arched marble bridge, ornamented with two rows of finely carved lions, stands beside a short section of renovated town wall. Some of the original flagstones remain, over the centuries their granite surface worn unevenly smooth to a fine gloss finish. Lamentably, this exquisite bridge shows signs of recent neglect. A mosque, built over 500 years ago, lies almost hidden in the middle of the small town. The branches of an equally old japonica tree shade the entrance to its courtyard. It is currently having an extension built and still serves a substantial population of Muslims—descendants of early traders along the Grand Canal.

······••●●●••······

The eastern sky is a wash of tangerine. The sun rises on a glorious autumn day with a handful of cotton wool clouds in a bright blue sky. A light breeze from the south-west stirs the leaves of the closely planted poplar trees that line the road, creating a wonderfully dappled shade for the cyclist.

South from Tongxian, the land changes little for hundreds of kilometres. On either side of the road the fields of maize and sorghum stretch to the horizon interrupted occasionally by kiln chimneys or a line of poplars. A whistle, a crack of a whip and a flock of sheep is hurried across a main road. Horse carts loaded with bricks clop lazily by. The town of Wuqing is not far away. Bricks are still made here but no longer do they make their way up the canal to the capital.

In fact, in this area, nothing at all makes its way along the canal. The wide grassy banks now slope gently down to the stagnant water, shallow and clogged with bright green duckweed. As sheep graze at the water's edge and a couple of horses feed under the shade of a row of trees, a young couple gathers the weed and shovels it into a small cart. Collected by means of a boom drawn across the surface of the water, the plant is used as fish food in nearby ponds.

This restful scene is in stark contrast to the picture painted by our earlier travellers, who talk of large junks and barges crowding the canal. Members of the Macartney expedition were ceaselessly amazed by the numbers of people that would line the banks to watch them pass, or that were encountered on their rare forays into towns and cities, and frequently commented on it in their journals. But here Staunton contemplates the not inconsiderable population that spent their lives on the water in this area.

Upon the deck of each of these large junks is built a long range of apartments, containing several families. It was calculated, that every one of these vessels contained not less than fifty persons; and that there were, between [Tongxian] and [Tianjin], at least one thousand such grain junks; thus containing fifty thousand inhabitants. An immense number of various other kinds of craft were continually passing to and fro, or lying before the towns bordering upon the river; and the number of people in them could not be less than fifty thousand more. So that upon a branch of a single river, the population of its moveable habitations amounted to one hundred thousand persons. *(Staunton)*

# TIANJIN 天 津

We entered the suburbs of the large city of [Tianjin], stretching, like London on the Thames, for several miles along each bank of the river... *(Barrow)*

The houses of this place are built of brick, and, in general, are carried to the height of two stories, with roofs of tiles: they were all of a lead colour, and had a very neat and pretty appearance. The place, however, is not formed on any regular plan: the streets, or rather alleys, are so narrow, as to admit, with difficulty, two persons to walk abreast; and have no pavement. It is, however, of great extent, and populous beyond all description. *(Anderson)*

On the outskirts of Tianjin, home of the famous 'Flying Pigeon' bicycles, the main road towards the city centre simply disappears and is transformed into a construction site. Cyclists, cars, buses and trucks compete with huge bulldozers with enormous knobbly wheels. Everybody follows everybody else, ploughing doggedly through the thick mud before this is scooped up by the earthmover. Buses hoot, bicycles tinkle and bulldozers growl. High above this confused cacophony, labourers in bright yellow hard hats work on the new concrete flyover. Beside the mire telephone engineers, aided by contraptions strapped to their feet, climb like monkeys up telegraph poles, and soon several cables fall across what is left of the road to add to the general mêlée.

Somehow though, in the space of about twenty minutes the whole chaotic scene seems to sort itself out. Nothing has stopped, the traffic has kept moving and all the time the construction vehicles continued to roar back and forth. But finally the bulldozers have cleared a path through the gravel and mud and before long the traffic is flowing more freely. It is the Chinese way. Somehow there is order amongst chaos.

Below its junction with the Grand Canal, the Hai River loops in an S-shape through the centre of the city. On either side, a surviving network of old streets and alleys that burrow their way through the buildings. Many of them are lively markets lined with small stalls and restaurants. The stalls selling fresh vegetables, meat and fish are at their most bustling early in the morning, when people clamour to buy the choicest produce. To satisfy the breakfast pangs of the market-goers, some people serve food out of what is little more than their front room. Some of the food is unique to Tianjin. *Guo ba cai* 鍋巴菜 is one such speciality served for breakfast. Like a vegetable pasta made from green beans, it is served in a kind of porridge and garnished with coriander leaves.

Because of its proximity to the ocean, an array of fresh seafood is available in Tianjin. At night, stalls lit only by strings of bare light bulbs offer fresh crabs and prawns and a variety of fish to be cooked and eaten in the open air.

The failure of Lord Macartney's mission to secure any form of trade concessions or even establish diplomatic relations, led indirectly to the First Opium War of 1839–1842, between Britain and China. The British East India Company, the largest of the trading houses at Guangzhou, had continued to ship increasing quantities of tea, silk and porcelain from China. Yet they had been unable to secure the import into China of more British products to balance the trade, and had found it increasingly difficult to obtain sufficient silver with which to make up the difference. Hence the introduction of opium, produced in India by the East India Company and traded as an alternative means of payment.

Growing resentment of the consequences of this drug on their population led the Chinese to attempt to stamp out the whole business. The British recourse to gunboat diplomacy ended with the emperor Daoguang 道光 being forced to sign the Treaty of Nanjing (*see* Chapter Four). The one-sided treaty led to further rumblings which were brought to a head, beginning with the Second Opium War in 1856 and culminating in China's signing of the Treaty of Tianjin in 1858 with Britain and France. This added Tianjin to the growing list of treaty ports and opened it to European trade. There followed the usual pattern of waterfront areas being divided amongst the various western nations.

The legacy of this treaty is still evident today. Strolling through the British, French, Russian, German or Italians quarters, along tree-lined boulevards, through porticoes and colonnades beneath shuttered windows and pink stucco and red-tiled roofs, one could quite easily imagine oneself in a European city. Thankfully, it has been preserved by the providence of the local government not, one imagines, through any desire to commemorate the signing of a lopsided treaty, but more from a wish to conserve an area of outstanding architectural history.

---

*The origins of Chinese opera can be traced back some 3,000 years to before the Zhou dynasty, when song and dance rituals provided the basis for many of the body movements seen today. However, the modern form of Beijing opera, or jing ju 京劇 as it is known in Chinese, is thought to have begun when opera troupes from Anhui Province visited Beijing in 1790 to perform for the imperial court. It was probably one of these early forms that was witnessed by the Macartney expedition in Tianjin in 1793.*

## CHINESE OPERA

The theatrical exhibitions consisted chiefly of warlike representations; such as imaginary battles with swords, spears, and lances; which weapons the performers managed with an astonishing activity. The scenes were beautifully gilt and painted, and the dresses of the actors were ornamented in conformity to the enrichments of the scenery. There was also a display of that species of agility which consists in tumbling, wherein the performers executed their parts with superior address and activity. The performance was also enlivened by a band of music... some of [the instruments] were very long, and resembled a trumpet; others had the appearance of French-horns, and clarinets: the sounds of the latter brought to my recollection that of a Scotch bag-pipe; and their music, being destitute both of melody and harmony, was of course, very disagreeable to our ears, which are accustomed to such perfection in those essential points of music. *(Anderson)*

On a stage in a small round community theatre in Tianjin, the exquisitely fragile Miss Zhao is arched backwards like a crab; with one outstretched arm she is whirling a sword above her head, round and round in ceaseless motion, about to kill herself. The rudimentary Chinese band at the foot of the raised stage has reached a climax of knocking and drumming. Wind, strings and percussion combine to produce a thunderous and impassioned cacophony that draws me straight to the heart of the drama. The audience of around fifty aged men is in uproar. This is fantastic, the best display they have had for weeks. Miss Zhao is killing herself because she has been wronged by an undeserving uncle. She plunges the sword under her arm, and sinks gracefully to her knees. The applause is tumultuous. The septuagenarian audience is cheering on its feet, but not to offer the accolade of a standing ovation—the old men are shuffling towards the exit. In a flash the hall is empty.

Every weekday afternoon this theatre in Tianjin's Nanhai Park is occupied by a knot of unkempt, whiskered individuals indulging their passion for China's highest art form—Beijing Opera. They sit on wooden benches in a smoky fug, crunching melon seeds and sipping tea out of jam jars. Between them they can lay claim to no more than one set of teeth. All wear home-knitted tank-tops, baggy cotton trousers and cotton shoes. They say they come to the bright warm theatre every day, if they can, for they love opera and also to escape their homes.

Dove-eyed Miss Zhao is completing her opera training (dance, gymnastics, singing, acting, acrobatics) at an institute in Tianjin. Performing with her on this occasion is an established star whose talent has taken him around the world on international tours. Today he is the Money God. Dressed in a baggy red suit with a wide sash round his middle and slices of gold paint covering his face, he struts across the stage in platform shoes singing lustily and delighting the crowd. The Nanhai Park theatre is rarely graced by professionals like these; amateur enthusiasts with maybe a dash of training are the standard fare.

It is fortunate for them that they are popular, for their earnings depend upon it. The theatre manager pays them a small appearance fee, the rest they must sing for. If one of the old men likes what he hears he 'purchases', for fifty yuan (US$6) and more, a basket of plastic flowers. This is placed on the stage in front of the singer, to a roar of approval from the crowd. The same twelve baskets are recycled for each

*A rudimentary theatre in Tianjin provides regular entertainment for a dedicated group of elderly men, who appreciate the finer points of this art form, banned during the Cultural Revolution. To the younger generation it remains an enigma.*

performance. Occasionally, a particularly enthusiastic spectator buys them all. The money taken for these tributes goes directly to the stars. A round sixty-five-year-old man dressed in a shiny blue-and-white shell-suit patrols the crowd, encouraging patronage and collecting the fees. 'Cuddly Chen' is one of my favourite people. He has a grin so huge and effervescent it leaves no room on his face for anything else. How can one not fill with laughter when confronted with a smile like this? His contagious sense of hilarity is not curtailed by his sketchy English. Pointing to himself he tries to look serious. 'Ugly man,' he says, then thrusts his finger in my face and follows it with 'beautiful girl'. He nearly chokes in convulsions of laughter.

After the show we sat with Miss Zhao while she took off her make-up. Performing in this 'amateur' environment was good experience, she said, and helped supplement her meager student's allowance, but she was anxious about her future. Beijing Opera, one of China's national treasures, is not popular with young people and attendance levels are falling. They complain that the pace is too slow and the stories too predictable. These days there are more 'hip' distractions, like karaoke and western music. The Tianjin audience is typical: aged and retired. Of course the tradition will survive, said Miss Zhao, but only a talented few can make a living from it. She is determined to try.

We found this Amateur Opera Paradise through our good friend Lao Wang— a.k.a. the Pedicab King—himself a big opera fan and, at thirty-five, a comparatively young one. We met late one night outside our hotel listening to a spontaneous street performance; two people were singing accompanied by an erhu. When they finished I turned to the crowd and asked where we could go to hear more. By a logic which Darwin would understand, Lao Wang became the medium through which all communication passed (he is the sort of individual who finds himself at the centre of any crowd). Everyone closed in around him and he was masterful.

'I know, I know,' he said. 'I can take you to two theatres tomorrow afternoon. I have a pedicab, we can go together.'

After the performance, Lao Wang pedalled us back through the drizzly streets of Tianjin. We asked him to eat with us.

A SCENE in an HISTORICAL PLAY exhibited on the CHINESE STAGE.

**Plate No. 2** *"The performers were habited in the ancient dresses of the Chinese. Female characters were performed by boys or eunuchs... The dialogue was spoken in a kind of recitative, accompanied by a variety of musical instruments; and each pause was filled up by a loud crash."* (Staunton)

'Yes, and can I bring my son?'
Why not invite your grandmother and six uncles as well, I thought, but smiled in agreement.

He lived opposite our hotel and after supper invited us back for a drink. We followed him into an alley and down a narrow dark passageway, barely wide enough for two people; we stumbled through a warren of unlit paths between high brick walls, turning left then right, up a short flight of steps and into his one-room apartment. The flat was empty; his wife worked evenings at a restaurant and would be back later. (Because of this Lao Wang went home to cook for his son William each night, which was of course why he had asked to bring him to supper with us). The twelve-year-old boy was straight away dispatched to buy beer and peanuts, and reminded that he still had to finish his homework.

'I encourage him to work hard. I want him to do well,' said Lao Wang. 'School for me was interrupted by the cultural revolution; I learnt nothing, no one did. Now all I can do is ride people around town. My son's life will be different, he can benefit from a good education in my place.' He was, however, an avid reader and showed us translations of Dickens, and Anna Karenina which he said he loved. William returned with beer, peanuts and his best friend, a girl from school, who wanted an English name.

The two of them giggled and chatted; she with spectacles and neat short hair, he tall, polite and full of humour. They were both bright. William was pushed hard by his father; he would interrupt to point out the importance of English and goad his son to work harder. William didn't mind; he seemed to have, at just twelve years old, the extraordinary perception to understand that his father behaved like this only because he wanted the best for him. 'I am working hard, I am trying,' he replied patiently. Mutual respect inspired them both.

One by one the Wang's neighbours arrived, calling in on their way back from work. The room next door was home to a Mrs. Li and her two teenage children, one a security guard and the other a student. The Wang's flat had no kitchen or bathroom— just one room with a bed, a sofa for William to sleep on and a cupboard supporting the television and piles of books. We breathed in and squeezed up. Living at such close quarters forced neighbourly solidarity; the two families seemed to share each other's lives and this was not resented. This involuntary intimacy seems to go a long way towards filling any vacuum left by the demise of the extended family, a result of China's one-child policy. The support networks between neighbours seem strong and effective.

It was an evening of laughter and questioning—Kevin and I producing the answers. The return of his wife from work prompted another round of beer. She was subdued and looked exhausted. The family album was produced with stark black and white pictures of a young Mrs. Wang and her two sisters, long plaits behind each ear and scarves round their necks like Young Pioneers. Fresh young faces of the cultural revolution. It was hard to place her amid the horror of that sinister time and, eager though I was to hear how it had involved her, she would not be drawn.

We talked until well past midnight. At one point a scuffle was heard on the steps outside; everyone was silent and cast questioning glances.
'Spies,' said Lao Wang and roared with laughter.
Mrs. Li from next-door shook her head violently and told him not to be so frivolous.

On our last night in Tianjin we were invited round to *bao jiaozi*—to make dumplings— something families do on holidays and feast days. Everyone wanted to give us a souvenir: William produced large plastic photo-frames, one for each of us; Mrs. Li a box of fluffy chicks; her daughter a glass ram (a ram represents my birth year). Of course we could not take any of them, not on bikes, so we had to find a way of leaving everything behind without giving offence. We simply accepted the pile with maximum gratitude and then announced that we could take none of it. Even when we walked down the steps they were still trying to press gifts into our hands... it was a serious breach of etiquette but I hope they understood. We had bought some English learning tapes for William. Both he and his father were delighted. 'You'd better get that tape machine mended as soon as possible,' commented William, knowing very well that nothing more would have to be said.

A.R.

# TIANJIN TO DEZHOU 天津－德州

The stream... was confined... between two artificial banks thrown up to a considerable height, and sloped down to the water's edge... The tops were converted into fine gravel-walks, shaded for many miles by rows of large willow trees, high poplars, and the quaking asp, interspersed with others bearing fruit, particularly of the plum kind. Along those banks, the country appeared cultivated as a garden, producing chiefly culinary vegetables. *(Staunton)*

Wherever possible the canal builders had used natural water courses, modifying or enlarging them when necessary. From Tianjin the Grand Canal adopts the course of the Wei River 衛河 , which follows a convoluted route south to the town of Linqing in Shandong Province. It wends its way through a landscape of rich, clayey soil the colour of milk chocolate, planted extensively with maize, sorghum and soya beans. Ripening sunflowers, their heads bowed as if in homage towards the south, grow in patches or strips filling in or dividing plots. Hebei Province and its neighbour Shandong are well-known for their fruit orchards. Approaching the town of Botou 泊頭 , hawkers become a common sight at the roadside. Often in long lines beside the same stretch of road, they sell boxes marked Tianjin or Botou pears. Others with modest baskets of fruit are in business on a smaller scale. Rows of wooden beehives sometimes stand beside the orchards, their occupants vital to the pollination of the nearby trees.

From Tianjin to the town of Dezhou on the border between Hebei and Shandong the Grand Canal runs side by side with the main road and railway line. Locomotives roll southward heaving columns of waggons stacked high with timber. Small herds of sheep and goats graze beside some of the many small irrigation canals that extend towards the horizon. Since leaving Beijing the landscape has been monotonously flat and would continue to be so for another 300 kilometres.

...the beauty of the scene makes some amends for the slowness of our motions. The banks slope gently down and are planted on the top with fine large shady trees, the fields neatly divided and admirably well cultivated, the farm houses picturesque, and every three or four miles are canals of different breadths either falling into the river or branching from it into the country. ...the general appearance of the country, give[s] it some resemblance to Flanders and Holland. *(Macartney)*

W of the SUBURBS of a CHINESE CITY.

**Plate No. 3** *"A view of the suburbs of a Chinese city. The double-roofed edifice on the right-hand side, is a temple of religious worship. The small building on four poles, to be ascended by a ladder, is a look-out house, one of which is erected at almost every military post; and that with a gateway through it, serves as a repository for arms, clothes, and other military stores. The method of fishing with a net stretched out by four pieces of bamboo, and suspended by a long pole, as in the hands of the figure sitting on the bank of the river, in the fore ground, is a common practice throughout the empire."* (Staunton)

Near [Cangzhou 滄州], in this part of the journey, wheat was perceived growing, for the first time in China, by the present travellers. It was about two inches above the ground; and, tho on a dry sandy soil, where no rain had fallen for the three preceding months, it looked remarkably well.

Beside the wheat flour for making the soft bread of cakes, by means of steam... much of it is used in forming the substance called in Europe vermicelli, much relished by the Chinese. *(Staunton)*

# Shandong Province

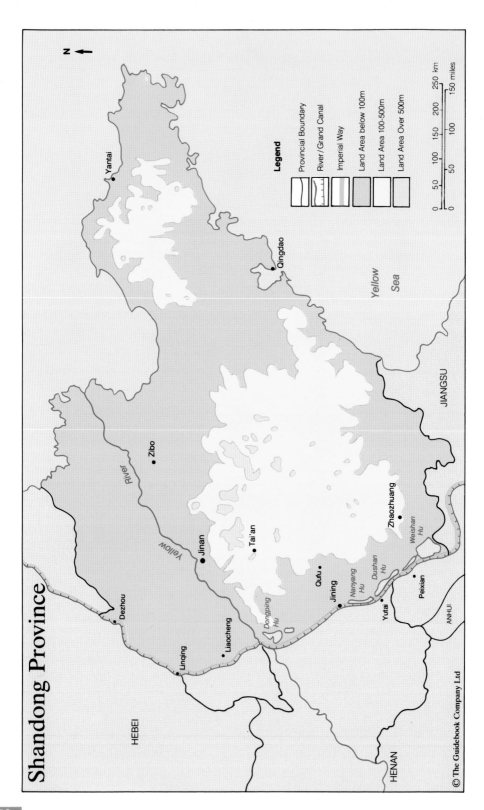

## Legend

- Provincial Boundary
- River / Grand Canal
- Imperial Way
- Land Area below 100m
- Land Area 100-500m
- Land Area Over 500m

HEBEI

HENAN

ANHUI

JIANGSU

Yellow Sea

Yantai

Qingdao

Zibo

Jinan

Tai'an

Zhaozhuang

Dezhou

Linqing

Liaocheng

Qufu

Jining

Yutai

Peixian

Dongping Hu

Nanyang Hu

Dushan Hu

Weishan Hu

Yellow River

0    50    100    150    200    250 km
0    50    100    150 miles

© The Guidebook Company Ltd

# Chapter Three

# Shandong Province
# 山東省

Shaped like one of those stone tortoises often seen in temples, Shandong Province sits on the east coast of China with its head, the Shandong Peninsula, jutting out into the Yellow Sea. Covering an area of 150,000 square kilometres, it supported a population of 24 million two centuries ago and ranked sixth among the provinces of the Middle Kingdom. Today, with almost 87 million people, it is the third most populous province behind Henan and Sichuan, averaging a density of almost 580 people per square kilometre, a figure exceeded only by Jiangsu Province.

The Yellow River surging through the heart of the province is both a blessing and a curse. Over the centuries it has behaved like a wayward hose pipe, wriggling first one side of the Shandong peninsula and then the other. Over many years of silt deposition the river bed has risen higher in many places than the surrounding land, leading to frequent disastrous floods. In the past these have covered vast areas, as much as 250,000 square kilometres, with waters reaching as far as Tianjin in the north and the Huai river to the south. Nowadays, with reinforced or reconstructed dykes and improved flood control the threat of flooding has been reduced.

At the time of Lord Macartney's journey, however, the river flowed much further to the south than today, cutting through the northern tip of Jiangsu Province (*see* map on page 80). It finally settled on its present course, reaching the sea north of the Shandong Peninsula in 1855, after a particularly devastating flood affecting four provinces: Hubei, Anhui, Jiangsu and Zhejiang. The immense amount of silt that it deposited clogged the Grand Canal and prevented navigation for more than a decade. This marked the beginning of the waterway's dramatic decline.

The Yellow River floods, devastating though they sometimes were, have resulted in a thick layer of fertile, alluvial soil covering the plains, thus allowing Shandong to produce a wide variety of food and cash crops such as wheat, maize and cotton. Although the province is one of China's major bread-baskets, it is perhaps best known for its vast areas of fruit orchards that grow delicious apples, pears, peaches and grapes.

The province was also the home of Confucius, known in Chinese as *Kong Fu Zi* 孔夫子 (551–479 BC). Deeply troubled by unstable political and social conditions he sought to implement his own ideas of moral reform. He was largely ignored during his lifetime and died in poverty. It was not until over 250 years later in the Han dynasty that his philosophy, kept alive by disciples, was finally accepted, and has remained a central influence on Chinese social and political thinking ever since.

# DEZHOU 德 州

## DEZHOU

The road to Dezhou is busy and fast. We were covering it at dusk. According to a blue sign hanging overhead there were twenty kilometres to go. I braced myself for the final stretch. Belting along beside me was a mini-tractor laden with brick-red tiles. Slap, slap, slap, slap... the hammering din from these vehicles is ear-shattering. (Forget pot-holes, stiff legs and saddle soreness; the greatest discomfort I endured on Chinese roads was noise—from these engines without silencers and the klaxon horns used by lorries). The driver sits on a saddle at the front, steering with handlebars attached to long metal poles sticking out of the engine like antennae. The man at the helm of this particular ear-shatterer saluted me as I passed. And so we started playing tag... each time he overtook he grinned and waved. I would then pick up speed and race ahead, turning back to smile. Another man was stretched out on top of the trailer. Hands behind his head he was gazing up at the sky, turning occasionally to spit. Suddenly he spotted me and sat up in surprise. He gawped for a moment and then started to laugh. Thankfully from then on he chose to deliver his saliva to the opposite side of the trailer. The game continued apace and helped me burn through the remaining kilometres, but a warm feeling at the top of my right knee-cap crescendoed with a buzz and a twang. Time I realized to stop showing off. And so, like a seagull coasting behind a ferry, I slipstreamed the tractor for the last five kilometres into town.

It was pitch dark by the time we reached Dezhou. Inadvertently we strayed off the main road and found ourselves passing down chaotic side streets: there were no lights, just pot holes and billowing clouds of heavy dust. We had passed caravans of mule-carts transporting wheat straw on the way in, and this was where they were heading. Whirling clouds of gritty clinging dust engulfed me. I screwed my face tight and tried not to breathe. Figures were darting around, heads bowed, picked out by the headlights of an oncoming vehicle whose beams sliced cheesecake wedges out of the ochre dust world. Never had I breathed such dust. It sat an inch deep on my face and bike bags and left my hair thick and sticky.

Finally passing out of the subterranean zone we moved on to tarmac roads peopled by families, three to a bike. One such assembly escorted us to the 'Electricity Guest-house'. This turned out not to be a neon palace but a standard hotel full of Chinese businessmen. The lobby of the main building was a brown marble-and-mirrors affair, with clocks displaying times in Moscaw, okyo and Weisingdon (sic). Across the courtyard was a cheap practical guest-house and we crossed to this unvarnished alternative.

The manager immediately took us under his wing. He loved our bikes. As soon as Kevin had unstrapped his bags, the twenty-one-speed mountain bike with front-wheel suspension was wheeled out into the courtyard for a spin. After a few hazardous attempts to hoist himself up onto the saddle the manager returned rather shamefacedly. Kevin obligingly lowered the seat and he set off again, this time with greater success, and managed to circle the courtyard several times, to the admiring coos of his employees. For this we were excused from paying a deposit. We were friends. It's never a bad thing to have the manager on your side given the arbitrary room rate system.

'You must eat,' he yelled, patting the bike and grinning from ear to ear. He ran the restaurant next door, a large high-ceilinged place, somewhat grander than our normal haunt. It was late and the staff were clearing up but he chivvied them into high activity on our account. The local speciality was flattened chicken known as *baji*. I had heard about it on the road: 'Oh you're going to Dezhou: you'll have to eat *baji*.' But, not for the first time, this was a delicacy that disappointed: once on a plate it revealed itself to be a brown greasy mass, all fat and skin. Appreciation clearly required a more seasoned palate than mine.

The guest-house's communal showers were timetabled: men between seven and ten, women when the men were done. Not so convenient for the women, but there were fewer of us. Still caked in dust I waited for an exasperatingly long time. At five minutes to ten a white-vested man in shorts strolled in to the shower room and set about his ablutions. Sulking, I waited some more, sitting in the corridor monitor's room. These *fuwuyuans*, as they are known, are mostly female and in their late teens. This one was dozing at her desk, head resting on some youth magazine printed on scratchy paper. In hotels like this guests are not given their own room keys, so the *fuwuyuan* has to open the door. We chatted as I waited. A sallow, unprepossessing girl, she told me she was disenchanted with her job but believed she could find something better. She realized she could take action to improve her situation—the first stirrings of self-empowerment, something many of her parents' generation have never had a chance to experience.

Lo Ying, my room-mate, was already in bed by the time I returned. This twenty-year-old marketing trainee from Tianjin was a curious mixture of brains, naivety and candour. She is of the first crop of the one-child policy and comes from a fairly sophisticated intellectual background, but had clearly been cosseted by doting parents. A recent graduate from university in Tianjin, a relatively chic progressive city, she was in her first job promoting 'Tasty Crunchy Instant Noodles' amongst the Dezhou hordes.

A twenty-four-hour building site was operating outside our window and our room was illuminated by floodlights aimed at the construction. Concrete mixers churned all night and cranes dangling huge metal girders swung through the bright night sky. It was a night of little sleep.

Like many Chinese, Lo Ying had an irrational fear of people who live beyond the confines of her own world. She worried about the 'bad people' out there who, she was convinced, were determined on giving us a bad time. 'They will cheat you, it's dangerous, there are many mean people,' she warned again and again. The Chinese tend to be protective over visitors and believe their country is a perilous place for the uninitiated. Unfortunately what she experienced of our luck only reinforced her opinion. When Kevin arrived the next morning bearing fruit and bread she asked him how much he had paid. 'This is much too much, they have cheated you, they are so impolite,' she said, apologetically. She was convinced that as we knew no better the bad people out there would always rip us off.

We spent the morning in the dimly lit, five-storey Dezhou department store. Every

(Left) With little to do in his old age, this man and his friends sit every afternoon by the Yellow River—entertained by watching the ferry unloading and loading.

(Above) Friendly characters in a small village close to the Yellow River, including a mother and her daughter (below). Some of the most abiding memories of my trip along the Imperial Way are of the people I met and their generous hospitality.

high-ceilinged store the length of the country had the same layout, floor by floor, and the same utilitarian stock: sensible shoes, gloves, caps, chunky cotton vests, padded flesh-coloured nylon bras, bolts of coarse material, pens, ink, tracing paper, biscuits, sweets. No frippery, all utilitarian and practical. The top floor always contained industrial products: stiff blue workers' jackets, thick black rubber gloves, cardboard welding masks with wooden handles held in front of the face with one hand like a pierrot mask. The industrial motifs occasionally found in high fashion in the west were contained in these products for real and their androgyny was compelling. Kevin was interested in a mask to preserve his lungs, after the Dezhou baptism of dust. We found white cotton doctors' masks—padded gauze with a complicated wrap-around string to hold them in place. The woman who served us found our confusion hilarious as we tried to put them on.

Dezhou itself is a modern middle-sized city with little that is old or characterful to recommend it. Its centre-piece is an artificial lake with a pavilion on an island. A wide paving stone path leads across the water and over a hump-back bridge with steps and a smooth slope for wheeling bicycles. A huddle had collected at the start of the path beside a ten-feet-high-structure blanketed in tarpaulin. I could make out a crude bamboo frame with four pointy legs and moved across to investigate. A dozen people were scurrying around it and on the ground lay trays of plants. They told me they were building a floral ram. The frame had been assembled but its foliage coat was not yet in place and I could see through its belly. It looked like a shrunken Trojan Horse. The flower-sheep was purely for decoration they said, with no significance as a town mascot or any relevance to the Chinese calendar. This was simply civic pride meeting local creativity in an effort to make Dezhou beautiful.

That night Lo Ying announced she would like to eat with us. We wandered on to the streets and picked on a restaurant round the back of the hotel, a shabby brightly lit room with urns of locally made 'Virility Wine' on shelves behind the maitre d's counter. No doubt the liquid would have easily triumphed over virility, as alcohol often does, but I couldn't bring myself to test its powers; the exotic, extraneous flesh parts (all animal, I was assured) floating in the liquid dulled my curiosity.

Meek Lo Ying grabbed the menu. What did we want to order? Aubergines, potatoes, snow-peas. She turned on the woman in charge, who deferentially put down her knitting and picked up her pen. After each dish Lo Ying looked firm and demanded, 'How much are you going to make them pay? At the end she asked for the list, added up the total and showed it to the boss saying, 'You must charge them no more than this.' She turned to us and gave her instructions, 'Pay no more than twenty-two yuan (US$2.67). Refuse to pay more.' And with that she left saying she had no intention of eating and had come only to ensure that we were not overcharged. Our restaurateur then lapsed into what was standard procedure: serious and business-like at first, she relaxed once reassured that serving two 'Big Noses' was not a cause for alarm. She asked where we were from. We exchanged a few words then she turned to the other diners and for the next hour or so they talked of all they collectively knew about Britain and foreign places in general. Initially the conversation focused on English weather, football and language then moved on to Hong Kong, freedom of travel and the varying sizes and shapes of foreigners.

The next morning we loaded up our bikes in the hallway of the hotel. A small group gathered to watch and marvel at our eccentricity. Kevin paid our bill. Lo Ying was hovering close by. Suddenly she blanched. She was paying twenty-seven yuan for her bed in our room; I was charged forty (US$4.85). Our 'special relationship' with the manager, who had so fancied our bikes, had clearly not been special enough.

A.R.

The Grand Canal skirts the city and nowadays is little more than a sewer. An outlet gushing putrid effluent flows into a small lagoon bordered by sandbags. A fine mesh screen filters the solids which are shovelled to one side by a young man wearing waders—and a rather grim expression! Loaded into a donkey cart, this is transported to the nearby fields to be spread as manure.

Creamy white froth and coffee-coloured water flow slowly down the narrow channel. About ten metres above are a series of four concrete piers each with a rusty hopper and chute, once used for loading barges with coal, stone, sand or grain bound for Botou or Tianjin. Around 1980 the water level in the canal dropped, making it impossible to navigate barges. These piers have stood redundant ever since.

# DEZHOU TO LINQING 德州—臨清

The canal follows the course of the Wei River from Dezhou to the town of Linqing, and marks the boundary between the provinces of Hebei and Shandong. About thirty kilometres to the south-west, just beyond the small town of Gucheng 故城 , a high bank thrown up to protect the town from floods forms a levee that overlooks a wide flood plain packed with maize, sorghum, cotton and soya bean.

On each side of the canal, the country, as far as the eye can reach, is one entire flat, but smiling with fertility. *(Anderson)*

A narrow cart track leads down to the canal where an old barge is being used as a ferry. A wire hawser, pegged to the bank on each side, stretches across the canal and runs in a metal roller mounted on the bow. A couple of old planks at the water's edge serve as a flimsy loading ramp for the few bicycles, motor-bikes and barrows that are waiting to cross the canal. The ferryman stands on the deck greeting the passengers as they embark cautiously. Several such tracks cross the canal in this area and other ferries can be seen in the distance. Barges carrying freight can no longer navigate along this section of the canal. As if to emphasize the point the water lies calm, its surface ruffled only occasionally by a slight breeze.

It is a warm, still afternoon. An ox and a couple of mules stand tethered nearby ready to be coupled up to waiting carts. Their owners are transporting a load of bulging sacks, heavy with grain, from the opposite side. A few sheep and goats graze on the grassy verge by the water. Swifts dart to and fro picking off insects that fly above the ripening maize. A hazy sun brushes everything in a soft watery light, painting a peaceful and idyllic rural scene.

*One of the countless small ferries that cross the Grand Canal.*
*This one, just beyond the small town of Gucheng in north-western Shandong Province,*
*typifies many in the north, where a complete lack of canal traffic allows a wire hawser to be*
*stretched across the canal. The ferryman pulls the boat across by hand.*

People tend their small vegetable plots, collecting water from the canal in a brace of pails hanging from a yoke across their shoulders. Others use a special kind of wheelbarrow: a metal box on wheels, with a funnel fitted to the top for filling it with water. As the sun sinks lower the track zigzags through large fields of cotton, dotted with men, women and children picking the crop. At a crossroads a ring of haystacks shaped like Mongolian yurts encircle a hard-packed area of ground that had been swept clean. In the centre a group of villagers winnows a small mountain of wheat by lofting shovelfuls of the grain high above their heads; the chaff hangs momentarily in the air before drifting slowly to one side.

## LINQING 臨清

On the twenty-second of October, the yachts stopped before [Linqing], near which stood a handsome pagoda of nine stories. (*Staunton*)

The Grand Canal runs north-south along the western edge of town and marks the provincial border, where two bridges cross the canal and enter Hebei Province. Just to the north, rising from fields on the flood plain beside the river, stands the pagoda with its distinctive lampshade top, looking for all the world like Alexander's drawing. It is said to have been built in the Ming dynasty, in which case it is the very same tower that Lord Macartney and his entourage passed 200 years earlier. A track leads along the levee and from this a narrow path drops down through fields of maize and towering sorghum. In the middle of a small clearing, there it stands—a sorry tower. When seen up close, it is a disappointment. Its blue-grey brickwork is crumbling in many places with no signs of any repair work ever having been carried out. What looks to have been a door in the base has been bricked up. Graffiti is scrawled on the outside, but then it seems to have been in this state for some time...

In the hope of finding within it some inscription, that might point out its designation, we mounted with some difficulty upon the first of its nine stages or roofs (for the little door on a level with the ground was walled up with bricks) but it contained only the bare walls, not even a stair-case remained nor any possible means of ascending to the top and the lower part was choked up with rubbish. *(Barrow)*

It looks a sad sight and it is not clear why such an historical landmark should not have been restored and preserved. We were later to pass many more pagodas, almost all of which had been left to crumble, looking tired and grey; in fact many had not only grass but whole shrubs growing from their roofs, giving them the appearance of lately having had a perm.

These pagodas (or as the Chinese name them Ta) that so frequently occur in the country, seem to be intended only as embellishments to particular grounds, or objects to terminate vistas or prospects. Whatever their intention might have been, it should seem the rage of building them no longer exists, not one of a late erection having appeared on the whole country, and more than two-thirds of those we saw being in ruins. *(Barrow)*

From a distance the Linqing pagoda still maintains some of its original dignity. On the opposite bank of the canal, one can sit late on a warm autumn afternoon and watch as the tower casts reflections on the still waters; behind, while swallows wheel overhead, the sun sinks lower in the hazy evening sky. As the pagoda stands ignored, a tall, red-brick chimney near town belches thick, black smoke which spreads in the breeze and drifts across the canal: a reminder, if one should be needed, that China's attention is now focused quite clearly on its future.

Back in the Ming dynasty Linqing became an important source of bricks, the soil in the area being especially rich in clay. In particular, they were used for the building of temples, tombs and palaces during the Ming and Qing dynasties. There was a total of 384 official brick kilns at this time and their bricks, once inspected for quality, were carefully wrapped in yellow paper and brought to the wharf to be transported north on the Grand Canal. The museum in Linqing incorporates an old gate, part of the original city wall, which was built using local bricks—a distinctive blue-grey with the manufacturer's stamp still clearly visible on some of them. The Ming dynasty poet Li Dongyang (1447–1516) wrote a verse about the view of the canal from the tower above this gate.

> *The ten-li households are separated on both banks,*
> *Their buildings are as high as the clouds of the blue sky.*
> *Official and merchant boats sail past thick and fast,*
> *And the banging of drums and gongs can be heard everywhere...*

Linqing, as the poem suggests, was an important and bustling trading centre on the Grand Canal. A place where merchants were said to outnumber the local population by more than

W. Alexander del.

A VIEW near the CITY of LIN-TS

**Plate No. 4** *A view of Linqing pagoda in 1793,*
*compare this with the photograph on the following page taken in 1995.*

Banks of the GRAND CANAL.

W. Byrne sculp.

*A shepherd tends his flock on the banks of the Grand Canal opposite Linqing pagoda. Built in the Ming dynasty, this is the same structure that was passed by Lord Macartney in 1793, and sketched by William Alexander, the expedition's artist. (see Plate No. 4)*

tenfold. It was also well-known for a local delicacy called *jiu cai hua* 韭菜花 , or Chinese chives. Their small white flowers pickled in oil and peppercorns were a special favourite of the emperors, who had them shipped to Beijing on the Grand Canal.

[Linqing] is one of the larger cities, and is surpassed in commerce by very few others. Not only the merchandise of the province but a great deal from the entire kingdom is handled here. Hence there is always a multitude of transients passing through. *(Ricci)*

## LINQING MOSQUE

After checking into a hotel on our first evening in Linqing we walked through a street market eyeing up the various restaurants. People nudged each other and pointed at us as we passed saying, 'They're the two that have cycled from Beijing, that's them.' The message moved down the line like a game of Chinese whispers. The news had travelled from the hotel round town in a few short hours.

There are few visitors to this historic but faded Shandong town and so, being conspicuous, we could not escape falling into the hands of the local foreign affairs department. They, too, knew all about us before we met them. The gentlemen from Linqing's *wai ban*—Mr. Zhang and Mr. Xu—are not overstretched and were understandably eager to seize this chance of exercising their hard-learnt skills. They were in general most obliging, if a little obsessed with mindless formalities. Mr. Zhang, the senior *wai ban* representative, had a pot-belly and a round pock-marked face. His features were frozen in a state of bewildered anxiety. With perplexed perspiration on his brow he was forever digging in his pockets for a handkerchief to mop up. He wanted to show us the town and arranged a tour of the sites, even providing a complimentary minibus. Dressed in a neat grey suit (with the designer's label still attached to the left cuff) he arrived for us early one Saturday morning accompanied by his sidekick Mr. Xu, a fresh university graduate with a luminous freckled complexion. Mr. Zhang was, at seven thirty in the morning, already bewildered and anxious.

We asked to see the mosque, a Ming dynasty relic. Accessible only via a quiet factory yard, it rests among a clump of secular, commonplace brick buildings. It is an extraordinary inconsistency, all around it the buildings are shoddy and workaday; only the mosque has grandeur. This exotic temple is redolent of all that is rich of Linqing's fabulous past, a hangover from times when the town was a multicultural trading entrepot with people from different nations and religions mixing freely in the pursuit of commerce. But today it seems a pocket misplaced, entirely at odds with its present circumstances.

The mosque complex is a striking mix of traditional Chinese and Islam. The eaves of the swooping tiled roofs of the main building jut out to spike passing clouds beneath three tall spires topped by onion-shaped finials. A wide red door opens into a high hall that disappears into dark recesses. It is faded inside, and smells of damp tangy carpets. The floor is covered in rugs which, we were told, are locally made, a matter of some pride. Huge wooden pillars support the roof. How unusual in China to see such a grand empty space, without clutter. My eyes were drawn to the circular emblems which covered the walls, extracts from the Koran in a florid Arabic script. They made an interesting maze for the eye to puzzle over. But the main attraction was a series of frescoes of pomegranate and pine trees, dating back to the Ming Dynasty, said to be unique. They were faded, and in some places rather clumsily restored, but added to the mystery of the mosque.

On an average Friday, 500 people worship here and at festivals the numbers swell to 1,000. But on this day it was deserted except for two people: an imam in a white skull cap, and his pupil. The fourteen-year-old boy was being trained in the ways of Islam and lived in the mosque compound. He attended a regular school but spent all his spare time with his tutor and rarely saw his family. He took us to his room where he had been practising his Arabic; his high wooden work desk was littered with scraps of thin tracing paper. Black ink curved across the pages. Biting his lower lip he bent over the desk and drew an inscription from the Koran. He can write well, he said, but still practises for several hours every day. The room he studied in had walls of dark wood panelling covered with gaudy pictures of Mecca and a hard stone floor. He shared it with another student and they both slept in a narrow cubbyhole adjoining the study.

The imam was just twenty years old, deeply polite and gentle, and seemed wise. He had been at the mosque all his life and planned to stay. These two were as curious about us as we were about them. Though diffident, the acolyte, in his round white skull cap, could not pare his wide eyes from me. He was perplexed by our appearance in his midst—our strange colouring and height, our cameras and gadgets. What could we possibly be doing in his town, his mosque? I felt that he found this unfathomable. We had come from somewhere far removed from his world, had landed in his ring, and he could not make it out. Whenever he was not being addressed by one of us or the officials his eyes were stretched open, seemingly incredulous, and plastered on us. The imam was so polite and deferential that he asked few direct questions but the young boy gave all away with his wide insatiable eyes. And I was no less transfixed by him and his teacher.

The gentlemen of the *wai ban* were the chaperones at this curious cultural encounter. They added their own ingredient—the official, humourless, secular frost. They looked on whilst eager, 'life-combing' Westerners met gawping sheltered Chinese Muslim, but their interest was only perfunctory and they seemed oblivious to the substance of both the encounter and the place; their only concern was to ensure that we thought well of their town. They put a damper on our exchange and the imam clearly felt he was being monitored. Yet being faintly ridiculous they did at least contribute a dab of comedy—so earthly and perplexed beside the mosque's spiritual, unworldly wealth.

During the Cultural Revolution the mosque had been used as a factory. Both the *wai ban* officials and the imam were embarrassed to talk about this. The grand building survived well and was reopened in 1980. It would seem that its future is secure as long as the small band committed to maintaining it are allowed to continue their work without interruption.

After supper on our last night we returned to our hotel to find Mr. Zhang and Mr. Xu in an unoccupied room waiting to unfold an elaborate leave-taking ceremony. Sitting on a pink and red satin bedspread, adorned with love-hearts, Mr. Zhang trotted off a succession of formal farewell speeches. Solemnly he told us that he hoped we would always think favourably of Linqing, that we would tell everyone of the excellent hospitality shown to us by the people of the town, and that it had been a great pleasure showing us around. His final wish was that we would always be prosperous and would return to Linqing soon. The oration lasted some twenty minutes and stuck to the correct formula. It seemed a quietly appropriate final act to Linqing: the garish surroundings made it farcical but it was quaint and touching.

A.R.

Nowadays Linqing is a producer of cotton, wheat, paper, light machinery and tools. One of the largest cotton spinning mills in the area is a joint venture with a company from Hong Kong. Using modern machinery from Japan and England, much of the process has been automated. Although it employs some 2,000 workers, one of the first things that strikes one, apart from the cleanliness, is the lack of people; the factory floor was deserted save for a handful of men and women monitoring the machines.

A sufficient quantity of cotton is not produced in China for the consumption of the inhabitants, among the lower orders of which cotton is universally worn by both sexes. The importation of that article from Bombay is very considerable. It is sold at [Guangzhou] for dollars... and the dollars returned to the Chinese merchants for the teas, silk, and porcelain, exported from thence for Europe. (*Staunton*)

Wood is now a rare commodity in most parts of China and often has to be transported long distances, adding greatly to its cost. The timber stacked in the local rail yard, for example, arrives here by train from the Dongbei region in the far north-east of China, and is used for building. However, Linqing is surrounded by fields growing wheat and cotton and is now using the wheat straw, and even the stalk of the cotton plant, to manufacture a reasonable quality of paper. The local paper mill is a laudable example, albeit a necessary one, of adaptation to local circumstances.

# Linqing to The Yellow River  臨清 - 黃河

Up to this point the Grand Canal, for convenience, had largely followed the course of natural rivers. From Linqing it branches south from the Wei River and enters the canal constructed by Kublai Khan as a short cut to the south (*see* Chapter One).

This morning the fleet entered a very noble canal... It is a work of great labour, and prodigious expence; and its sides are faced with masonry throughout its course. *(Anderson)*

This enterprize, the greatest and most ancient of its kind, was found to extend from hence to [Hangzhou]... not only through heights and over vallies, but across rivers and lakes...

This canal has no locks, like those of Europe. The flood-gates are simple in their construction, easily managed, and kept in repair at a trifling expence. They consist merely of a few planks let down separately one upon another, by grooves cut into the sides of the two solid abutments or piers of stone that project, one from each bank, leaving a space in the middle just wide enough to admit a passage for the largest vessels employed upon the canal. *(Staunton)*

The flood or sluice-gates of the canal enabled the quantity of water within the canal itself to be regulated. By effectively reducing the width at certain stages they allowed the water to back up behind them thereby maintaining sufficient depth, provided there was an adequate water supply. Rivers crossed the canal flowing from west to east. Their waters would be allowed to flow into the canal to maintain the necessary level, and sluices on the opposite banks would then drain surplus water back into the rivers flowing away to the east. If the level in the canal became too high, for example at times of flood, then other sluices would also act as a safety valve and allow water to escape into channels irrigating the surrounding farm land. At the onset of the dry winter and spring seasons the water level in the rivers supplying the canal began to drop and all but the smallest boats on the waterway were brought to a standstill. As a means of alleviating this situation some emperors forbade irrigation on the upper reaches of northern rivers during the spring. As water was funnelled through these sluice-gates it naturally accelerated, therefore causing potential problems for the barge crews.

Some skill is required to be exerted, in order to direct the barges through them without accident. For this purpose an immense oar projects from the bow of the vessel, by which one of the crew conducts her with the greatest nicety. *(Staunton)*

At times it happens that the rush of water is so high and so strong, at the exit from one lock or at the entrance to another, that the boats are capsized and the whole crew is drowned. *(Ricci)*

We passed through at least thirty of these locks in the course of this day's voyage...*(Anderson)*

W.ᵉ Alexander del.ᵗ

CHINESE BARGES of the EMBASSY

London, Pu

**Plate No. 5** *"The flood-gates... consist merely of a few planks let down separately one upon another, by grooves cut into the sides of the two solid piers of stone that project, one from each bank, leaving a space in the middle just wide enough to admit a passage*

*35*

*B.T. Pouncy sculp.*

*rough a Sluice on the GRAND CANAL.*

*by G. Nicol.*

*for the largest vessels employed upon the canal. Men are stationed on each pier with fenders,
made of skins stuffed with hair,
to prevent the effect of the vessels striking immediately against the stone."* (Staunton)

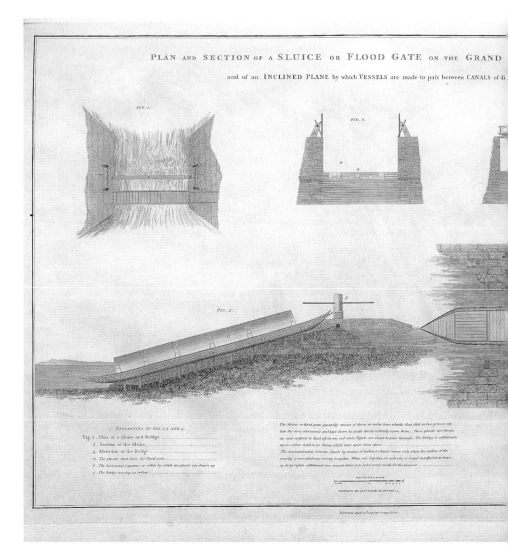

PLAN AND SECTION OF A SLUICE OR FLOOD GATE ON THE GRAND

and of an INCLINED PLANE by which VESSELS are made to pass between CANALS of di

The flood-gates are only opened at certain stated hours, when all the vessels collected near them in the interval, pass through them on paying a small toll, appropriated to the purposes of keeping in repair the flood-gates and banks of the canal. The loss of water occasioned by the opening of the flood-gates is not very considerable, the fall at each seldom being many inches; and which is soon supplied by streams conducted into the canal from the adjacent country on both sides. *(Staunton)*

Towards the end of the eighteenth century, at the time of Macartney's journey, the canal systems of Europe were perhaps at their height. Here Staunton draws a comparison.

This great work differs much from the canals of Europe, which are generally protracted in straight lines within narrow bounds, and without a current; whereas that of China is winding often in its course, of unequal and sometimes considerable width, and its waters are seldom stagnant. *(Staunton)*

Until the 1960s the Grand Canal was in use along its full length from Beijing to Hangzhou,

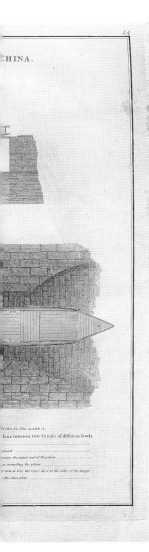

**Plate No. 6** *"In passing from an upper to a lower canal, the vessel lifted over the cross beam slides down by its own gravity; and to prevent the water from flushing over the decks, or her plunging into the canal below, a railing is fixed at the head of the vessel about to be launched, before which is placed strong matting. To draw up a large vessel... along the glacis into the upper canal, requires sometimes the assistance of near a hundred men, whose strength is applied by the means of bars fixed in one or more capstans. Round the capstans is a rope [which] is passed round the vessel's stern, which is thus conveyed into the upper canal with less delay than can be done by locks."* (Staunton)

carrying both passengers and freight. Since that time this northern section has become largely silted up. The problems of water supply to this, the highest point on the canal are, as we shall see later, enormous.

There are no plans to reopen the canal for its original purpose. Instead, it is used today as a means of flood prevention—as a conduit to channel flood waters that periodically surge down the major rivers following heavy rains in provinces further to the west. As evidence of this, just outside Linqing, a gang of labourers work against the clock at a canal crossroads. They are attempting to complete preparations for anticipated flood waters from the Yellow River 100 kilometres further to the south. A huge black rubber boom, like a section of a giant inner tube, extends across the dry muddy bottom of the canal that heads back towards the town. It is connected to a pumping station that will 'inflate' it with water—an eight-hour process—to form a barrage and prevent the water from inundating the recently revetted canal. The foreman says they have three days in which to complete the work before the waters are due. Looking south along what is the continuation of the Grand Canal, a narrow strip of shallow water extends in a straight line as far as the eye can see. Under a clear blue sky, in the still heat of the mid-day sun, with a few trees overhanging its gently sloping grass banks, it presents an innocuous scene. It is hard to imagine the flood waters surging up this channel.

## QING DYNASTY POSTAL SYSTEM

It was in the area of Linqing that Anderson wrote in his journal:

We this day saw the Chinese post pass along the road, on the side of the canal, with great expedition. The letters and packets are carried in a large square bamboo basket... it is locked, and the key is given to the custody of one of the attendant soldiers, whose office it is to deliver it to the post-master: The box is fastened on the courier's shoulders with straps, and is decorated at the bottom with a number of small bells, which being shaken by the motion of the horse, making a loud gingling noise, that announces the approach of the post. The post-man is escorted by five light-horsemen to guard him from robbery or interruption. The swiftest horses are also employed... which are renewed at every stage; so that the posts of China may vie in expedition with the English mail. *(Anderson)*

The official postal service of the Qing dynasty, seen here by Anderson, had a history of more than 2,000 years, stretching back to the Spring and Autumn period (770–476 BC) of the Zhou dynasty, by which time an efficient system was already in place. Under the Han dynasty there are references to both ordinary and express despatches, the latter carried on horseback. The Tang dynasty saw the system, called *yi zhan* 驛站 , develop still further with 1,639 postal stations, including 1,297 on land used by mounted couriers, and 260 on waterways. These stations were run by postmasters, *yi zhang* 驛長 , with postmen, *yi fu* 驛夫 , working under them.

In the Song dynasty an express system was developed to deliver urgent communications between feudal officials. Riders on horseback would carry the messages by relay, running day and night. The horse had a bell hung around its neck and pedestrians and other road users had to make way when they heard it approaching.

During the Yuan dynasty, under the Manchus, the service was called *zhan chi* 站赤 . Friar Odoric describes a series of hostelries situated in all towns and cities which he calls *yam* in which, 'everything necessary for the comfort of the traveller is provided.' Even, so he writes, 'two meals without payment'.

And when any matter of news arises in the empire messengers start incontinently at a great pace on horseback for the court... And when they come near those hostels or stations, they blow a horn, whereupon mine host of the hostel straightway maketh another messenger get ready; and to him the rider who hath come posting up delivereth the letter, whilst he himself tarrieth for refreshment. *(Odoric)*

Riders would use a system of tallies or tags, called *you fu* 郵符 , which entitled them to certain horses or other conveyances and privileges on their journey. The relay continued from post house to post house across the length and breadth of the country until it reached the capital.

And in this manner the emperor receiveth in the course of one natural day the news of matters from a distance of thirty days' journey. *(Odoric)*

Between the post houses, situated at shorter intervals, were a series of beacon towers, known as *feng* 烽 or *sui* 燧 , and, more importantly, a system of express stations called *ji di pu* 急遞舖 . Manned by four messengers and a postmaster, these were, according to Odoric, 'at about three-mile intervals'. Each messenger, he continues, 'was provided with a portfolio, bells, a spear with fringes, three feet of oiled silk, a cover in soft silk for the post parcels, a cap and an overcoat for the rain, a secret red stick and a return ticket'.

... appointed runners abide continually in certain station-houses... and these have a girdle with a number of bells attached to it. ... when a runner approaches one of those houses he

A QUAN or MANDARIN *bearing a* LETTER *from the* EMPEROR *of* CHINA.

**Plate No. 7** *A mandarin carries a letter from the emperor Qianlong along the Imperial Way, the yellow silk decorating the scroll indicating that it is a communication from the throne. Other road users have to dismount and, together with pedestrians, kowtow as the letter passes by.*

causes those bells of his to jingle very loudly; on which the other runner in waiting at the station getteth ready in haste, and taking the letter hastens on to another station as fast as he can. And so it goes from runner to runner until it reaches the great Khan himself. *(Odoric)*

> *At dusk the rustling red leaves give sigh after sigh*
> *While at the Post House I drink my gourdful of wine.*
> *Evening clouds float back to Western Mountains high;*
> *Across the Middle Ridges sails a rain so fine.*
>
> *I see the brilliant trees colour the city wall;*
> *I hear the River[1] rumbling to the distant sea.*
> *Tomorrow I'll reach the Imperial Capital;*
> *Yet fisherman or woodsman I still dream to be.*
> By Tang dynasty poet Xu Hun 許渾 . Inscribed on the post house at Tong Pass
> (one of the Great Wall passes in Shaanxi Province) on an autumn trip to the capital.

The Yuan dynasty network of postal stations stretched from the central station in Beijing throughout the empire along four main routes or post roads called *yi dao* 驛道 . The central route ran from Beijing through Henan and from there to either Hubei,

---

[1] Yellow River

Hunan and Guangxi, or to Guizhou and Yunnan. The western route went through Shanxi and Shaanxi and from there to Gansu and Xinjiang in the far north-west, or into Sichuan and Tibet. Another ran from Beijing to Jilin and Heilongjiang forming the north-eastern route. And finally, there was the route to the south and south-east, which extended through Shandong to either Anhui, Jiangxi and Guangdong, or to Jiangsu, Zhejiang and Fujian.

A rider on horseback carrying an express document was expected to travel at a rate of 300 *li* per day. (a *li* 里 is an ancient Chinese measurement usually equivalent to half a kilometre; 300 li would be about 150 kilometres. To put these distances covered by the post riders into a modern-day perspective, on good roads riding fully laden bicycles, our record for a day's ride was just over 160 kilometres which we covered in a little under eight hours). By 1742 it is recorded that the maximum speed had been raised as high as 600 *li* per day, although this was later reduced and was resorted to only in special cases. This speed may well have been found impossible in certain mountainous areas, for example in Jiangxi and Guangdong provinces where sometimes horses could not be used. However, by 1842 a speed of 800 *li* was occasionally being achieved.

From historical records it can be seen that postmen travelling on foot could regularly achieve distances of 100 *li* during a twelve-hour day, while on horseback riders could cover at least twice that. Express documents were required to travel both day and night and could therefore easily sustain a pace of 300 *li* or more. In the mid-19th century documents were regularly being transmitted between Beijing and Nanjing in five days (about 440 *li* per day) and between Beijing and Guangzhou in fifteen days. The difficult terrain in the south of the country clearly slowed things down.

When a document was despatched, its expected date of arrival, based on the speed set out in the regulations, was written on the outside. On arrival at its destination this date was compared with the actual date of receipt. If the document was late then the reason for the delay was discovered and the officials concerned were fined one year's salary.

Towards the end of the Qing dynasty this system gradually gave way to the modern postal system of today.

K.B.

The countryside continues much the same. There is not a hill to be seen in any direction. About twenty-eight degrees Celsius during the hottest part of the day and very dry, the weather is ideal for the harvest that is now in full swing. Everywhere either maize is being cut or cotton picked. And wherever there is space on the ground, including in many cases the road itself, the crop is spread out to dry. Small rocks or logs are spaced out around the area of grain or cotton to prevent vehicles running over it, but pose a serious hazard to the unsuspecting cyclist.

The Yellow River is near. Apple orchards cover extensive areas on either side of the road. Some of the trees are so heavy with fruit that their boughs have been propped up with poles. Along the road are numerous substantial villages, stretching back amongst an impressive array of leafy trees. The houses, nearly all brick-built, have flat roofs with just a slight curve— enough to allow rain water to run off, but flat enough for maize cobs to be laid out to dry.

From a distance this gives the appearance of bright golden-tiled roofs like those of the imperial palaces in Beijing. Each village is seemingly self-sufficient with its own timber yard, grain mill and coal press, the latter turning out the small cylindrical blocks of compressed coal powder used in most homes for cooking.

More and more fields are planted with soya bean—a low, somewhat straggly plant. The leaves and pods are allowed to yellow in the field before they are harvested and spread out over the roads to dry. Vehicles passing over them crush the pods, releasing the hard beans inside. The farmers later simply fork away the plants, which are stored for silage, leaving behind the creamy-white soya beans which are swept up and winnowed.

# THE YELLOW RIVER 黃河

*Don't you see the Yellow River's waters descend from Heaven,*
*Rushing seaward, never to return?*
Extract from a poem by Tang dynasty poet Li Bai 李白 , (701–762).

About a kilometre before the Yellow River, the road rejoins the Grand Canal—now a very different sight. Milk chocolate-coloured water, obviously heavy with silt, churns along very fast and very high between stone embankments. It swirls violently round the concrete pillars of a bridge, pushing up great waves and all but submerging them, the water only a couple of feet below the level of the road.

At the junction with the river a series of sluice gates, about 200 metres long, has been thrown across the canal. These are only partially open, the water forcing itself through the narrow openings, surging and eddying with frightening force. One can easily imagine the destruction that the unchecked flood waters of this river can wreak.

... travelling by fresh water channels... I came to [the Yellow River]. This river passeth through the very midst of [China], and doth great damage to that country when it breaks its banks. *(Odoric)*

Its source is beyond the border of the kingdom, to the west, on the mountain called Kunlun, which they say is the same mountain, or at least is near the mountain, from which the Ganges takes its rise... This Yellow River has no respect at all for Chinese law and order. It comes from a barbarous region and... it frequently ravages whole districts of the realm when it fills up with sand and changes its course at will. There are certain magistrates who try to control it with religious rites, offered to the river, or to its spirits. *(Ricci)*

This river runs through the heart of China, for a distance of six months' journey... It is bordered throughout with villages, cultivated plains, orchards, and markets, just like the Nile in Egypt; but this country is still more flourishing, and there are on the banks a great number of hydraulic wheels. *(Batuta)*

Members of the Macartney expedition describe their approach to the Yellow River. It must be remembered, however, that in their time the river crossed the Grand Canal some 380 kilometres to the south-east. The large city referred to by Barrow is Huaiyin 淮陰 in Jiangsu Province, which we will reach later in our journey.

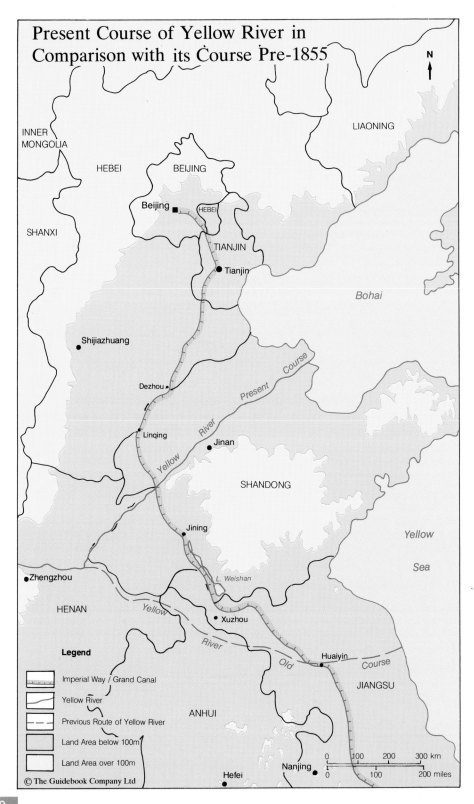

# Present Course of Yellow River in Comparison with its Course Pre-1855

N

INNER MONGOLIA

LIAONING

HEBEI

BEIJING

Beijing ■

HEBEI

SHANXI

TIANJIN

Tianjin ●

Bohai

Shijiazhuang ●

Dezhou

Present Course

Linqing ●

Yellow River

Jinan ●

SHANDONG

Yellow

Jining ●

Sea

● Zhengzhou

L. Weishan

HENAN

Yellow

Xuzhou ●

River

Old

Huaiyin ●

Course

JIANGSU

**Legend**

Imperial Way / Grand Canal

Yellow River

Previous Route of Yellow River

Land Area below 100m

Land Area over 100m

ANHUI

© The Guidebook Company Ltd

0     100     200     300 km

0           100        200 miles

Hefei ●

Nanjing ●

The canal at this place is, perhaps, the grandest inland navigation in the whole world, being nearly a thousand feet in width and bordered on each side by stone quays, built with [massive] blocks of grey marble mixed with others of granite; and this immense aqueduct, although forced up several feet above the surface of the country by embankments thrown up by the labour of man, flowed with a current of three miles an hour towards the Yellow River, to which we perceived we were fast approaching, by the bustle and activity both on shore and on the numberless canals that branched out in every direction from the main trunk; on whole banks, for several miles on either side, one continued town extended to the point of junction with this large river, celebrated in every period of the Chinese history. *(Barrow)*

... a continued chain of towns and handsome villages, an immense number of vessels of all kinds, and a most thronged population, announced the approach of the Yellow river... Several of the largest barges were waiting in this neighbourhood till the ensuing season, to convey the Imperial revenues to the capital. *(Staunton)*

Here Staunton refers to the barges which carried the grain tax to Beijing. It was now the beginning of November and already the water level in the canal to the north had dropped, making it impossible for these large barges to pass. At the time of the Qing dynasty there were said to be just over 10,400 of these grain ships operating on the canal. Their cargo however, had to be transferred to smaller barges when sailing through shallower sections or negotiating locks.

Macartney's party had to hurry their journey for the same reason. Many of the rivers and canals further north became frozen over in the winter effectively halting all traffic until the spring thaw.

The canal appeared now to have assumed the form of a considerable river, and brought us to a very large city... it is washed by large canals, and, on the south side of it, there is an extensive bay which communicates with the Yellow river. This bay is of great extent, and would contain the proudest fleets of Europe... *(Anderson)*

The width of the river at this place was full three quarters of a mile; and the stream, where strongest, ran with the rapidity of seven or eight miles an hour; and the water was thick and muddy as if the heaviest torrents of rain had just descended, whereas, in fact, there had not fallen a shower for many months. *(Barrow)*

The Yellow River is certainly an impressive sight. The water rips past, churning violently, heavily laden with silt and with the consistency of soup. It carries with it thirty-four times more sediment than the River Nile—more than any other river on earth. The members of the Macartney embassy were understandably awed by what they saw. Particularly Mr. Barrow, who went to town with his mathematics. Taking a conservative estimate of the average width, depth and velocity of the river, he calculated:

...that in every hour, there is discharged from that river into the Yellow sea, a volume of water equal to 418,176,000 solid feet, or 2,563,000,000 gallons of water, or eleven hundred times as much as appears to be furnished by the Ganges. *(Barrow)*

Observing the amount of sediment that settled in water samples, he further determined the amount of mud that must be suspended in the river:

...a quantity equal to 3,420,000,000 solid inches, or 2,000,000 of solid feet of earth is wafted to the sea in every hour; or 48,000,000 every day, or 17,520,000,000 in a year. *(Barrow)*

With the bit now firmly between his teeth, there was no stopping him. He continued to surmise that given these figures and the depth of the Yellow Sea (they had sailed through it on their way to Beijing, taking meticulous soundings as they went), it would take seventy days to accumulate enough earth to deposit an island of one square mile. Multiplying this by the estimated surface area of the Yellow Sea he calculated that to fill it in would take 8,750,000 days, or 24,000 years!

—····•◉•···—

A group of old men gather on an embankment, overlooking a bend in the great river. They have come to watch the loading and unloading of the ferry that is approaching gingerly against the boiling current, to dock below. Some of them have brought small folding chairs to sit on. It was to be a process that took a couple of hours.

The slip road down to the ferry is an unmade road, rutted and thick with dust. There is no proper loading ramp to the ferry. Instead a makeshift affair of lengths of wood and pieces of steel plate are thrown down in a haphazard way. The loading ramps on either side are often washed away by floods; these clearly had been recently rebuilt. It takes a while for the load of mainly small tractors and trailers to disembark. Sometimes as many as six of these tractors are lashed together in a convoy, their engines spluttering in chorus, as they pull the heavy trailers up the slope. Several men perch precariously on the axles, or anywhere else they can find a foothold, and bounce up and down to add weight as the tiny wheels fight for grip, spinning and digging themselves deeper and deeper in the dust. Once the offloading is complete then the whole process has to be repeated in reverse, as trailers piled high with teetering loads of bricks are hauled on board.

*(Opposite page) Millet ready for harvesting. Shandong is one of China's most important grain producers with large crops of wheat, maize (left), rice, soybeans, sorghum and millet. Several crops now widely grow in China were originally introduced from overseas, mainly around the sixteenth century.*

Once the comedy of the loading has been completed the situation becomes very serious. The coxswain's face sets with a look of intense concentration, muscles taut, as he wrestles with the wheel while stretching to make frequent adjustments to the throttle levers of the two engines. At one point, approaching the opposite bank, he holds the ferry steady, side on against the vicious current, lining it up with the ramp. Of course, engines have not always been available to help steer across this unforgiving river.

... there were a variety of currents running with great violence, and in opposite directions... and the skill of navigating [the barge] consists in being able to get into that individual current which runs towards the place of the vessel's particular destination. *(Anderson)*

## YELLOW RIVER VILLAGE

*When crops are worked at noon,*
*It is sweat that moistens the soil.*
*Who stops to think, before a bowl of food,*
*That every grain comes only through long toil?*
By Tang dynasty poet Li Shen 李紳 (772–846).

Mrs. Yang ushered us into her new home and switched on the television. She pulled out two stools and invited us to sit and gawp at the huge blaring box, putting the volume up high. For a few minutes we hovered in a semi-circle around the overly large screen, in reverential silence, as if it were some kind of altar. After a decent pause I intimated that we would rather drink our tea outside in the sunny courtyard and our hostess smilingly acquiesced.

We were in a compact village on the banks of the Yellow River. The settlement snakes around several small hills—the first rising ground we had come across in a month along our southward route from Beijing. The hills rise out of a fertile plain. The area often floods and the slopes offer some kind of protection to local farmers: a perfect place to build homes. The fields are thick with ripening crops. At this time, September, they are a ferment of activity, dotted with people working all hours to bring in the harvest.

Narrow cobbled pathways lead up between the houses. The buildings have high walls and small windows—on account of the floods—and are made of grey stone blocks, not unlike a fortified medieval European village. But the similarity stops with the gently rounded roofs. At this time of year they are a gleaming yellow, scattered with corn cobs lying out in the sunshine to dry. Chickens and pigs roam the streets at will, together with a few children and packs of dogs, while pockets of people sit under the dark leafy trees chatting. Several old ladies dressed in pale grey hobble up the hill, their feet maimed from being bound seventy years ago. Now balancing on sticks they wobble and totter but manage somehow to move quite rapidly, seemingly defying natural laws of physics which would suggest they must tumble.

We happened upon Mrs. Yang and her husband one lunch-time. The large courtyard in front of their house was full of the spoils of harvest. They had both been in the fields cutting maize and Mr. Yang was just chopping wood, in warm sunshine, preparing to light a stove to boil water for tea; he invited us in. He had big lips and a round stomach, noticeable only because the shirt he was wearing was unbuttoned to his navel revealing a white cotton vest that accentuated the bulge. His hair seemed to be running in circles chasing its tail round his scalp. His grey trousers were rolled up above his ankles. Mrs. Yang, petite and quietly spoken, was wearing a floral print shirt and black nylon trousers, and of course the ubiquitous short black gum-boots favoured by Chinese farmers. She had white straight teeth and a nose that wrinkled when she smiled, and she smiled often. Her hair was straight and in a bob, framing her lovely warm face.

The television that gave us an audience was in the new home they had just finished building. The high-ceilinged rooms were sparsely furnished, the floors bare concrete, the walls freshly painted a bright light blue and covered with calendar pictures of fluffy white dogs. Next door, fronting on to the same courtyard, was the old house they had inherited from Mr. Yang's family. They have built their new home not because they did not want to share with Mr. and Mrs. Yang senior (who are no longer of this world), but to symbolize their assumption of the family property. This was a rite of passage, and a mark of their prosperity. Even so, at the moment all their living is done in the old building, the new home housing only the television.

Our arrival provoked much neighbourly interest. The courtyard was soon teeming with people; crowds of children were racing around hither and thither and laughing. In a village such as this everyone marches freely in and out of everyone else's property; there is no sense of jealously guarding what is private and neighbours share their lives with each other.

Lunch took two hours to prepare. I sat on a low wooden stool and watched the process through. The kitchen was small and dark, lit only by a narrow window above my head. Against one wall was the cooking range—a wooden board with two large holes in which sat woks. The fire was inside the 'sideboard', at one end of which was a narrow opening and a handle. Mrs. Yang squatted down beside it and using a long barbecue fork she fed the flames with straw; with the other hand she pumped the handle which fanned air over the embers. Every few minutes she stopped to tend the fire, dropping what she was doing elsewhere. Organizing the heat necessary to cook lunch everyday consumed a great deal of time and effort: how much easier to turn a knob, light a match and stand back for a flame of gas.

All her utensils were simple and bare, mostly hewn from local materials. A short plank of rough wood supported on bricks served as a shelf on which all chopping and preparing was done. A grainy rolling pin sat on pegs knocked into the wall above that. Vegetables lay on bare earth underneath the shelf. Flour was stored in a dried gourd, cut in half, which rested on the plank shelf.

Instant noodles take just a few minutes to fix; the ones we had for lunch that day took an hour. Flour and water was mixed and kneaded, round and round, in a large bowl. Mrs. Yang then sprinkled flour, from the gourd, over the plank and rolled out the dough, over and over, for twenty minutes or more. Finally she judged the dough to be fine enough and it was folded layer upon layer like a concertina and sliced. The chopped noodles were put into a shallow bamboo basket. She then returned to the plank to crunch the sharp blade of a large knife through crisp vegetables, the blade

Sporting a perfect hexagonal hat, as worn by many farmers in Shandong,
an old man is busy threshing his crop of soya beans. Allowed to dry in the fields after ripening,
the plants are then spread across a nearby road where passing vehicles
crush the pods to release the hard, creamy-white beans.  During the peak harvest month of
September, the country roads are covered with all manner of crops—
drying in the sun, or being threshed or winnowed. The air is filled with choking dust.

thumping down on to hard wood. Potatoes, chillies, leeks, carrots. These were fried in one wok, along with some beancurd. In the other wok space a cauldron of water was steaming a dozen *mantou*—soft bread rolls—lying on a bamboo mat. Every few minutes she had to move to the fire to feed the flames and pump the bellows. Soft dry smoke mixed with the sizzling smell of onions and garlic, the kitchen was full of the sounds and smells of soon-to-be-satisfied hunger. As she stirred the frying vegetables she would dip her ladle into spice jars set out beside the wok— salt, chilli, garlic, ochre and scarlet powders—scraping her spatula against the side of the wok as she did so. Once the vegetables were ready, boiling water was brought in from the stove outside and the noodles were thrown into the pot. Finally, wreathed in clouds of steam, Mrs. Yang drained the noodles with a spoon-like sieve and, dividing them between five bowls, she motioned for me to follow her next door.

We ate in the living room of the old house. Black and white photos of earlier generations hung on one wall; on another clung pictures of Mao and Zhou En Lai. But larger than these and far more garish were posters of blonde, blue-eyed overly-bonny babies, and beside these the ubiquitous shots of scantily clad Chinese women leaning provocatively on motor-bikes. It was a peculiar mix of taste, and a peculiar mix of cultural influences.

The Yang's fifteen-year-old son joined us for lunch, home from school for the meal. He did not register too much surprise at finding two foreigners feeding their faces at his mother's table, but no doubt would have won incredulous stares from his classmates when he recounted his tale later that afternoon. There were two other children, the eldest a mechanic working for an uncle in Jining, and a daughter who was a factory worker in a small town close by. The youngest son said he was not yet certain what he would do, but I could sense parental hope that he would stay in the village, work in the fields, and occupy the family home. I feel sure that if he does so he will imprint his seal of ownership by fitting the kitchen with modern appliances and a gas ring. There was great charm in the preparation of our meal: we ate only local produce and nothing came out of a packet; admittedly the flour had already been ground in the village mill but every other stage of the process happened before my eyes. This is to me incredibly special, yet so labour-intensive and time-consuming that under these circumstances the work is nothing but a burden, especially given the other essential tasks like harvesting that swallow time. The arrival of that aspect of 'Progress' which releases people, especially women, from such daily toil can not come too soon.

Our time with this family was unusual. The Yangs did not bombard us with questions, were not pushy; they went out of their way to show us hospitality, but discreetly. Normally in such encounters there is a frisson of exchange, verging on confrontation, both sides greedy for something. The Yangs were totally undemanding; they simply fed us, with great charm, and neither required nor requested. Their hospitality was great and by opening their unadorned doors in such a candid way offered us an unprecedented close-up of what life in rural China is all about.

A.R.

# HIGHEST POINT OF GRAND CANAL

... the yachts arrived at the highest part of the canal, being about two-fifths of its entire length. Here the river, the largest by which the canal is fed, falls into it with a rapid stream in a line which is perpendicular to the course of the canal. A strong bulwark of stone supports the opposite western bank; and the waters striking with force against it, part of them follow the northern, and part the southern course of the canal. *(Staunton)*

It was around this area that Macartney's party passed the highest point on the Grand Canal. The river Staunton writes of does not exist today and I believe that the Yellow River, when it re-routed itself further north, took over its course. The bed of the Yellow River has been raised by years of silt deposition sometimes leaving it higher than the adjacent land. It is still prone to periodic flooding. Water now flows north and south away from the Yellow River into the Grand Canal.

During the Ming dynasty, the emperor Yongle ordered his Minister of Works, Song Li 宋禮, to solve the navigation problems on the Grand Canal, in particular those in Shandong Province. Although Song Li drafted some 160,000 labourers to dredge the waterways and to rebuild the embankments, he had no idea how to overcome the problems of water supply. It was the brilliant water engineer, Bai Ying 白英, a native of Shandong Province, who provided the answer. His scheme involved building a dam of approximately two-and-a-half kilometres across the river. From here a feeder canal diverted water into the canal at its highest point. A bifurcation gate was built to divide the water, sixty per cent to the north towards Linqing, and forty per cent to the south towards Jining. This provided an adequate water supply to enable the largest barges to pass and ensure the smooth passage of the grain supply to Beijing to the north. It was Bai Ying who also suggested the construction of a system of locks and sluices to overcome the problems caused by the relatively steep gradient along this section of the canal. The ingenuity of this scheme did not escape the inquisitive eye of Sir George Staunton.

It is, no doubt, from this elevated surface, that the author of this canal saw, with the comprehensive eye of genius, the possibility of forming this important communication between the different parts of the Chinese empire, by measuring from thence the inclination of the ground to the north and south, and uniting the devious streams which descended from the heights of every side, into one great and useful channel... *(Staunton)*

# JINING 濟寧

Saturday 26th October 1793

The air was this morning extremely cold; the thermometer having sunk so low as forty degrees [Fahrenheit]... At seven o'clock we passed a lock, whose current bore us into the city of [Jining], which, from the great number of junks laying there, must be a place of immense trade. Indeed, the water was so entirely covered with them, that our fleet was obliged to come to anchor, in order to give time for a passage to be made between them. The canal took a winding course through this place, which is elevated above it, and its banks fall in beautiful slopes to the water. *(Anderson)*

*This restaurant, typical of many rural roadside establishments,
serves 'fast food' such as noodles or, as here, bao-zi. The restaurant owner and his son
are stuffing dumplings with a vegetarian mixture.
Once the bamboo tray is full it is placed at the bottom of a stack
of similar trays steaming on a wok of boiling water.*

23rd September 1995

It is six o'clock and the eastern sky is brightening as the day dawns clear and bright. Ming dynasty buildings cluster beside the canal throwing reflections across the still water. Grey-tiled roofs sweep above white-washed walls. Nearby in a mosque, richly decorated with glazed tiles of gold and green, a small group of Muslims kneel in silent prayer.

The ghostly hoot of a steam engine echoes through the chilly morning air. A bus clatters past with a blast of its horn as it passes cyclists pedalling their way to work, reminding one that this is a contemporary scene.

The Ming dynasty buildings are a reconstruction—an indoor market area of shops and restaurants. They stand beside the original canal as it loops through the city centre. The sides of the canal have been recently faced with stone and lined by narrow grass banks. Young willow trees droop their branches over flower beds. A marble bridge arches across the canal to a promenade.

Across the road, on the north bank of the canal, stands Tai Bai Lou 太白樓 . Originally built in 1391, this two-storey colonnaded pavilion with its green-tiled roof stands to commemorate the Tang dynasty poet Li Bai , also known as Li Po, perhaps the most famous of all the classical Chinese poets. He lived in Jining for fifteen years, during which he resided on the second floor of a wine shop whose products he made ample use of. It was in the spring of AD 747, while he was travelling to what is now Nanjing in Jiangsu Province, that he composed a touching poem dedicated to his two children whom he had left behind in Jining. His wife had previously passed away. It is a long poem but the first few lines read thus:

> Here mulberry leaves grow green,
> The silkworm is ready to shed its skin.
> I left my family in the east of Shandong,
> Who sows our fields there on the dark side of Mt. Gui?
> Spring chores too long unattended,
> River journeys that leave me dazed.
> South winds blow my homing heart,
> It soars and comes to rest before the wine shop.

Alongside the canal, beyond the 600-year-old mosque, a bustling street market wends its way between rows of ageing warehouses and merchants' stores. Their white-washed stucco greyed and peeling, their signs faded and barely legible. The exotic aroma of dried spices mingles with dank smells of fish. A short cheery lady behind a butcher's stall chats to shoppers as she carves meat from a fresh pig's carcass, her sharp knife slicing smoothly between the ribs. A small shop sells an array of delicious honeys, clear and light, thick and dark. Another woman, with a small trolley, pushes her way between the noisy jam of people and bicycles distributing steaming bowls of porridge to warm hungry stomachs on a chilly morning. She returns later to gather the empty bowls.

But for the most part this city is one of tidy tree-lined boulevards and clean, modern buildings, banks and offices. One in particular, a sleek, thirty-five-storey tower topped with a revolving restaurant and a structure that can only be described as looking like a giant portable telephone complete with aerial, would not appear out of place in any major city in the world.

## EXECUTION PARADE

The man's head is lowered over his chest, his arms bound behind his back. A rough placard round his neck tells me his name, his crime and his sentence. A condemned man about to die. Forty of these condemned men are being paraded through the streets of Jining. With shaved heads they stand four abreast behind the cab of a lorry, an armed policeman in green uniform beside each man. One truck carries helmeted soldiers with rifles across their chests—the firing squad. This is designed as a procession of evil. Criminals on display, their guilt to be witnessed by all who see them. Driving through the pale morning sunshine they screw up their faces to keep the dust from their eyes, the placards around their necks swinging in the breeze.

The parade has passed my hotel twice by half past eight. Wailing sirens draw people's attention to the macabre procession of slow-moving vehicles. Motorbikes with side-cars hover alongside the lorries, in each perches another trussed up felon, shell-shocked and blinking. People on the streets turn to look, stare for several

PUNISHMENT of the TCHA.

---

### Plate No. 8

*Common punishments of the day included flogging with a bamboo cane and the cangue—
a type of stock consisting of a heavy wooden framework secured around the neck,
with the hands often confined as well. Thus prevented from reaching his face or head,
the resulting irritation often drove the prisoner crazy.*

---

moments, but as the cortege passes they turn their backs and move on; no one registers any shock, no one reveals disquiet at this image of soon to be extinguished life.

If punishment is considered an effective deterrent to crime, then advertising the penalties to be met by criminals is logical. Authorities want to publicize the misery of the consequences of evil. And these men look miserable enough. The first time round most of the convicts were staring blankly ahead, by the second circuit almost all heads were bowed low, unseeing. The shame and humiliation of what they were being forced to endure combined with terror at the sentences on their heads made these men less than human. By any standards it is barbaric and inhumane to taunt people in this way. But, argues Chinese logic, if they are guilty of atrocities then what compassion do they deserve?

A.R.

# JINING CHEF

One-metre-high flames furl from the wok. The white-frocked chef stands outside his restaurant on the pavement working the pan handle. Food leaps up and down in and out, sometimes rising a foot into the air as he spins and shakes and flips the deep-bowled pan. People are racing all around him, but he never lifts his eyes. He flings chopped meat and peppers together, mixes spices and tosses the lot in the air. Bubbling brown juice trickles down the side.

His kingdom is unadorned. Narrow benches only a foot off the ground fill three bare rooms joined by connecting doors. Tables are shared like an old 'singles bar'. Bottle tops and cigarette butts cover the floor together with the crunching husks of melon seeds. The rooms have white walls and bare bulbs, there are no posters. Chopsticks wrapped in paper stand in empty jars on each table. A greasy screen covers the corner of one room and behind this the preparations are done. Vegetables and meat are chopped (provisions lying in buckets on the floor), dirty plates are rinsed in oily water with an oily cloth.

The chef, with a faceful of grin, stands outside with his wok on an old oil drum stove. Servers hand him food on an oval plate. He tosses it into the wok, adds garlic, coriander, chilli, cumin—all manner of spices—from bowls lined on a shelf in front of him, dipping his spatula in each receptacle and inching a line of ground powder along its edge. As he stirs the metal wedge grates against the wok. Burning chilli smoke bites the eyes and back of the throat. 'Too much of this, not enough of that, bring more,' he shouts, eyes down. He loves the drama, the great showmanship, and the hectic pace. Dish after dish, that is his thrill. His wife is a bundle of smiles and wants to show us everything. She shares his pride in their set-up. They open for breakfast at six and carry on cooking for sixteen and a half hours every day of the week. He is seventy and thriving. The restaurant is his retirement project. He is the static pivot, everything kaleidoscopes from him; the others weave patterns round him, running hither and thither. Wiping his arm across his

*A common sight along many city streets all over China—a chef cooking on a simple oil-drum stove. This seventy-year-old man runs his restaurant with his wife as a retirement project. Serving breakfast, lunch and dinner, they work over sixteen hours a day.*

forehead he shouts orders, laughs, demands, encourages.

There are at most twenty people, all male, crammed into the three rooms. They are mostly friendly, some overly so; all are drunk. They spit on the floor. Others sit at tables on the pavement. But they suddenly burst through the doors holding beer bottles and chopsticks, giggling: the police are patrolling and they are not allowed to eat out on the street. Their tables are dragged inside and we all shunt down along our benches to make room. Everyone is laughing, especially the chef's wife.

A.R.

Today, Jining stands at the northerly limit of navigation on the Grand Canal. Small fishing boats with one or two people on board putter their way towards Nanyang Lake 南陽湖 to the south; a handful are still sculled by oar.

In a boat-building yard next to the water the steel skeletons of two much larger barges are being welded. One of the workers squats beside the rusty steel ribs. Sparks fly from a brilliant white flash as the welding rod touches steel with a crack and a buzz. The figure stands, short and slight in drab blue overalls. As the Mao cap is lifted cascades of silky black hair fall around a pretty young face; her cheeks flushed, she wipes her brow. Zhao Lan Fang 趙蘭芳 began working at the yard six years ago at the age of thirteen. About a third of the workers in her yard are women and together with the men they complete about twenty-four boats per year. These particular barges, when finished, are destined for Hangzhou and will spend their working lives hauling loads of coal, bricks or other building materials. This is one of more than 100 such boat-building yards along the length of the Grand Canal.

Barrow describes the scene to the south of Jining where a series of lakes bordered the Grand Canal. It is along this section that without doubt the greatest engineering feats of this waterway were accomplished; quite astonishing considering it was achieved by manpower alone. Here he also describes the sluices (mentioned earlier in this chapter) which acted as a safety valve for the canal.

... we came to an extensive lake [Nanyang Hu]... navigated by a great number of sailing boats. From the east side of this lake the canal was separated only by an immense mound of earth. To the westward the whole country, beyond the reach of sight, was one continued swamp. The morass being several feet below the surface of the water in the canal afforded the means of regulating the quantity; and, accordingly, at certain distances, we observed stone arches turned in the earthen embankment to let off the superfluous water that might be occasioned by the swelling of the feeding rivers. *(Barrow)*

In this area today, pump houses draw water from the canal and discharge it into stone channels that disappear through the paddy fields. They are driven by electricity from the nearby power station. The farmer no longer has to resort to using his own efforts. At the time of Staunton's journey, the water sometimes ran level with, or even beneath, the level of the fields, and then the farmer had to fall back on sheer strength.

... two [men] stood opposite each other on two projecting banks, holding ropes fixed to a basket, which swinging to and fro for a considerable time, they gave it a velocity that assisted in throwing the water into a reservoir dug near the river's bank; from whence it was communicated, where wanted, by small channels. *(Staunton)*

# JINING CANAL

There is no suburbia round Jining. Riding southwards out of the city, along the canal, the urban centre is behind us in no time. After only a few kilometres of countryside we pass the skeleton of a huge bridge, part of a new highway network linking this relatively remote area to China's industrial powerhouses nearer the coast. The tapering contours and magnificence of its frame speak volumes about the ambitious plans nurtured by bureaucrats for that mythical place of wealth and prosperity, 'Modern China'. But it is a prophetic symbol—part of a system linking developed areas and bypassing rural backwaters that are falling further and further behind. The shell of this new bridge slammed home the gulf between the future, as the planners see it, and the extant reality of rural life as we witnessed that day on our ride from Jining.

The canal flows through a complex network of flats and ponds and much of the region seems to be submerged. Villages thread along the banks of all this water. The low houses are made of packed ochre earth and each has a walled yard where animals live, equipment is stored and a myriad chores are done. These settlements can be reached by car but the only traffic we pass on the packed earth levee is on foot, or bicycle, or has four legs.

Much of life is driven by the canal. There is a great deal of fishing; green nets and bamboo shrimp pots clutter most yards. Wherever there are nets there are people sitting under trees mending them. Under the roof of a workshop, beneath a canopy of tall trees, a small group hammers together ten feet long wooden boats. We could buy one for 800 *yuan* (US$100).

We follow the path through village after peaceful village. Whenever we stop a large crowd immediately gathers round us. I pull up beside a travelling shirt seller; he uses a loud hailer to draw potential customers from their afternoon siesta, but unfortunately for him interest in his floral prints quickly dries up when we appear. We are bad for business and the peddler wanders off. A roving ice-cream man fares better. His wares are endorsed by the foreign devils who delight in his rocket-shaped pink confections and his sales soar as a result. The ice-cream is covered in a paper wrapper, an unusual concession to the vagaries of marketing, (though of course rather essential for ice-cream distribution). The existence of this one wrapper draws my attention to how litter-free this place is. There is no rubbish anywhere. Goods do not come 'packaged' to such an unsophisticated market; in addition most of what is consumed is home-produced and not much needs to be brought in from outside the community.

Between villages the path is lined with tall silvery trees throwing dappled shade on the warm dry earth. Large wooden crosses rise above many ponds, suspending huge nets that sit like bowls just beneath the surface of the water. On a bank beside one of these ponds three boys are feeding a campfire. Lying on their bellies, knees bent, they throw twigs on to the flames. Resting on the fire is a pan containing their bubbling lunch of fresh fish. They jump up as we pass and scuttle down the bank to hide in long grass, but soon come charging back, laughing all the time.

Further along we come across a posse of octogenarian goatherds, working as a team. Between them they are looking after more than eighty animals. They sit on

*A group of elderly men watch over their herd of goats,
grazing on the bank of the Grand Canal, south of Jining.*

*This flat landscape, with its reed beds beside lakes and waterways,
is typical of this area of Shandong and large regions of Jiangsu Province to the south.*

the bank in long grass, their backs to the path, with the canal stretching before them. Two of their number are posted at the outer reaches keeping a wandering eye on the flanks of their flock to ensure the animals do not spread too far as they graze. The rest sit on low fold-up stools at the top of the bank, chatting. All are dressed in faded blue cotton and large pointed bamboo hats, their wrinkled walnut skin glowing, beards whiter than the fleece of their flocks. Several wear dark spectacles with glass half an inch thick. The smell of sun-baked earth and dry grass, the buzz of murmuring goats and the intermittent low chatter of the old men fills the air. As jobs for pensioners go, this must be one of the more pleasant, when the weather is good: hours of patient watching out in the company of friends.

A quest for water is fruitless. We inquire in several shops, nothing more than dusty dark counters in a front room offering an identical supply of cigarettes, biros, notebooks and playing cards. But one shop-keeper offers us tea. He produces a tiny earthenware pot and three thimbles. We stand on one side of his glass counter in the small room that also contains his bed, whilst he occupies the other together with his two grandsons, all the time re-filling our pot. People follow us and before we have drained two cups, the shop is crammed with curious faces. Soon they fill the room and spill onto the track outside, pressed in a tight semicircle around the door. My back is against the wall, I have a foot's space in front of me; except for that the room is solid with bodies. We laugh and laugh. Hilarity gradually spreads through the crowd. The old man has cheekbones like towel rails and a smile that rises up each side to meet them. His head is shaved and his eyes burn out of his face like comets. We talk about tea, what we are doing in China, where we have come from, what he thinks of Jining (he has been there only a few times) and towns in general, about his grandchildren and particularly his pride that they are now learning 'that foreign language' at the local school. Laughing raucously he grabs my high-tech, vulgar mirror sun-glasses and places them on his bald head. He is a sensation. We all roar. With those cheekbones and bone structure he is an exquisite model. His bed, his possessions, everything, is being trampled by the enthusiastic crowd but he is unconcerned, revelling in his showmanship. Eventually someone falls and the whole mass tumbles forward amid peals of laughter. We right ourselves and dust each other down, but clearly it is time to go. I survey the goods on offer in his shop, wanting to make a purchase in lieu of payment for the flagons of tea we have consumed. Behind his head in a large jar are some peanuts, home-roasted. We take these, a strong favourite at any time, and he charges us double and seems well-pleased. Before I can go he tugs at my arm imploringly, telling me I can not depart without leaving a souvenir. I feel his demand is reasonable; given the etiquette of souvenir distribution in China his hospitality certainly warrants some token of remembrance. Of course he has his eye on my glasses. All I can offer in their place is a yellow baseball cap, given to me by a friend in Beijing on the day of departure. I am loath to part with it, yet knowing how much delight the sight of old 'Laoye' in a baseball cap would cause his grandsons and assembled fans I pass it over the counter. I hope he still has it.

On the way back we met a party of three on a fishing expedition—an uncle and his two nephews. It is Sunday and they have ridden out from Jining for a day of rural quietude. They chat about their lives in the disorderly city and speak nostalgically of the gentle world here in the countryside. Theirs is a typical urban-dwellers' longing for the peace of the simple life. I am amazed that the circle has turned so quickly for some in China; many rural lives totally lack modernity and, I would have thought, were not fit to be romanticized, but the pace of development in the cities is clearly alienating some.

A.R.

*The vast majority of farming in China is still labour intensive, with planting and harvesting done by hand and animals often used for ploughing or harrowing.*
*In the north of the country oxen are used, like the pair here harnessed for ploughing.*

The lakes along this part of the Grand Canal, as it approaches the border with Jiangsu Province, have shrunk markedly in recent years. Receding in some cases several kilometres to the east, away from the canal, they now present a very different scene to the one that confronted the diplomats two centuries ago. Here Staunton also describes some interesting and ingenious ways that were used to control the water level.

On the western side of this lake, is a high and thick embankment of earth, which separates it from the canal, the surface of whose waters is considerably higher than that of those which fill the lake. [These embankments] of earth were supported on each side by walls of stone; and to prevent the column of water in the canal from becoming too heavy for the embankment to support it, sluices are cut at certain distances, by which the superfluous water passes off, either immediately into the lake, or upon the low lands, and sometimes into ditches made into the middle of the embankment, to serve as reservoirs. *(Staunton)*

Barrow writes about the canal to the north passing through rising country, which, although flat to the human eye, had passed through cuttings as deep as ten or even twenty metres in order to maintain an acceptable gradient. He may have become slightly carried away with his measurements as Staunton, conservative as ever, estimated six metres at least. They now found themselves heading south through country that steadily descended toward sea-level.

... they have been obliged to force up the water between immense banks of earth and stone, far above the level of the flat surface; consisting almost entirely of lakes, swamps and morass. *(Barrow)*

It struck Staunton that it must have presented a strange sight to the farmers in their fields to see the masts and sails of their barges seemingly floating along high above them. He also gives an interesting insight into the size and construction of these embankments.

The canal which had hitherto been embanked only on one of its sides, was now so on both. It was a curious spectacle... to see a vast body of water, forced up by human skill and industry, into a narrow channel, several yards above its former bed, and flowing along in that airy state... The earthen embankments in this part of the canal, were supported by retaining walls of coarse grey marble, cut into large blocks, and cemented together with a kind of mortar. Those walls were about twelve feet in thickness; and the large stones on the top were bound together with clamps of iron.

The canal was here, in fact, an aqueduct much elevated above the adjoining country, which, wherever it was dry, was crowded with villages. The grounds beneath are inundated during a considerable part of the year, and were cultivated in rice, whose stems shot above the water. *(Staunton)*

The amount of sweat and toil that must have gone into this project and the means by which it was mustered did not escape them either.

The quantity of human labour that must have been employed, in amassing together the different materials that compose this immense aqueduct, could not have been supplied, in any reasonable length of time, except in a country where millions could be set to work at the nod of a despot. The greatest works in China have always been, and still continue to be, performed by the accumulation of manual labour, without the assistance of machinery... *(Barrow)*

The reason it was necessary to build the Grand Canal between embankments to such a height was due to the water level of the Yellow River. Because of heavy silting, its bed had been raised high above the surrounding land, and thus the canal had to be constructed likewise in order to connect with it. Since this time, the Yellow River has changed its course and settled to a much lower level making such feats of engineering unnecessary nowadays.

Just before the canal crossed into Jiangsu Province it passed Weishan Lake 微山湖, again separated by an embankment. Lord Macartney was reminded of the similarity between this and the great canal of Russia where it passed Lake Lagoda, with which he was well acquainted, having spent some three years there as a diplomat.

Continued our course on the canal, which is now supplied from a very extensive lake [Weishan Hu] on our left hand. The bank here between the canal and the lake occasionally varies in breadth being in some places not less than half a mile thick, and in others scarcely more than two hundred yards. Though the lake is very extensive I could see its extreme boundaries from the deck of my yacht. The prospect of it this morning at sunrise was most delightful, the borders fringed with wood, houses and pagodas on the sloping grounds behind, and the lake itself covered with numberless vessels crossing it in different directions, according to all the various modes of navigation that poles, paddles, oars and sails can supply. On our right are many villages on the bank, which is here and there pierced with sluices, in order to turn the water for the purposes of agriculture. *(Macartney)*

# Chapter Four

# Jiangsu Province
# 江蘇省

The coastal province of Jiangsu has been known for centuries as 'the land of fish and rice'. It is a land of abundance—vast plains dotted with lakes and criss-crossed by rivers and canals amidst a sprawl of intense agriculture. In Chinese, the word Jiangsu is composed of two characters: the first meaning river and the second, meaning 'to revive', contains the two ideograms representing fish 魚 and rice 禾 . Jiangsu is the most densely populated province in China with more than 700 people per square kilometre. It spreads across the lower reaches of the Yangtze and Huai rivers and along the east coast bordering the Yellow Sea, covering an area of over 100,000 square kilometres. It is also the flattest and lowest-lying province. Rice has been grown here for at least 4,000 years. It became a major rice-growing area in the Tang and Song dynasties.

Since the implementation of economic reforms a few years ago, the irresistible influence of the industrial giant of Shanghai 上海 , which sits cupped beneath the estuary of the Yangtze, has had a great impact. Its industrial and commercial suburbs are fast spreading westward towards the cities of Suzhou 蘇州 and Wuxi 無錫. Their small village and township enterprises, which benefit from its capital and expertise, are more prevalent and better developed than in many other areas. These small industries are mainly funded by private enterprise and in some cases are eligible for modest government grants to help them get started. Others are joint ventures with companies from outside China—Hong Kong or Taiwan for example. Largely as a result of this kind of industrial activity, Suzhou now ranks third behind Beijing and Shanghai in per capita production. Jiangsu as a whole has the highest industrial output in the country. The province is a major producer of silk and cotton and its textile industry ranks first in China in terms of output.

## PEIXIAN TO XUZHOU  沛縣 – 徐州

Having passed the lakes and swamps, we entered suddenly upon a most delightful part of the country, crowded with temples and villages and towns and cities. The surface of the country was now broken into hill and dale, every inch appeared to be under tillage... *(Barrow)*

The greatest part of the land was under cotton, of which the pods were now opening, and ready to be gathered. *(Staunton)*

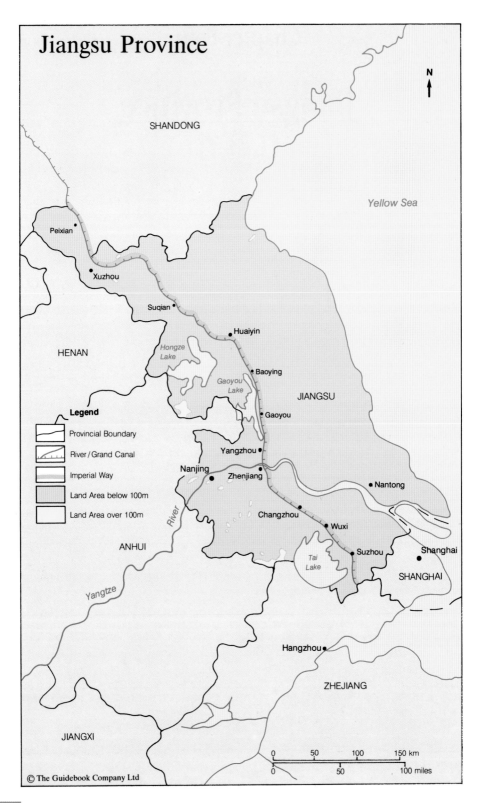

# Jiangsu Province

N

SHANDONG

Yellow Sea

Peixian

Xuzhou

Suqian

Huaiyin

HENAN

Hongze Lake

Baoying

Gaoyou Lake

JIANGSU

**Legend**

Gaoyou

Provincial Boundary

River / Grand Canal

Yangzhou

Imperial Way

Nanjing

Zhenjiang

Nantong

Land Area below 100m

Land Area over 100m

River

Changzhou

Wuxi

ANHUI

Tai Lake

Suzhou

Shanghai

SHANGHAI

Yangtze

Hangzhou

ZHEJIANG

JIANGXI

| 0 | 50 | 100 | 150 km |
|---|----|-----|--------|
| 0 | | 50 | 100 miles |

© The Guidebook Company Ltd

*Fifteen-year-old Dong Xiao Ni works on her parents' farm helping to harvest their crop of cotton. As with many children, once old enough to work in the fields, they sacrifice their school education to work long hours on the family farm.*

A landscape of maize and cotton is etched by a maze of irrigation channels. Wider canals, dotted with small fishing skiffs and staked with flimsy nets, stretch lazily and unbending to the horizon. Occasionally a larger barge loaded with sand splutters past men in straw hats sitting motionless beside long fishing rods. Farmers in this region still plant large areas of cotton as a cash crop. At this time of year the ranks of straggly, waist-high bushes appear dead, their sparse leaves turning to brown. Whole families take to the fields to help gather in the harvest.

Dong Xiao Ni 董小妮 is fifteen and in the mellow autumn sunshine she helps her parents and elder brother. Her nimble fingers, their nails artlessly dabbed with a crimson nail polish that matches her jacket, deftly pops the fluffy white bolls out of their bursting pods and drops them into a pouch wrapped around her waist. Like many farms in the area, their crop of maize and sorghum has already been harvested and after ploughing the fields will be planted with winter wheat.

It is still common to see two or three oxen pulling ploughs or drawing harrows. With one hand controlling the reins and the other on the wooden handle the shiny steel blade cuts through the heavy clayey earth. Calling to the animals the ploughman only occasionally needs to stroke their flanks with the whip to keep them on line. To break up the clods the farmer then couples the oxen to a harrow, a large rectangular frame covered with long metal teeth on the underside. His wife stands on the implement to add extra weight and rides along as though on a surfboard. It seems, however, an increasing number of farmers are able to afford small tractors or even rotavators.

Approaching Xuzhou the landscape begins to throw up slag heaps along a hitherto flat almost featureless horizon. This area provides Jiangsu with virtually all its coal. This is distributed to the south along the Grand Canal, which has become an increasingly important artery supplying the energy-starved province and its giant industrial neighbour, Shanghai. This is supplemented by coal transported by rail from the northern provinces of Shaanxi, Shanxi and Inner Mongolia to Xuzhou, where it is loaded on to barges. In 1995, the canal was used to transport 24.5 million tonnes of coal to the southern hinterland and this is expected to increase significantly in the future.

From behind a high brick wall, through a pair of rusty green gates, a group of miners emerge onto the road, their shift ended for another day. Some are still wearing their hard hats and head-lamps, their faces smudged with black, their clothes grimy.

An apparently seamless succession of small towns run along the main road—satellite towns and suburbs of the sprawling industrial town of Xuzhou. One such town straddles the wide road with ranks of two- or three-storey, newly-whitewashed buildings. Against a blue sky, swept clear by a fresh breeze, they radiate a relaxed, Mediterranean atmosphere. In the centre of a roundabout at the main intersection looms a sculpture of two gigantic bulls. Both strain forward, muscles rippling, one with its head bent to the ground, the other with its head stretched high, as though hauling some immense load. Typical of many similar town-centre sculptures in the area they symbolize the striving of the town to pull itself out of the poverty that, about ten years ago, used to engulf this area.

A rumple of low hills surrounds Xuzhou. Wide new boulevards lead towards the city centre. Treeless, they look stark and bare, exposing their modern office buildings and shops of white tiles and blue-tinted glass. Its large population seems to throng the streets, tottering on bicycles beside buses and cars.

Xuzhou serves as a railway hub for the region with a network of lines radiating in all directions: north to Tianjin and Beijing, south through Nanjing, east to the coast and west through Xi'an and into the mountains beyond. The Grand Canal, which passes the city a few kilometres to the north, relieves some of the burden from the already overloaded railways by supplying an alternative means of transport for enormous quantities of coal destined for the heart of the province around the giant basin of the Yangtze River.

—··•◦●◉●◦•··—

A thick grey mist obscures all but the closest detail. Morning presents a drab world without sun or shadow. Hundreds of cyclists pour out of the city towards their factories in the suburbs. All are smartly dressed in clean and fashionable clothes. Women wear trouser suits or new jeans, the men in casual trousers with pullovers or blousons. Many of the factories masked by the deadening mist are weaving mills or chemical plants—the north of Jiangsu is rich in mineral resources for the chemical and fertilizer industries.

To the south, away from the clamour of the city centre, under dappled avenues of plane trees, lies an older section of town. Alongside a narrow canal, old men sit talking and admiring each other's songbirds that perch in frail bamboo cages hung in the branches above. Squeezed between dilapidated apartment blocks, their balconies draped with washing, is a Catholic church. Built in red brick at the turn of the century, it musters about 400 wor-shippers for Sunday mass. A middle-aged man with a greasy mop of black hair and wearing a crumpled brown suit  walks along the street dangling a hedgehog by one of its hind legs from a piece of string. The other three legs flail helplessly in the air as the man calls to a group of women who stand nearby, enquiring whether they fancy his little delicacy for their cooking pot.

A car park on the corner of a busy junction becomes, by night, an open-air restaurant. Stalls festooned with bare light bulbs display an array of fresh food. Small clay pots hold combinations of noodles, eggplant, bean sprouts, quail eggs and tiny salted fish, ready to be boiled on a gas stove. Platters of chicken and pork are displayed beside an assortment of vegetables and whole pink fish. A couple of tables form the kitchen and the food is cooked on an 'oil-drum' stove. An electric fan at its base forces air through the burning coals and sends a blast of flames roaring around the large wok in which the chef expertly tosses and stirs the steaming contents.

A bright young lady in a scarlet sweat-shirt and black ski-slacks, her shoulder-length hair twisted and pinned neatly up at the back of her head, acts as hostess and waitress. She busies herself carrying dishes between kitchen and table, taking orders and opening endless bottles of beer for the customers seated on small stools around circular tables. A little black purse dangles from her wrist in which she keeps the night's takings. During the day she works in a factory making cigarette-lighters and in the evening helps her friend, the chef, to run his restaurant.

This form of alfresco dining has become very popular in many cities in China, especially with younger people who now can afford to eat out. Many of the customers in these restaurants are young professional women. Whereas before they had only eaten in restaurants when taken by their boyfriends or husbands it is common now to see groups of two or three young women enjoying a night out together.

# ROAD TO SUQIAN 宿遷

Heading south-east the Imperial Way leaves behind the coal-mining and industry of Xuzhou and the canal winds once more through a flat agricultural landscape dominated by rice fields. As the low hills and slag heaps of northern Jiangsu sink into the early morning mist, the dew settles on bundles of rice, cut the previous day, that lie in the fields. It is the end of September and the rice harvest has begun.

## RICE HARVESTING

Mr. Su had just bought a Japanese rice harvester with the help of friends, and he was now recouping his investment by hiring it out to wealthy farmers in central Jiangsu Province. It cut, separated and bagged the rice—doing in just fifteen minutes a job that would have taken a dozen people three days. It was the only machine of its kind that I saw in China. A crowd had gathered to observe its progress, thus negating its impact as a labour-saving device.

*A Japanese made rice-harvester being used on a farm in Jiangsu Province.
Operated by three men–a driver, and two others sitting at the back–
it cuts the rice and feeds the stalks along a conveyor into the machine,
where the grain is separated and is fed into sacks.*

*Archaeological evidence in the lower Yangtze basin shows rice has been cultivated in China for some 4,000 years, although more recent discoveries suggest this period could be doubled. Here, not far from the town of Xuzhou, at the end of September, rice stands ready for harvesting.*

*At harvest time everybody in the village, young and old, must pull their weight.*

Almost everywhere in China harvesting is done by hand. In a village in northern Jiangsu I met a primary school teacher called Liang Haimei who was working in the fields. She told me she had come back to her village for a few weeks to help her parents. Everyone pooled resources and worked together at this time of year, she said. Each family had its own plot and could hold on to as much grain as it wanted; what was left was sold to the state. The people of this village were great fans of Deng Xiaoping and his economic reforms which they said had improved their lives a hundredfold: they now had full stomachs and cash in their pockets—profits from what they sold on the open market—whereas before they had been starving. Even so all were adamant that their children should move to the cities where they imagined they would find good jobs, earn a decent wage and lead more comfortable lives. No one wanted his child to remain on the land.

Conditions of rural life vary. In prosperous parts of the country some farmers have accumulated considerable wealth. In Zhejiang we were joined at lunch one day by a nineteen-year-old lad who had tailed us for an hour or more on a black Japanese motorbike. His father, a farmer, had bought it for him. I asked him what he did. 'Not much,' was the answer. He had left school and was in theory helping at home but I had a feeling that this lad, in his natty black jumper and baggy trousers, did not spend much time in the fields getting his hands dirty. Village dwellings in this part of the country are often two-storey brick houses with large gardens. Countless windows and balconies are currently being fitted with blue glass; this is the most popular manifestation of prosperity.

Machines will gradually make agricultural tasks less arduous but this process has hardly started in most parts of the country; it is, anyway, a double-edged sword, for mechanization will leave a great many people with not much to do, which could be

*Stalks of rice straw are twisted and tied to bind a sheaf of harvested rice.*

dangerously destabilizing. For the most part though the rural Chinese (seventy-five per cent of the total population) will continue, for quite a few years more, to toil from dawn till dusk and to do everything by hand. And travellers (like me) will continue to be amazed by their stoicism, strength and resilience, and be naively charmed by the sight of a blue-clad farmer walking home from his fields with a hoe over his shoulder at twilight.

A.R.

A great proportion of the surface of the country is well adapted for the production of rice, which, from the time the seed is committed to the soil, till the plant approaches to maturity, requires to be immersed in a sheet of water. Many and great rivers run through several provinces of China, the low grounds bordering on those rivers, are annually inundated, by which means is brought upon their surface a rich mud that fertilizes the soil, in the same manner as Egypt receives its fecundative quality from the overflowing of the Nile. *(Staunton)*

In his journals Sir George Staunton wrote extensively on the methods of rice cultivation and harvesting, showing how these techniques have changed very little since he passed through the country.

He described how the seed, which had previously been soaked in dung diluted with 'animal water' to promote growth, is planted in paddies which were divided and enclosed by banks of mud thrown up by hand.

A thin sheet of water is immediately brought over it... In a few days the shoots appear above the water. As soon as the shoots have attained the height of six or seven inches, they are plucked up by the roots, the tops of the blades cut off, and each root is planted separately, sometimes in small furrows turned with the plough, and sometimes in holes made in rows by a drilling stick for that purpose. Water is brought over them a second time...

As the rice grew, the water, through evaporation and absorption, disappeared entirely until the ground was dry. Having matured it was then harvested by means of a sickle. For the first crop this happened towards the end of May or beginning of June. There were various methods of threshing and it is here that some recent changes have taken place. A flail was sometimes used and occasionally can still be seen in use by a few farmers today...

... or by cattle treading the grain, but sometimes also by striking it against a plank sit upon its edge, or by beating it against the side of a large tub scolloped for that purpose; the back and sides being much higher than the front, to prevent the grain from being dispersed.

*Traditional winnowing is still carried out almost everywhere in China—a method unchanged for centuries. Sometimes, when there is insufficient breeze to separate the chaff, huge electric fans are used to generate an artificial wind.*

Cattle, if used nowadays, usually trudge round in circles pulling a large concrete roller, being far more effective than just hooves alone. But perhaps the biggest change to have taken place is the use of small tractors which, replacing the cattle, now roar round in dizzying circles like a demented go-cart with the concrete roller in tow.

Another popular alternative is to use an electric threshing machine, which closely resembles an upturned lawnmower. Bundles of rice are held with their heads against the whirling blades and the grain flies off and lands in a loose pile, which once swept up is then ready for winnowing. This is largely carried out by the age-old method of hoisting shovelfuls of grain into the air and letting the wind separate the chaff, or else by means of a large sieve held between two people and shaken. When there is little or no wind this can be difficult, in which case giant fans that resemble World War I aeroplane propellers are used to provide some strong artificial wind.

The labour of the first crop being finished, the ground is immediately prepared for the reception of fresh seeds. The first operation undertaken, is that of pulling up the stubble, collecting it into small heaps, which are burnt and the ashes scattered upon the field. The former processes are afterwards renewed. The second crop is generally ripe late in October or early in November. The grain is treated as before; but the stubble is no longer burnt. It is turned under with the plough and left to putrefy in the earth. This, with the slime brought upon the ground by inundation, are the only manures usually employed in the culture of rice. *(Staunton)*

In the harvested fields in Jiangsu, the stubble is being burnt off and ploughed back, ready for the planting of winter wheat. Dusk is approaching. The sun has already sunk into the brown-tinged haze that skirts the horizon—a combination of dust from the dry earth and smoke from burning fields. There is still plenty of activity on the Grand Canal as several barge-trains of ten or twelve boats coupled to a tug chug lazily beneath the sweeping span of the road bridge in Suqian. Their red and green navigation lights glimmer in the fading light. Much larger individual barges also splutter past, husband at the wheel, wife standing on the bow frantically waving a tattered white flag, bludgeoning oncoming vessels into giving leeway.

From the north, emerging out of the gloom, comes a line of much smaller, slower boats sprouting what appears to be a number of antenna-like appendages. As they come closer it becomes clear that these appendages are alive. Occasionally one flaps its wings and continues preening. Others, their grooming completed, have already tucked their heads beneath their wings in sleep, each roosting on its own perch. These are the fishing cormorants, *Pelicanus Sinensis*, or in Chinese, *lu ci* 鸕鷀, used for centuries by fishermen on lakes and rivers all over China. Having sold their catch at the market, the fishermen row their boats into a narrow creek where they moor for the night. The men chat and joke as they cook their simple supper of fish, beans and rice on small charcoal stoves sitting in the bottom of their boats. Smoke spirals languidly into the chilling evening air. Food and even a book passes from boat to boat by means of a net on the end of a long pole. During the winter fishing season the fishermen live and sleep on board these compact, neatly made wooden skiffs which cost about 1,500 yuan (US$180) when new. The men have to find other work in the summer when heavy rains make fishing difficult.

The boat used by these fishermen is of a remarkable light make, and is often carried to the lake together with the fishing birds... *(Staunton)*

The usual practice is to take ten or twelve of these birds, in the morning... and to let one or two at most at a time dive for fish, which are taken from them the moment they bring them to the surface. *(Barrow)*

...it is astonishing to see the enormous size of fish with which they return, grasped within their bills. They appear to be so well trained, that it did not require either ring or cord about their throats to prevent them from swallowing any portion of their prey... *(Staunton)*

In the course of three days' navigation, we saw several thousand boats and rafts employed in this kind of fishing.*(Barrow)*

About four-and-a-half centuries earlier Friar Odoric had been shown the technique of using cormorants for fishing. He recounts how his host had led him onto a bridge to watch as the birds dived repeatedly...

... catching great numbers of fish... putting them of their own accord into the baskets, so that before long all the three baskets were full.

Although Staunton claims that cords around the birds' necks were not necessary, Odoric mentions their use...

And mine host then took the cord off their necks and let them dive again to catch fish for their own food. And when they had thus fed they returned to their perches and were tied up as before.

And one can almost hear the friar's lips smacking with relish as he recalls...

...And some of those fish I had for my dinner. (Odoric)

*The morning's fishing completed, a fisherman wheels his small craft home.*
*His trained cormorants perch obediently on the boat preening themselves.*

# JIANGSU CHURCH

The provinces of Jiangsu and Shandong are littered with the shells of broken-down churches. These coastal areas were accessible to missionaries at the turn of the century and Christianity spread, though only in patches. Almost all places of worship were shut down during the Cultural Revolution and most have not re-opened, though a few are gradually being rehabilitated by small aging congregations. Government suppression of religious activity is well documented and only state religion is condoned, but Christianity, both government-sanctioned and clandestine, clearly has a hold in some communities.

One Sunday morning we were led to a new brick church on the edge of the small canal town of Suqian by an elderly man who informed us with a grin that in the 1930s he had known many people as tall as Kevin and myself. 'All missionaries,' he said, 'long since gone.' The church he attended was spartan and unfinished, its bare brick walls dotted with a few pink notices. The congregation sat on splintering school chairs and there were no walls along one side, enabling a large part of the assembly to gather outside and still consider themselves to be participating. The congregation numbered some 500 or 600; most were sitting on their haunches in the sunshine, chatting and disregarding the sacred meeting taking place over their shoulders.

We were hustled into a 'vestry' tacked on to the side of the building and given tea. Moments later the plain-clothes vicar appeared at the door, hymn book in hand, having deserted his flock momentarily in order to inspect his visitors. Suddenly he made an alarming request.

'Please come to the pulpit and lead our prayers,' he said.

I smiled weakly. My Chinese vocabulary is a bit sketchy in the piety department. I followed him with trepidation as he led me up into the pulpit whereupon a prayer book was thrust into my hand.

The vicar introduced me and handed over the microphone. I was standing face to face with 500 Chinese Protestants. They stared up expectantly. Trawling my church-going memory for suitable sentiments, I turned up two familiar themes: prayers for 'Christians around the world persecuted for their faith' and for 'those less fortunate than ourselves'. I scanned the congregation before me and realized that its members fitted nicely into both categories. I settled instead for something more secular: an explanation of what I was doing in China. I also thought I would enlighten them as to what churches in England are like. My Chinese became increasingly garbled and unintelligible. By my side in the pulpit was the lovely old gentleman who had brought us to the church. He managed somehow to comprehend what I was trying to say each time and paraphrased my speech for the greater understanding of the congregation. One or two things did, however, get a little confused in translation: my comment that numbers attending church regularly in Britain are falling came across as a proud statement that Catholicism in the UK is waning whereas Protestant congregations are swelling, producing a roar of approval from the crowd. Given the rapturous response I decided not to disabuse my audience.

After five minutes I felt I had done my duty before God and his supporters in Suqian. I looked at the chaplain hoping he would let me relinquish my spot in the pulpit. Alas, he had another plan.

'Annabel,' he said smiling, 'now you must sing a hymn.'

This time I really did falter. How merciless to inflict my voice on a crowd of decent churchgoers. I warned that I did not know any hymns in Chinese. In the end, however, I had no choice but to throw back my head and sing. The only thing that came to mind was an old Sunday School favourite, beloved of my brother and myself: 'The Foolish Man Built His House Upon The Sand'. The congregation, with good reason, looked bored and unimpressed. I, however, had tears streaming down my face, so helpless was I with the hilarity of the scene: singing that old favourite to 500 Jiangsu Christians. The idea of my brother sniggering from the back of the church and making faces at me was so hilarious that my knees turned to jelly.

When the service was over we retired once more to the vestry and resumed our tea. Several people crowded round the entrance to stuff prayer requests for sick relatives in my palm. As I left I passed a frail stooping old lady weeping inconsolably. She was distraught and said she wanted to die. Two friends and one of the church organizers were with her, trying to restrain her, encouraging her to persevere. I hope she did.

A.R.

# COAL BARGE TO HUAIYIN 淮 陰

## COAL BARGE TO HUAIYIN

The captain of the 160-metre-long coal barge was waiting to greet me with a nervous smile. I climbed gingerly down a rickety metal ladder built into the wall of the lock and landed heavily beside him. 'Please feel free to wander around as you wish,' he said, chuckling, 'we have nothing to hide.'

I watched as the crew lowered my bike on deck with a rope, and my toes curled with excitement. Negotiating this leg of the journey had been a game of snakes and ladders. First to help us was a Mr. Xu who was in charge of a neighbourhood committee in the small Jiangsu town of Suqian. He was introduced to as a kind of 'fixit' wizard. Xu was delighted by the perversity of our desire to travel the canal by barge and we became his crusade. At our third interview he announced that he had a friend who was a lock-keeper at a gate just out of town who might be able to arrange things.

I was touched by his obliging enthusiasm. He explained that just five years before he could not have dreamt of such free contact with foreigners and so this was a novel and tremendous source of fun. His willingness to act without fretting about accountability to a higher authority was something new, evidence perhaps of an emerging sense of personal freedom.

At six the following morning we went to his office and were told to bundle our bikes up on to the roof of a small minibus. This was the first time we had eschewed leg locomotion. Twenty-five kilometres out of town we met Xu's friend, the lock-keeper. Not having been forewarned as to our demands or even of our existence, he

*The leviathan of the Grand Canal. This empty barge, passing through Huaiyin lock, is returning to Xuzhou in the north of Jiangsu Province, where its vast containers are filled with over 3,000 tonnes of coal. The cargo is then shipped 150 kilometres south to the Yangtze River. Over 24 million tonnes of coal is transported in this way each year.*

was somewhat taken aback to find us in his courtyard seeking his protection. But nonetheless, after reading our letter of introduction from Mr. Xu, he assured us that he could assist. In the meantime we explored the lock. An incessant stream of barges glided in at one end and out the other. The opening mechanism was housed in a glass-walled watch tower controlled by two ladies who were busy knitting. It was a fine vantage point revealing a rash of activity both on and off the canal. The knitters spent some time explaining their drill and pointing at various buttons until a message on the internal tannoy warned them we had to be ejected immediately as the area was out of bounds to the likes of us.

Straight after this four officers from the local Public Security Bureau Foreign Affairs Section arrived, brandishing the 'How To Deal With Aliens' rule book. They had followed us from Suqian, and were carrying our registration forms from the hotel in which we had passed the previous night. We were told we were in a part of China closed to foreigners and were liable for a large fine. I began to feel we could be in for quite a bit more if they were so inclined. We were escorted to the lock guest-house and subjected to several hours of questioning, all of which was relayed down a mobile phone to someone important in an office in town. We had to account for our being in such a remote place. My passport was examined minutely and every visa and stamp had to be explained. I also had to furnish them with full details of my time as a student in China some eight years before. Eventually they moved to meatier matters: what did I think about Hong Kong's return to China in 1997? Wonderful, I said. But we all agreed that Shanghai was the city of the future.

Our chief interrogator was a pudgy, pear-shaped man. His companion, a quiet amiable gentleman with a grey flash sparking through his hair from temple to crown wanted to talk about the Northern Ireland peace process. At last the officers retired to consider their verdict over lunch, leaving us under 'guest-house arrest'. Several hours later they returned, in a cloud of rice wine and garlic, to inform us that we were being given special dispensation to pass through this remote part of China. I was amazed: rules are rules, after all, and Chinese officials generally like to abide by them. There was, though, one proviso: we would have to be chaperoned. I told them that was unnecessary. 'Miss Annabel,' came the reply, 'the People's Republic of China has been established for forty-six years. In all this time not one foreign friend has travelled by barge down this canal. You are the first. It is my pleasure and my honour to offer you a guide.'

This is how we came to be accompanied by the slouching Lao Fu: a less willing companion you could not wish to find. He sulks and he scowls-but is irresistibly droll. Scuffling along at the pace of a snail, with his dishevelled hair, he was the picture of truculent sloth. But once aboard the coal barge his true colours were revealed: a master of wry humour and devilish tales. His antics delighted the crew, who sat round him as he regaled them with tall stories about fellow bargers. His disrespect for all was manifest, but the scoundrel was undeniably charming.

We were granted a free run of the barge; the captain did not even bundle us into life jackets. Two huge container 'pits' lashed together formed the cargo hold, and were shunted from behind by a three-tier tug. The eighteen-man crew was well-dressed and polite: the company operating this particular barge was considered an excellent employer and clearly picked off some of the brighter talent from its town base Huaiyin. The young crew seemed content and bonds of friendship stretched across the dividing line of rank and age. Their day is split into four six-hour shifts. The whole team goes up and down the canal for two months at a stretch, followed by one month off. Their load is always coal, 3,341 tons of it, transported from Xuzhou in the north to Zhenjiang in the south. The holds are empty on the return trip.

At the very front is a little cabin occupied by a couple of crew members, posted to keep an eye on the water ahead. So far are they from the tug that the thud of the engines is lost. I felt I was adrift on a free-floating peninsula. The captain, up in the wheel-house, has to grab his binoculars to see into this part of his realm and there is an air of the junior common room down here. To combat the silence the lads have rigged a small tape recorder to some large speakers and they pump music across the placid water. At night it is especially blissful, once the music has died away, leaving only the peace of lapping gliding water. At three o'clock one morning I went and sat with the two men on night duty. They were wielding a powerful spotlight from bank to bank to check for oncoming vessels. When one comes into sight they yell at it down a loud hailer entreating it to keep to one side. Everyone must move for this mighty vessel. For the rest of the time there is no sound but the silver canal drifting by. These were precious moments of peace.

When the time came for us to depart, Lao Fu produced a masterful display of coquettish insolence. The three of us were due to disembark at the next lock but during supper in the galley, in front of the captain and half the crew, he announced that he believed Kevin and I should stay on board, because at three in the morning it would be dangerous for us to cycle into town to look for a hotel. The captain paled. He recognized that depositing us at a lock at that early hour was not ideal and that he could be held responsible for any misadventure that might befall us; but the deal struck in Suqian stipulated that we would get off at this place.

After supper I engaged in a stint of shuttle diplomacy. First I had a lengthy interview with Lao Fu perched on top of a bollard on deck. He did not want to extend his responsibility for us beyond what had been asked of him. He would not be moved. My next port of call was the neat cabin of the captain's mate. The captain himself was not to get involved in all this, his deputy had to do the unseasonable stuff of negotiating. After twenty minutes of small talk on the design features of this particular barge (it was even equipped with a pool table) we turned to the gritty stuff of our predicament. His final position took some time to establish, but eventually he acknowledged it could be difficult for us to find somewhere to stay, yet he was 'not sure how convenient it would be' for us to continue on the barge. The truculent Lao Fu reappeared. A three-way discussion ensued. I had a feeling I was missing an important point somewhere along the line; yet I could not believe that they were both unable to tell me to my face exactly what was going on. Having made no headway after half an hour, we took a break. Finally I went back to the captain's mate with a new approach. 'I speak this language badly so I am going to be blunt.' Taking control of the situation worked. He admitted he was abashed to order us off the barge but it would be better for all if we went.

In the end getting rid of us proved not so easy. We drew into the lock after four o'clock. The canny Lao Fu shinned up a ladder and disappeared to rouse the lock-keeper. This gentleman soon appeared, a green padded army coat over his pyjamas, holding a lantern, with a grinning Lao Fu at his side.

He shook his head. No we could not disembark at his lock. What was he going to do with us? We were not his problem and must stay on the barge. He added there was nowhere for us to stay because he didn't have a key to the guest room.

A heated dialogue commenced: the captain pleading from the deck, the lock-keeper yelling down from above. Beside him Lao Fu grinned and refrained from getting involved. I sensed stalemate so decided to pitch in.

'We have inconvenienced the captain enough,' I said, 'and don't want to hold him up. He has work to do and must not fall behind schedule. It would be best for him and everyone else if you would let us ashore.'

Five minutes later, after an impressive display of grumpiness, the lock-keeper assented. We were hustled up the ladder, palming our companions off with hasty farewells, regretting that a bad feeling was colouring our final moments with them. We followed the lock-keeper across a dead garden to some dark buildings. He threw open a door and kicked a strip light into life, exposing a four-bedded room containing one poor man who, mole-like, rubbed his sleepy eyes and tried to sit up. This was a peculiar dream for him. We wheeled our bikes into the room.

'I'll be back at seven, for breakfast,' and with that the lock-keeper turned on his heels and left. I clambered on to the wood-framed bed that seemed to lack a mattress and slept.

A.R.

*Cruising both day and night on the Grand Canal, these giant coal barges use powerful searchlights to navigate in the dark. With their days split into six-hour shifts, the crew of eighteen work two months on and one month off.*

# Huaiyin to Yangzhou 淮陰–揚州

At the time of Lord Macartney's travels through China the Yellow River, as we saw in the previous chapter, passed through the north of Jiangsu crossing the Grand Canal at the city of Huaiyin.

On the second of November, the yachts arrived at that part of the canal where it forms a junction with the Yellow river... Upon the nearest coast... is a very extensive and populous town. The canal here is about three quarters of a mile in width, and forms an excellent harbour for shipping. *(Staunton)*

This day just before we came to [Huaiyin] we passed through the largest sluice I have as yet seen in China. The fall was between three and four feet. These sluices which in some districts occur at the distance of a few miles from one another properly form locks of that distance. The boats collect in great numbers at the sluice, the valves open, and in a few minutes the whole fleet passes through, the flood gates are then let down and the canal soon recovers its former level.

[Huaiyin] is an immense town; from its extent on both sides of the water and the prodigious number of vessels and people, I should suppose it to be nearly equal to [Tianjin]. *(Macartney)*

Huaiyin stands at the northern end of the Hong Gou Canal, the oldest section of the Grand Canal that has flowed for almost twenty-five centuries. Built in the Qin dynasty (221–207 BC), the city was so named because it was established on the south bank of the Huai River.

According to ancient Chinese custom the south bank of a river is referred to as the *yin* 陰 , (the feminine or negative principle in nature) and the north bank as the *yang* 陽 , (the masculine or positive side). After the Sui dynasty it developed rapidly, and became a major commercial centre in Jiangsu during the Yuan, Ming and Qing dynasties, when the Grand Canal was at its zenith. More than 30,000 builders were employed in four large shipyards which, during the reign of Emperor Yongle, produced annually 680 large grain ships, each with a capacity of fifty tons. During the Ming dynasty the grain boats on the Grand Canal were said to number 11,775 and were crewed by a total of 121,500 officers and sailors. They carried some four million *dan* 擔 of grain north to the capital each year. One *dan* is equivalent to just over fifty kilograms.

In his journals, Barrow describes how the continuation of the Grand Canal from the Yellow River (at Huaiyin) to the Yangtze River was constructed on the same principles as it had been in southern Shandong Province. This is corroborated by Staunton and clearly shown in Alexander's drawing.

*VIEW of the LAKE*

The country being level and abounding with lakes and marshy grounds, it was carried upon a mound of earth kept together by retaining walls of stone the whole distance, which is about ninety miles, being in parts not less than twenty feet above the general level of the country; and the sheet of water it contained was two hundred feet in width, running sometimes at the rate of three miles an hour. Canals of communication supplied it from the westward; and the superfluous water was let off upon the low marshes. The tops of the walls of [Baoying] were just on a level with the surface of the water in the canal, so that if the bank opposite to it were to burst, the whole city must inevitably be inundated. (*Barrow*)

From these circumstances some judgment may be formed of the strength of the embankments which contained it, and the immensity of labour such a work required. (*Staunton*)

*re it is separated from the GRAND CANAL by an embankment of Earth*

*London. Published April 11 1796. by G. Nicol.*

**Plate No. 9** *"[The Grand Canal] was carried by the margin of [Gaoyou Lake], whose surface was much lower than that of the canal, which was separated from the lake by a strong embankment."* (Staunton)

Town now succeeded to town; the country offered the most beautiful views, of which no adequate idea can be given by written description. And when I mention the country as one scene of varied cultivation, divided by well-planted enclosures, peopled with farms that are surrounded by orchards, enriched with villas, and their ornamental gardens, a very inadequate picture is given of the expansive scenery on either side of the navigation which bore us through it. *(Anderson)*

*Heavily laden barges, water washing over their gunwales, prepare to exit a lock at Huaiyin.
Normally two gates operate in tandem, one for upstream traffic
and the other for downstream. Lock breakdowns can lead to
long queues building up, when barges may wait days to pass through.*

# BARGE-TRAIN TO YANGZHOU

## BARGE-TRAIN TO YANGZHOU

Most barges plying the canal are lashed into teams of ten or twelve, and pulled by a tug. An endless line of barge-trains snakes through the water, with a top speed of six knots, hauling all manner of commodities: bricks, timber, tiles, earthenware urns, tightly packed rubbish, and occasionally livestock. This is the core of canal life. Thousands of people are permanently settled in this watery world, moving backwards and forwards along the ancient route. We tasted a slice of this life when we travelled on one of these barge-trains from Huaiyin to Yangzhou, a 150-kilometre journey which took three days.

Life on the canal has its privations. Above all it is gentle but monotonous. Only when the train comes to a lock is there a call for urgency. Then there's an explosion of activity as everyone reaches for ropes and hooks to make the boats fast to the walls and prevent collisions. Often the train has to be untied and broken up to allow all members to squeeze inside together. Everyone is on deck, dogs and children too, while the business of ropes and fenders is the only concern. When the lock gates ease shut and the water level starts to go down, peace returns. Passing through a lock is hard work: apart from this there is little to be done bar the simple life tasks of cooking and cleaning.

I spent most of our journey in the company of Li Ping, a trim, square-shouldered woman with a deep-seated sadness and melancholy eyes. Her two children stay with her husband's parents in a town to the north of Jiangsu in order to go to school. Living apart from them distresses her but it is her choice to accompany her husband. Occasionally she leaves him for a month to fend for himself but as he admits to having a girlfriend in one town along the canal this also makes her distraught. She says she's trapped. Her roses are her distraction. Li Ping nurtures a crop of blooms under a canopy behind her cabin. Red buttons with many petals and fresh whites with large drooping heads sit in terracotta pots, turning a pocket of the grey, commercial barge over to something personal, earthy and human.

Kevin was billeted with the bachelor boys in the hold of the tug beside the engine-room. He had to share the small bunk space with six lads who were working shifts and passed the night playing mah-jong, their gambling bouts fuelled by ceaseless cigarette smoking. I was rather more fortunate: Li Ping gave me her bed and the whole of the downstairs cabin whilst she and her husband slept on a narrow shelf in the steering house. Her hospitality included the use of a potty—triggering a chain of dim recollections and unlikely throw-backs.

Li Ping's husband is a kindly, good-looking man. It was he who rescued us from our thirty-hour purgatory at Huaiyin lock. Streams of barge-trains passed through every hour but no one had wanted to take us on board so the spartan station became our home for several days. A more unlikely corner to be holed up in one could not wish for.

Li's husband had appeared on the morning of our second day of waiting. The responsibilities of his position included collecting all log books from his fellow bargees

(Above) With most of his sixty-five years spent on the canals, Huang Bing Zhang
retired a few years ago. But bored with life on dry land, he returned to work on the water as
first mate on this barge-train— and still plays a more than active role in the duties on board.

(Opposite) Occasionally, Li Ping will spend a month at home with her two children,
but most of the time she accompanies her husband on the barge-train—she knows about the
girlfriend he visits when she is away. She finds solace in tending the roses that
she grows on the back of their barge—they remind her of her children, she says.

and taking them to the lock-master's office for registration. He listened to our request, then said he thought his captain would take us. Five minutes later he returned with the captain in tow, a husky-voiced ruddy man with arms that hung woodenly at his side. The crowd of 'advisers' that had collected around us at this remote outpost quickly began slapping his back and pumping his hand encouragingly. He was thus bamboozled into stowing us away on his train.

Once aboard the wily captain turned us into an asset. Queues lasting several days sometimes build up at lock gates, more often than not because the operating mechanism of one of the two channels has broken down. On account of his unusual cargo of foreigners our captain managed to wheedle permission from the lock officials to jump to the front. Over the ship's tannoy he apologized to the other barges lined up along the banks saying he was carrying two foreign guests and it would be unseemly for them to have to wait. We all laughed like devilish conspirators.

Those living on the train form an extended family and treat each other's property as their own. Many were born to this existence and have had relations working on the canal for generations. The crew consisted of chain smokers, bar one young lad with a lisp who rejected tobacco on health grounds. This was the only committed male non-smoker I met in China. Second in line to the captain was a raucous old devil with a wild grin and tin whistle which he blew whenever he could. He had retired from the canal once but missed the life so much he won special dispensation to rejoin his team for another few years on reduced wages. His wife, elfin and spry, beamed all day long and seemed to welcome her extended working life as much as her husband. The far end of the train is a silent world unto itself. It was occupied by several younger couples, with babies, who rarely came up to the front and had nothing to do with the management or piloting of the barges. We walked down to meet them one liquid dusk as the barges were crossing Gaoyou Lake. Far from the thump of the tug, in the midst of so much water, the tranquility at the tail-end of the train was immense.

One thing all bargees seem to have in common is dissatisfaction with their falling pay. The standard wage is 800 yuan a month (US$100) and this, they say, is dropping year on year because the value of their cargo (in this case cement gravel) is falling. In addition competition is getting tighter. One evening as we waited at a lock to register, a crowd of people from neighbouring trains collected in Li's cabin. They all said they were dissatisfied, that they disapproved of Deng's reforms opening the economy to market forces, that life had been better for them under Mao and that they were worried about the spread of corruption. These were the least satisfied people I met.

Li Ping was an astonishingly willing and candid interlocutor. She was clearly bored by her circumstances—a somewhat friendless round of cooking, cleaning, knitting

*The mist of a cool, early October morning dampens the sun's first rays as a string of ten barges makes its way down the Grand Canal towards the Yangtze River. Each time it passes through one of the many lock gates on the way, the barge train must be split in two—a busy time for the crew who otherwise have little to do apart from play mah-jong.*

and singing, broken intermittently only by the urgency of the locks. We talked about her life, my life, her husband and her country; it is thanks to her that I absorbed a technicolor impression of life on the canal. That she was happy to let me sleep in her own bed is an indication of her unfettered outlook. Hardest for her to accept was that I, through choice rather than misfortune, was at twenty-eight still single. This goes against the most fundamental precept of her life (and almost every woman in China). 'Wasn't I worried? I was now too old to get married, there was no hope for me.' I have promised to return in two years with a child and a husband, to prove that anything is after all possible.

'What do couples do in the West when one partner cheats on the other?' she asked.

'Separate,' I replied, confident that she would never do such a thing, for she knew her husband could not be without her, nor she without him. In spite of their problems their relationship was by far the most demonstrative that I have seen in China; their closeness was striking.

The hours of frankness and friendship with Li Ping were golden. There were other crisp moments. Feeding time was sensational. On the first day Kevin and I were instructed to sit at a circular metal table built on the deck at the front of the tug. The food that arrived from the galley was delicious: fresh river fish in the spiciest most exquisite sauce imaginable. This was accompanied by large wedges of rice, piquant soup, fried cabbage and radish, all rich with flavour. A banquet eaten whilst gliding through peaceful bamboo-fringed calm—I still revel in its magic.

Those days on the barge were an unbeatable insight into life on the canal. While this is not about to disappear, one wonders what the future holds for the canal and particularly those who live off it.                                                                          A.R.

# YANGZHOU 揚州

*Green mountains dim, and waters wide:*
*Unwithered yet by autumn's end, the grasses in the south.*
*Along Bridge Twenty Four, bright moonlit nights,*
*Does jadelike beauty still provide instruction on the flute?*[1]
By Tang dynasty poet Du Mu 杜牧 , (803–852)

The city, originally known as Hancheng, was built in the fifth century BC by Fuchai, the king of the state of Wu in the Spring and Autumn Period. Its fortunes were closely linked to the Grand Canal and the movement of the Yangtze River. During the Tang dynasty a government official reformed the transportation system so that all the grain from the south would first concentrate in Yangzhou before being shipped north. Some 240,000 tons of grain and an even greater volume of other goods passed through Yangzhou every year and the city became a major trading centre between the north and south. Ten official shipyards were established for the construction of grain ships.

Because Yangzhou was only ninety kilometres from the sea and the Yangtze formed a natural harbour it also became a major trading port for foreign vessels from such countries as Korea, Japan, Persia and India.

In the ninth century the Japanese monk, Ennin[2] wrote:

*Market places dot a ten league thoroughfare; when night markets open, a myriad lights glow under the azure sky.*

... the very great and noble city of [Yangzhou], which has twenty-seven other wealthy cities under its administration; ... a city of great importance... and Marco Polo himself did govern this city for three full years, by order of the Great Khan. The people live by trade and manufactures, for a great amount of harness for knights and men-at-arms is made there. And in this city and its neighbourhood a large number of troops are stationed by the Khan's orders. *(Polo)*

This city is a noble city... This city hath also a vast amount of shipping. *(Odoric)*

Yangzhou began to lose its status as a sea port when, over the years, the Yangtze silted up on its northern side where the city stood, and it was no longer near the great river.

The canal, on proceeding somewhat farther ceased to have a current; and the ground rising to the southward, it was found necessary, in order to gain a level, to cut down about twenty feet deep for a tract of seven or eight miles; at the end of which the yachts reached a city of the first order, bearing marks of great antiquity. Some of the walls and buildings were in ruins, and overgrown with mosses, grass, and shrubbery. It still had the appearance of carrying on a considerable trade; and there were not fewer than a thousand vessels of different sizes lying at anchor close to it. *(Staunton)*

The old Sui and Tang dynasty city stood on a plateau to the north-west of present-day Yangzhou and it may well have been these ruins that Staunton and his companions saw. Some of the old city walls as well as a museum and various reconstructions can still be seen

---

[1] The last two lines refer to a bridge in Yangzhou where legendary beauties used to meet to play the flute.
[2] A Japanese Buddhist monk, he visited Tang dynasty China between AD 838–847 in search of new scriptures and enlightenment, and kept a detailed diary of his travels.

today. One can stand on the reconstructed ramparts of the Tang city and have a magnificent view over the modern city below. A museum now stands on the site of the palace of the emperor Yangdi who, during the Sui dynasty, was responsible for the construction of sections of the Grand Canal. His tomb, a simple mound of earth surrounded by a recently added white marble wall, can been found amongst rice paddies just outside the small town of Huaisi 截泗 to the north of Yangzhou. Regrettably, the wall and an accompanying stele have been daubed with black paint and graffiti.

# YANGZHOU FUNERAL

### YANGZHOU FUNERAL

In parts of China five decades of communism have effaced, in theory, any idea of an after-life and done away with funerary pageantry. In reality the funeral rite is in many places still very colourful and important. Mourning traditionally does not take place behind closed doors. Honour and respect are measured by the volume of wailing; the more public the grief the better. This probably accounts for our inclusion in a funeral spectacular. It seems extraordinary to invite two camera-toting tourists to join the fun of your favourite uncle's funeral—but this is what happened.

Whilst straying along some narrow back streets in an old part of Yangzhou, my ears were diverted by a peculiar instrumental mix. Rounding a corner we met a band, set up in the courtyard of a house, consisting of several classical Chinese wind instruments, a trumpet, a couple of drums, an electric keyboard and bass guitar.

*The second of three days of mourning ends with a four-hour Chinese opera attended by about 150 relatives, friends and neighbours, squeezed into the family's courtyard. A mixture of comedy and tragedy, it is performed in the local Yangzhou dialect.*

*Relatives try to comfort Mrs. Wang as she is overcome with grief on the morning of her husband's cremation. Her husband's body, under a red satin cover, can just be seen lying inside the house.*

This is not an especially harmonious combination. Gaggles of people were milling around but no one was paying much attention to the players, all of whom looked decidedly bored. In no time at all we had been invited to sit down and join the party which, it transpired, was a funeral. The celebrations were stretching over three days, the band played throughout the extravaganza whilst mourners came and went.

The deceased gentleman had spent his life working as a pilot on the Grand Canal. He left a widow, three brothers, four sons, two daughters, numerous grandchildren and countless nephews, nieces, great nephews, great nieces. He had been the head of a large clan still based in Yangzhou that has lived by the canal for generations. Eager smiles and a warm welcome soon dispelled any anxiety about being spectators at such an emotionally charged occasion. We were led to believe that by witnessing the old man's funeral we would be honouring his memory, and so we stayed.

Several branches of the family lived in the same courtyard and it was here that commemorations took place. That evening a local opera troupe performed outside the house under street lights for four hours. A crowd of 150, young and old, gathered to watch. The story that unfolded told of impoverished greedy brothers and sisters trying to divide the wealth of their one prosperous relation. The cast of five was in costume and fully made up. Humour was slapstick and bawdy and hinged on an effeminate simpleton with upright pig-tails, pink cheeks and scarlet bloomers. Across the audience faces were rapt. Even though most had seen the performance many times before they still subsided in genuine howls of laughter and shed genuine tears when a beautiful innocent daughter died. How amazing that traditional shows are still so popular with young and old alike. This is community theatre at its purest: in dialect, performed under street lights on a scratch of pavement in celebration of a major family event, the audience squatting at the performers' feet. Only the widow Wang stayed out of the excitement, remaining instead in the front room of her house where her husband's body was stretched out.

*A sketched portrait of Mr. Wang is carried by one of his four sons.*
*A granddaughter moves to lead the procession as the mourners, followed by a*
*brass band, march down the street to waiting vehicles.*

The third day of the funeral party began at the family home with breakfast. Mourners were dressed according to rank: sons and widow with swathes of white cotton tied round their heads and covering their shoes; daughters and spouses with white arm bands and skull caps; the next generation of grandchildren and great nephews and nieces with red arm bands and white skull caps. The rest of us—the casual mourners—wore black arm bands. More than sixty people had gathered for this day of high-octane mourning. In the background caterers were already at work skinning eels and gutting fish for the feast that was to be the culmination of the 'laying to rest'.

The body of the old gentleman had been lying in state in his front room for the past two days. He was togged up in a blue silk padded jacket and a dark peaked cap, his face nicely touched up and his browned skin stretched tightly over his features. He looked exceedingly hale and hearty. On this final morning he was stretched out on a bier and covered by a red silk cloth. His sons and daughters circled his body, wailing. His wife also wept loudly but was so overcome with emotion she found it hard to move herself around the room and for most of the time lay in a heap by the door. An expert of some denomination, there to administer luck, jumped around, seemingly casting spells. He wrote some calligraphy, black ink on stark white paper, and burnt paper money. When these necessary attentions were complete the bier was carried out of the house onto the street and up towards a waiting van. The crowd surged in front of it towards a table set out in the alley covered with 'lucky' fruit, sweets and biscuits. The neighbours pushed to grab as much as possible. Ten metres up the lane another table had been set out. Again everyone scrambled to stuff their pockets, pushing rivals out of the way. It was a jumble of scuffling elbows. A doleful row of four sons followed, one carrying a black and white portrait of their father, their white head-dresses dragging along the street. In front of them was a line of grandchildren; behind walked Mrs. Wang the widow supported on all sides

*One by one the four sons, following tradition, jump into the grave, squat momentarily there and climb out. Then their father's ashes, contained in a small wooden box, are passed down and placed inside an earthenware pot. Mr Wang, who spent his life working as a pilot on the Grand Canal, is being buried next to an old friend, within sight of the ancient waterway.*

by daughters and daughters-in-law, so bowed with grief that she had hardly enough momentum to move forward. A large crowd of friends and relatives drifted around the chief mourners, but most showed little emotion, many even seemed disinterested. Grief was expected only from the immediate family; everyone else could treat the occasion as a jolly get-together with no call for mock solemnity. Three tables later we arrived at the end of the alley where we clambered into waiting trucks, the bier was already installed in a bus. Throughout the forty-five minute journey across town to the crematorium the band continued to play on top of its float, no doubt the trumpeter losing a few teeth on top of the jolting vehicle.

[The procession] would sometimes extend for nearly half a mile. The train was usually arranged in the following order. In front marched a priest uncovered, next a group of musicians with flutes, trumpets, and cymbals; after these the male relations of the deceased in long white frocks and behind them the chief mourner, supported by two friends, whose exertions to prevent him from tearing his cheeks and hair appeared to be truly ridiculous. Then followed the coffin, covered by a magnificent canopy and borne generally by four men, sometimes by eight. After the canopy the female relations proceeded in chairs, or more generally in the little covered carts, wearing white frocks like the men, their hair dishevelled and broad white fillets bound across their foreheads. On approaching a bridge or a temple the procession always halted while the priest burned little images of tin foil, or let off a few crackers, upon which the noisy gong and the rest of the band made a flourish. *(Barrow)*

When the body was in situ on its slab, prior to being shunted into the furnace, we were permitted one last walk-past. We were ushered into line by a white-coated man blowing a whistle. 'Advance,' he cried and marshalled us up the steps and into the presence for the last time. Canned music oozed through the hall. White-tiled and spacious, the crematorium was modern, airy and bright, but too clinical to be reassuring. Mrs. Wang's knees buckled as she was herded round like an octopus, her supporting daughters providing extra arms and legs. No one was allowed to linger; the marshal blew his whistle and the music stopped abruptly in mid-bar.

We moved to a plastic-cushioned waiting room where we sat for half an hour. Voices were low but there was some laughter and levity. Across from me the immediate family looked exhausted, slate faces grey with grief. They sat back deep in their chairs, mentally deflated, eyes puffy and strained, skin shiny from the wash of tears. Finally we climbed back into our vehicles. A wooden box with a red ribbon was in the arms of Mr. Wang's eldest son; he held it tightly but with little apparent emotion.

Once again the band played us across town. We were delivered to a path leading beside the canal not far from the Wang's house. Here we formed a magnificent procession to the family burial ground. We walked first along a narrow silvery tree-lined path above the water, then through a jigsaw of buildings, allotments, fields, and apartment blocks. A line of grandchildren led the way bearing tall wispy bamboo rosettes, like catherine wheels of tissue paper. The band followed, marching single-file, and we tripped along noisily behind. Finally we reached a tree-lined bank at the edge of a field. Chief mourners and the keener onlookers pushed forward to where a hole had been dug and formed a circle around its mouth, the rest hung back and continued chatting. One by one the four sons jumped down into the grave, squatted down, then clambered out again. Then the man responsible for administering luck finished some calligraphy, burnt paper money, and then also descended into the hole. The casket was lowered into his hands and placed in an earthenware pot. Then, together, we scattered handfuls of earth from above, and coins to ensure that Mr. Wang's spirit could get to where it needed to go.

The casket was soon covered. Abruptly the band stopped playing, turned on their heels and sauntered off. Clearly, they were contracted to perform until the ashes were in the earth and would do no more. Mysterious to the end, they faded away across the fields. And so we wandered back to the family home, a couple of hundred metres away. Before entering the courtyard every person had to step over a mound of burning straw, and once inside we were all given sugary water and a handful of boiled sweets. Then we settled down for a feast. We sat in warm sunshine at large round tables under the shade of a tall leafy tree. All family members showed up. Children were back from school for the banquet and adults who had worked in the morning took the afternoon off. It was a huge gathering, but there was no ceremony, no speeches, no public acknowledgment of why we had all come together or a word of thanks or consolation for the widow. The four sons sat round their mother who was smiling lightly but looked dishevelled and exhausted. Much of the rest of the family was buoyant and light-hearted; this was just another opportunity for the clan to meet up. The likenesses were striking: different combinations of similar features sitting in a circle across a white table cloth covered in round plates of seafood and vegetables.

A few days later we returned to the Wang clan headquarters and were greeted with profound warmth. We had gone to give some photos of the day. Once again we met unstinting hospitality and total acceptance. I was told I would be accepted into the family as the deceased man's new daughter, and that he would have been happy to have us at his funeral, that it was a kind of honour. The ceremony we had been part of had been traditional and steeped in superstition. The Wang family were not rich but its members had gathered to mark the passing of their clan leader in an honourably lavish fashion: all requisite respect had been shown. The pageantry and panache were striking, as was the tepidity of those from the further reaches of the extended family who remained wholly unmoved. The comfortable ease with which the passing of this life was acknowledged demonstrates a realistic acceptance of the workings of mortality. This is the norm in much of the Third World. Often the Chinese are criticized for seemingly undervaluing life, but this is only a manifestation of an attitude to life and death very different to that in the West.

A.R.

They burn the bodies of the dead. And when any one dies the friends and relations make a great mourning for the deceased, and clothe themselves in hempen garments, and follow the corpse playing on a variety of instruments and singing hymns to their idols. And when they come to the burning place, they take representations of things cut out of parchment, such as... horses, male and female slaves, camels, armour suits of cloth of gold [and money] in great quantities, and these things they put on the fire along with the corpse... And they tell you that the dead man shall have all these slaves and animals... alive in flesh and blood, and the money in gold, at his disposal in the next world. *(Polo)*

The Chinese are infidels and idolators, and they burn their dead after the manner of Hindus. *(Ibn Batuta)*

From these quotes it was obviously general practice, certainly in these parts of China, to cremate the dead around the thirteenth and fourteenth centuries, for both Marco Polo and Ibn Batuta remarked on it as it was in stark contrast to the customs they were used to. However, towards the end of the sixteenth century, Ricci talks about the dead being buried. At some stage during the intervening period the practice of cremation had fallen out of favour.

The Chinese place their dead in wooden coffins, which are made of incorruptible wood, when that is obtainable, sparring no expense in the making.
They place the body in a wooden box, and then hermetically seal the box with a glossy bituminous substance. Thus sealed the casket will remain absolutely impenetrable to fetid gases for years. The Chinese frequently keep the bodies of their deceased in the home, sometimes for years, until they have built or discovered a suitable place for burial. *(Ricci)*

It is interesting to note too, that the casket containing the body of Father Ricci himself was kept for almost a year from the time of his death beside the altar of his chapel in Beijing, before his eventual burial outside the walls of the capital.
Burials were still common practice at the time of the Macartney expedition 200 years later. Although Ricci made no mention of the burning of paper effigies it frequently crops up in the journals of the members of the Macartney expedition. So it seems safe to assume this continued unchanged from Polo's time. Barrow also touches on a far more brutal practice concerning the burials of royalty about which he had learned.

Formerly it was the custom to bury slaves with emperors and princes and sometimes also their concubines alive; but this cruel practice has given way, in modern times, to the more harmless one of burning representations of their domestics in tin foil, cut into the shape of human beings, and of placing their statues in wood or stone upon their graves. *(Barrow)*

About ten years ago, because of a chronic shortage of space available for cemeteries, the government instructed that, in the cities, dead people had to be cremated and relatives receive a box containing the ashes. Only in rural areas where there is more space can people continue to be buried in the traditional way. One can often see graves dotted around allotments or paddy fields, the small mounds topped usually with a simple concrete dome or headstone. Occasionally, depending on the wealth of the family concerned, a more elaborate structure is erected, surrounded perhaps by a low wall, within which relatives burn offerings or leave food at the time of the important annual grave-cleaning festivals in spring and autumn.

# Nanjing & The Yangtze River 南京，長江

The following morning being the 5th November, we launched into the grand and beautiful river called the [Yangtze], which at this place was about two miles in width... The numerous islands rising out of the river and covered with verdure, the multitude of ships of war, of burden and of pleasure, some gliding down the stream, others sailing against it; some moving by oars and others lying at anchor; the banks on either side covered with towns and houses as far as the eye could reach, presented a prospect more varied and cheerful than any that had hitherto occurred. *(Barrow)*

The face of the country was here entirely changed. Instead of flat country... the ground rose gradually from the margin of the river, enriched with various kinds and tints of culture, interspersed with trees, temples, and pagodas. In the river were islands skirted with shrubbery, and rocks rising abruptly from the surface of the water.

A vast variety of vessels were moving on this large river. The waves rolled like those at sea, and porpoises are said to be sometimes seen leaping amongst them. *(Staunton)*

The Yangtze River dolphin or baiji is the most endangered dolphin in the world today. A combination of illegal fishing, water pollution, habitat loss and increased river traffic have had a devastating effect on the population of this rare cetacean. Current estimates put the number at less than 100. The Chinese government has declared the baiji a national treasure and is working with scientists in an effort to prevent the species from becoming extinct. However, with the serious impact on the environment brought about by construction of the Three Gorges Dam Project further upriver, it is difficult to see how this dolphin, unique to the Yangtze River, will be able to survive.

The Yangtze River, or in Chinese Changjiang (literally, Long River), is the world's third longest river after the Amazon and Nile. Stretching 6,300 kilometres from its source in the Tibet-Qinghai Plateau to the Yellow Sea, it narrows to only one to two kilometres when approaching Nanjing, where it is constricted by

*The sun struggles to penetrate the blanket of smog that lies over Nanjing as barges pass under the Nanjing Changjiang Bridge. Built in the 1960s, with a span of more than one and a half kilometres, it is the longest double-deck, road and rail bridge in China—and the only bridge across the Yangtze River for hundreds of kilometres.*

hills. Further east it widens gradually to eighteen kilometres near the city of Nantong 南通 , before entering the sea close to Shanghai.

Although the Grand Canal crosses the Yangtze to the east of the town of Zhenjiang 鎮江 the present-day road must take a detour through Nanjing, 100 kilometres to the south-west, and across the monstrous Nanjing Changjiang River Bridge. Built between 1960 and 1968, it is the longest double-deck bridge for rail and road traffic in China. The span alone is more than one-and-a-half kilometres and along with its sweeping approaches totals nearly seven kilometres. Above the railway line, supported by massive Stalinesque columns where callow-faced soldiers stand guard with fixed bayonets, its two lanes of traffic thunder day and night.

Nanjing, the capital of Jiangsu, was made the capital of the Middle Kingdom in 1368 by the first Ming emperor, Hongwu 洪武 . This was after he had driven out the Mongols from Beijing, effecting the demise of the Yuan dynasty. It remained the capital until 1402. Situated on the south bank of the lower reaches of the Yangtze River and backed by mountains the site was first settled some 5,000 years ago. The city itself dates back some 2,400 years.

The history of Nanjing was closely linked to that of the Grand Canal in 1842 with the culmination of the Opium War. One by one the coastal ports from Guangzhou (then known to the outside world as Canton) to Shanghai fell to the powerful British navy. Finally they sailed up the Yangtze to seize Zhenjiang. Their aim was simple—to force the Chinese government to open their ports to European trade.

5th August 1842

... anchor again near the opening of the northern portion of the Grand Canal—the southern entrance is close by [Zhenjiang]. The river is about a mile and a half wide. Of course we have blockaded the canal and stopped the supplies going through to Pekin. *(Edward Cree)*

The choice of Beijing as capital had always proved to be a serious burden on the empire. Its total dependence on the Grand Canal to transport food was its Achilles' heel. The Grand Canal, as one official noted, was like a man's throat: if it was unable to supply the southern grain tax for a single day, the capital would die. This fact had obviously not been lost on the British Navy, who used it to great effect. It was this blockage which quickly forced the signing of the Treaty of Nanjing on 29 August 1842. Not only were the five major ports opened for trade but the seemingly insignificant island of Hong Kong was also ceded to the British.

10th August 1842

[Nanjing] is about 250 miles from the sea. The river here is wide, like a lake, but still deep and swift. On the northern shore is the royal Hunting Ground of the emperors of the Ming Dynasty, a fine large park walled round, said to be filled with game. It is hilly and well wooded. *(Cree)*

13th August

Lord Saltoun [commanding the 1st or Right Brigade] has established his headquarters at a large village outside the northern wall, where they found some extensive farm buildings and rich mandarins' houses and stabling for the ponies of the Madras Artillery. Some of the men came upon a warehouse full of raw silk and, not knowing what it was, used it for swabs to clean out their quarters and even for litter in the stables till they found the ponies got into such a tangle that they could not extricate their legs and it was found they had destroyed hundreds of pounds' worth of raw silk. *(Cree)*

## PARK LIFE

'Just stretch your leg on this bench, and lean forward gently. That's right.'
Pain shoots up my thigh. My ninety-three-year-old personal trainer twinkles, greatly amused that I am so stiff and unsupple. Zhou Wen rises at four every morning. Rain or shine he meets his friends in Nanjing's Xiuqiu Park and, as day breaks, they can all be found stretching and twisting their bodies, part of an exercise regimen that successfully preserves them; like the delectable Hundred Year Old Eggs, time seems only to have increased their strength. Zhou has witnessed life in Nanjing since he was fifteen. A mechanic by profession, he retired some thirty years ago and now lives with his grandchildren in a suburb backing on to the Yangtze River. His companions in the park are mostly twenty years younger than he but Zhou keeps up with little difficulty.

Next we try the swivelling arm trick. I chase his lower arm as he rotates the limb in front of his chest. I can just about keep up and then he pounces, clenching my wrist with a grip like a vice, and twists. I squeal with pain and again he laughs. His strength is astonishing. He is frail and looks shaky on his legs, but the power in his hands is extraordinary. We try again, I follow his moves, but always he is too quick for me and when my wrist is seized in that grip he has the power to topple me. This is all very jolly for him. He chuckles then shakes his head at my physical inadequacy. But all the same he pulls out four tangerines from his cloth bag and offers me two; he has decided I have earned them and there is absolutely no question of my refusing.

Strains of 'The Carpenters' float across the park lake. Within the confines of a circular roller-skating rink two hundred people are dancing. It is seven o'clock in the morning. A coil of spilling skirts rocks around the ring. The majority are soberly dressed

*Every morning at seven o'clock, people gather at this park*
*to enjoy an hour of ballroom dancing before going to work. This is just one of a host of*
*different forms of exercise that begin the day all over China.*

*Ge Ben-ling, a fifty-five-year-old retired car mechanic,*
*rises at four-thirty each morning before going to teach tai-chi at a playground*
*near his home in Nanjing. This slow motion exercise is said to have been developed*
*by a monk who lived some time during the thirteenth or fourteenth century.*

couples avoiding eye contact, but there is the odd all-female pairing and an occasional man stepping out on his own (with arms stretched around his invisible partner). There are few smiles. This is a serious business, not an occasion for a vain parade of nimble footwork meant to impress but the considered pursuit of graceful exercise. Rumba, waltz, foxtrot, two-steps, three-steps and the rest—all are performed with generous but considered panache. Skirts wheel; men rise on tip-toes and twist women under their arms, a river of undulating motion. The woman in the wide scarlet skirt seems to rotate faster than most. Looking through the rink railings I find her movements mesmerizing. With the confidence and tautness of a flamenco dancer, she lightly spins her way past the other couples, demanding a large space for the fullness of her movements. At eight o'clock the Carpenters are switched off and the rink empties. The dancers, flushed from their exertions, retire chattering for work.

Imagine dancing at dawn, outside, sober—surely an exhilarating way to start a day. Dancing in many cultures is so often a sexually loaded exchange: we do it in the dark, quite probably a preview to more intimate activity, an exercise of our freedom to attract any partner we choose. For the Park Dancers, on the other hand, the occasion is totally asexual: they dance for exercise, for fun, for fresh air, for the pleasure of movement to music. It is absolutely not a question of sexual adventure before a day's work. The popularity of this kind of dancing is partly due to widespread curiosity about such western pastimes that were until recently censured as being too decadent. Now sanitized (the Carpenters are hardly going to incite rebellion) they are condoned, and people love them. How ashamed I am that my ballroom dancing is no good. How the Park Dancers would have laughed had I joined them for a spin on the rink.

Elsewhere in the park more traditional Chinese physical disciplines are being practised: tai-chi, sword swinging, fan dancing, tree hanging (a lesser known endurance test involving swinging your legs whilst holding on to a branch above your head). Then there is robotic movement-follow-my-leader with stiff legs and jerky arm extensions in a figure of eight between trees, synchronized by a clicking tongue. All these and more have their devotees. For the most part though the local population is engaged in arm swinging and leg stretching, or making music. A group of six or seven sit in a pavilion beside the lake jamming on traditional Chinese instruments-erhu, qin, flute. Some sing as well, and others dance. Only the elderly hang out in this corner and many of them stay all day. Those who are retired say they are here because they want to be out of their homes which are small and are shared with their daughters-in-law. They would rather be in the park happily in the company of friends.

Mr. Ge, a tai-chi master, takes us under his wing as rather lame protégés. Moving with a straight spine and erect head he swoops low to the ground in a flow of motion while gradually rotating round to face us. He wears a loose white cotton pyjama suit with knotted braid buttons and loops. There is a heaviness to his body underlying his physical strength; he is not wiry but full-jowled and powerful. Mr. Ge is keen to demonstrate movements and explain the philosophy of tai-chi. People gather in a circle around him, the numbers swelling when we bashfully try to follow his demonstration. Every morning he leads a troupe in the park. His interest is piqued by my video camera and he would very much like a copy of my recording to show to his pupils, he says. It seems a relatively fair trade-off. Later he took us to his house, shared with his eldest son's family, and fed us noodles. The apartment seemed comfortable, but maybe not for five people. His son owns a huge karaoke player which we linked up to the video camera. The whole family gathered to watch his expertise in the park. He glowed with pride.

Under trees along the banks of the lake are several stone tables where groups of four or five hunch down to play chequers and cards, often with a crowd of advisers at their shoulders. At one a watch repairer sets up his tray. He squints through an eye-piece and fiddles with the clock in his hands then reaches into a compartment spilling over with silver instruments for a tool, clinking through the pile of junk as he fumbles for what he is looking for, dropping it back with a ping when the job is done. Without looking up he tells me he is a retired mechanic and has to do this work to supplement his state pension which, he complains, goes nowhere. Four friends sit round him as he works. He acknowledges them all and converses warmly but never raises his eyes from the employ of his hands.

By the main gate in the shade of a tree a man is standing on his head on a narrow wooden bench. He is distracted as I move in close to film the concentration used to summon such balance and comes tumbling down. As he hustled me off I guiltily acknowledge that I deserve his cold shoulder.

There are many such parks throughout China where municipal space is intensely cultivated by a large number of people. Generally elderly Chinese of both sexes·are far more nimble and better preserved than their Caucasian counterparts. It is widely believed they have grown up on an inferior diet and have toiled harder, have to suffer inferior medical services and live in less hygienic environments, yet unquestionably they ride the passage of years with much less physical cost. The inherited culture of the gentle workout, be it swinging from a tree or a lifetime of tai-chi, must go a long way to account for this. No doubt the communality of the Chinese plays a part: they are rarely alone, and thus loneliness, one of the great afflictions of the aged in the developed West, does not work to destroy the elderly as it does elsewhere. Even though the average age of the dawn exercisers in the Nanjing park is high, the energy and laughter brewing within it is extraordinarily vital.

A.R.

# ZHENJIANG 鎮江

... in the middle of the river, there stands a rocky island on which there is an idol-monastery containing some 200 idolatrous friars, and a vast number of idols. And this Abbey holds supremacy over a number of other idol-monasteries... *(Polo)*

In crossing the river the attention was particularly attracted by an island situated in the middle of the river, called [Jin Shan], or the golden mountain, which rose almost perpendicularly out of the river, and is interspersed with gardens and pleasure-houses. Art and nature seemed to have combined to give this spot the appearance of enchantment. It belonged to the Emperor, who had built upon it a large and handsome palace, and on the highest eminence several temples and pagodas. The island also contained a large monastery of priests, by whom it is chiefly inhabited. *(Staunton)*

Jin Shan 金山 , or golden mountain, is no longer an island. The silting of the Yangtze has grafted it to the south bank of the river where it stands just to the west of the modern town of Zhenjiang. The temple is still there, a working Buddhist monastery, and is undergoing extensive renovation.

Zhenjiang was a ferry crossing on the Yangtze River as far back as the third century BC. About six hundred years later the city of Tiewengcheng was built on the site of Beigushan 北固山 (this hill still stands overlooking the Yangtze) by Sun Quan, the ruler of the kingdom of Wu in the Three Kingdoms period. With the opening of the southern section of the Grand Canal in the early seventh century Zhenjiang grew into an important port on both the canal and the Yangtze. It was most prosperous during the Northern Song dynasty (960–1127). Xijindu Street 西津渡古街 , a one-kilometre-long, busy shopping street dating from the Song dynasty, and said to have been visited by Marco Polo, is still preserved today. Previously it terminated at the river where there was an important ferry crossing, hence its name—West Ferry Crossing Street.

This city hath shipping finer and more numerous peradventure than any other city in the world. And all the vessels are as white as snow, being coated with whitewash. And on board of them you find halls and taverns and many other conveniences, as handsome and well ordered as are anywhere to be found. Indeed it is something hard to believe when you hear of, or even when you see, the vast scale of the shipping in those parts. *(Odoric)*

## ZHENJIANG TO SUZHOU
## 鎮江 - 蘇州

The ground to the southward of the [Yangtze River], gradually rose to such a height that it was found necessary to cut down the earth in some parts to the depth of near eighty feet, in order to find a level for the passage of the canal. *(Staunton)*

The Grand Canal was now on its final leg between the Yangtze and its terminus at Hangzhou as it headed south through the famous canal cities of Changzhou 常州 , Wuxi and Suzhou.

*The interior of Jin Shan Temple. Over the last few years it has been undergoing extensive renovation and re-decoration. On the site of an important working Buddhist monastery, the temple is visited daily by hundreds of visitors .*

VIEW of the *TCHIN-SHAN*, or *GOLDEN ISLA...*

*Alexander delt.*

*London...*

**Plate No. 10**
*"The river begins to narrow and is divided into numerous channels by beautiful islands.
The banks are more hilly and still rich in cultivation. At a sudden bend of the river
to the west we came in sight of... the fairy-like Golden Island [Jin Shan]*

## 39

*G-TSE-KIANG, or GREAT RIVER of CHINA.*

*Nicol.*

*Wilson sculpt.*

*in the centre of the river with its tall pagoda on the top and its sides covered with temples,*
*gardens and trees, the walled city of [Zhenjiang] on the left hand and*
*high blue mountains beyond. Farther up the river is the entrance of the Grand Canal."*
*(Edward Cree on passing up the Yangtze River in 1842)*

W. Alexander. del.

CHINESE BARGES of the

London P.

**Plate No. 11**

"[This plate] *shows a view of Chinese barges preparing to pass under a bridge.*
*On the left hand side of the print appears a communication under the bridge,*
*between the grand canal and another branching from it, without any inconvenience to*
*foot passengers, or to the people employed to track the barges.*
*Solid and permanent bridges are thrown over the canal in many parts of this province.*
*Some of them were built of reddish granite... and some of a coarse grey marble.*

## 40

*W. Byrne sculp.*

*paring to pass under a Bridge.*

*Nicol.*

*The arches of some of those bridges are of a semicircular, and others an elliptical form.
Some are in the form of a horse shoe, the space being widest near the top of the arch.
For passing under these bridges the strong single masts of the yachts and barges were
taken down... Those masts were readily lowered to pass under the bridges, some of which,
however, were so lofty as to allow the vessels to pass under them in full sail.
Those bridges were here necessary for a communication between the opposite sides of the canal,
along which was an uninterrupted chain of towns and villages." (Staunton)*

*Just as modern vehicles now clog the many old narrow roads in historic cities like Suzhou, the same is true for barge traffic.*

Nor was the canal on the opposite side less lively; for two whole days we were continually passing among fleets of vessels of different constructions and dimensions, those belonging to the revenue department being the largest, each capable of carrying at least two hundred tons. Cities, towns and villages were continued along the banks without intermission: and vast numbers of stone bridges were thrown across the canal, some having one, some two and others three arches. The face of the country was beautifully diversified with hill and dale and every part of it in the highest state of cultivation. *(Barrow)*

Nowadays it is quite a different picture. The growth in importance of the railways by the 1920s, and to a certain extent the expansion of the road network, saw a decline in the use of the canals. It is only along this stretch from Xuzhou through to Hangzhou, in the north of neighbouring Zhejiang Province, that the Grand Canal is still heavily used; a constant procession of barges carrying mainly coal and building materials such as sand, gravel, cement and bricks.

Many factories and industries have been sited alongside the canal to be easily supplied

*Here, in an old street in Zhenjiang dating from the Song Dynasty,*
*a game of Chinese chess is in progress.*
*Known as* xiang qi 象棋 *or 'elephant game,'*
*a form of Chinese chess is known to have existed in China*
*at least as far back as the second century BC,*
*when there are clear references to it in ancient literature.*

by means of barge. The industrial suburbs of the cities extend like tentacles along the Grand Canal as they do along the main roads and railways. For much of the distance between Zhenjiang and Suzhou the canal runs parallel with both the railway line and the road creating an industrial corridor some two hundred kilometres long.

Nevertheless, there is still some respite, areas where the farmland takes over. A quilt of rice paddies, now shorn of their crop; a country of short brown stubble interrupted by shallow lakes. Here and there a line of willows or poplars traces a smaller canal as it disappears into the haze.

# Suzhou 蘇州

*Those coming to Gusu [Suzhou],*
*Find people dwelling on riversides,*
*Ancient places are many with little land to spare,*
*Over canals span bridges in large numbers,*
*Water chestnuts, lotus roots are offered in evening markets,*
*And in spring boats sail laden with silk.*
By Tang poet Du Xunhe 杜荀鶴 (846–904).

Suzhou has its origins 2,500 years ago when He Lu, the father of King Fuchai, built a city on the site. Enclosed by a twenty-four-kilometre-long wall of compressed earth it had eight road gates and six canal entrances. One, the Panmen gate 盤門 in the south-west corner of the city, has been restored and is still there today.

When the Grand Canal opened in the seventh century the city grew in wealth. The poet Bai Juyi became governor and had eight gateways constructed along with sixty streets and 300 crimson wooden bridges mentioned in his poem. He also had a canal built to link

*(Above) This photograph of whitewashed canal-side cottages in Suzhou, taken in August 1994, shows the kind of scene that has been synonymous with the town for centuries. In November 1995 these cottages had been demolished—and were just piles of rubble and timber beams.*

*(Below) These recently finished, still vacant apartments in Suzhou indicate the widespread construction, both residential and industrial, that is now taking place in the city. Many stand empty as still only a small percentage of the population can afford to buy their own flat.*

CHAPTER 4 : JIANGSU PROVINCE

*Beisi Ta or North Temple Pagoda was first built more than 1,700 years ago in the Three Kingdoms period. The original eleven storey tower was destroyed by fire during the Southern Song dynasty, but was later rebuilt with nine storeys during the Ming dynasty.*

the city directly with the Grand Canal. Called the Shantang Canal 山塘河 it passed through the city's west wall to Tiger Hill and the site of He Lu's tomb.

In his journals, Father Matteo Ricci relates that the canal in this area was so narrow and so crowded with boats that it was impossible to make much progress on it in either direction. Knowing this, he took another mode of transport—apparently common in China at that time as well as, so he claims, comfortable—to continue his journey. It was thus that Ricci arrived in Suzhou.

They use a cart, built over a single wheel, on which one person sits astride in the centre, as he would on a horse, with two others sitting, one on either side. This cart or wagon is pushed by a driver by means of two wooden shafts. It affords a safe and a speedy means of travel...

People move about here on land and on water, as they do in Venice, but the water here is fresh and clear... The city is all bridges, very old but beautifully built...

Both the streets and the bridges rest upon wooden piles of pine, sunk deep into the river, after the European fashion. A great part of the merchandise from Portugal, by way of Macao, and from other foreign countries, passes through this river port. The merchants here carry on a heavy trade throughout the whole year with the other trading centres of the kingdom, with the result that there is scarcely anything that one cannot purchase at this mart. *(Ricci)*

The streets of the city of [Suzhou], through the suburbs of which the yachts now passed, were divided, like Venice, by branches from the principal canal. Over each of these branches was erected an elegant stone bridge. The fleet of the Embassy was nearly three hours in passing the suburbs of [Suzhou], before they arrived at the city walls, under which was drawn up an immense number of vessels. In one ship-builder's yard were sixteen upon the stocks close to each other, each of the burden of about two hundred tons. In the walls of the city are turned several arches, through which the canal passes.

[Suzhou] appears to be an uncommonly large and populous city. The houses were generally well built and handsomely decorated. The inhabitants, most of whom were clad in silk, appeared cheerful and prosperous...

The gentlemen of the Embassy also thought the women of [Suzhou] handsomer, fairer, and dressed

145

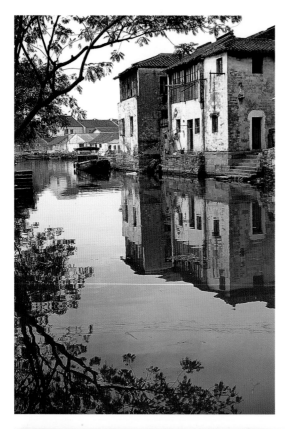

(Left) An old tea house in Tongli
同里. This quaint old town
possesses an excellent example
of a classic Chinese garden,
completed in 1887 as part of a
private residence.

(Below) The ancient canal town
of Tongli has been preserved by
routing a new road some distance
away, alongside which a
new town is growing.

*The sun sets behind Ruiguang Ta, the Pagoda of Auspicious Light, in Suzhou—the oldest surviving pagoda in Jiangsu Province. It was originally built with thirteen storeys in the Three Kingdoms period, but later reconstructed in the Song dynasty as the seven storey tower seen today.*

in a better taste, than most of those they had seen to the northward. The ladies are sometimes distinguished by a small cap on the forehead brought down to a peak between the eyebrows, made of black satin, and set with jewels. They likewise wear ear pendants of crystal or gold. *(Staunton)*

The whole face and neck were washed with a preparation of white lead and the cheeks highly rouged; and two vermilion spots... were particularly conspicuous, one on the centre of the under lip and the other on the chin. Their feet were universally squeezed down to an unnatural size. *(Barrow)*

Suzhou, touted for centuries by poets, writers, scholars and, in recent years, by tourist guidebooks as the city of gardens, is fast becoming the city of parks—industrial parks. To the east of the city vast acreages alongside a new highway unfurling towards Shanghai, have been cleared and set aside for industrial development. Much of this is being financed by joint-venture projects with Singaporean companies. Huge areas of agricultural land have been laid waste and now sit, demarcated with simple wooden stakes, awaiting construction.

Ten years ago, claims a resident of the city, Suzhou was still a beautiful city. The air was clean and clear. Now chimneys belch yellowish waste. In some corners of the city unidentified acrid aromas assault the nostrils. Many of the quaint, two-storey, white-washed cottages that once jostled higgledy-piggledy beside the narrow canals, and often appear in artists' representations of the city, are gone. Many more are earmarked for demolition. Now modern town houses, rows of apartment blocks or sometimes much larger commercial developments sprawl alongside stinking canals. The once spectacular panorama of the city, visible from the top of the Bei Ta 北塔 or North Pagoda, has disappeared beneath a smog-tinged haze.

*Rice lies cut but ungathered, coated with early morning frost—as a sudden cold snap early in November catches farmers in the middle of the harvest. Although the temperature is barely above freezing, this woman is out in her field at dawn preparing the ground for winter vegetables.*

At a short distance from [Suzhou] is the beautiful lake of [Tai Hu], surrounded by a chain of picturesque hills. This lake, which furnishes fish for the inhabitants of [Suzhou], serves them also as a place of public resort and recreation. Many of the pleasure-boats were rowed each by a single female. Every boat had a neat and covered cabin; and the rowers were supposed to follow more than one profession. *(Staunton)*

To the west of Suzhou is Lake Tai 太湖 , one of the largest lakes in China, covering an area of 2,425 square kilometres. Until a few years ago it was common to see large fleets of fishing boats with tall, rectangular sails drifting across the water, but because of overfishing they have been restricted to two seasons around May and October each year. Recently the lake has been beset by a far more serious problem. Choked with blue algae caused by the high phosphate content brought about by the pollution of agricultural fertilizers, the water has become starved of oxygen, threatening not just the valuable fish stocks but the whole ecosystem of the lake.

# Chapter Five

# Zhejiang Province
# 浙江省

Hills and mountains make up almost three-quarters of the total area of Zhejiang Province, while its fragmented coastline is peppered with thousands of islands. Its major river, the Qiantang 錢塘江 , is central to our theme of the Imperial Way. The Grand Canal terminates at the provincial capital of Hangzhou, so to continue further south along the Imperial Way, we must change from this to a succession of rivers that carve their way through the mountainous terrain of southern China. Although roughly similar in size to Jiangsu Province, Zhejiang has a much lower population density—averaging around 430 persons per square kilometre—but is nevertheless one of the wealthier provinces in China. To the south of Lake Tai, the low-lying fertile plains of northern Zhejiang bordering the Qiantang River are in fact an extension of the landscape of Jiangsu. As such it has been an important grain producer over the centuries, sending its annual tribute of grain tax north on the Grand Canal.

This area, along with the coastal plains, has always been prosperous and accounts for most of the province's wealth. The Southern Song dynasty (1127–1279) established its capital in Hangzhou, then called Lin'an, in 1127, and from then on the production of silk, pottery and porcelain developed apace. After the Opium War, Ningbo 寧波 was one of the ports opened to foreign trade, contributing greatly to the region's prosperity before the town was overshadowed in recent decades by Shanghai.

Although cotton is widely grown in this part of the country, it is silk which is the most important cash crop. Over 4,700 years ago, people began growing mulberry trees, raising silkworms and producing silk. Largely produced in the north of the province, where growing conditions are perfect for mulberry, its silkworm cocoon production is perhaps the highest in China. Concentrated around the towns of Hangzhou 杭州 , Jiaxing 嘉興 and Huzhou 湖州 , it produces approximately one-third of the nation's raw silk and satin.

The hilly country to the south is ideal for tea production. It is the most productive of the tea-growing provinces, accounting for almost one-quarter of the nation's total. The well-known Longjing 龍井 or Dragon Well tea has been grown on the slopes surrounding Hangzhou's West Lake 西湖 for over 1,200 years.

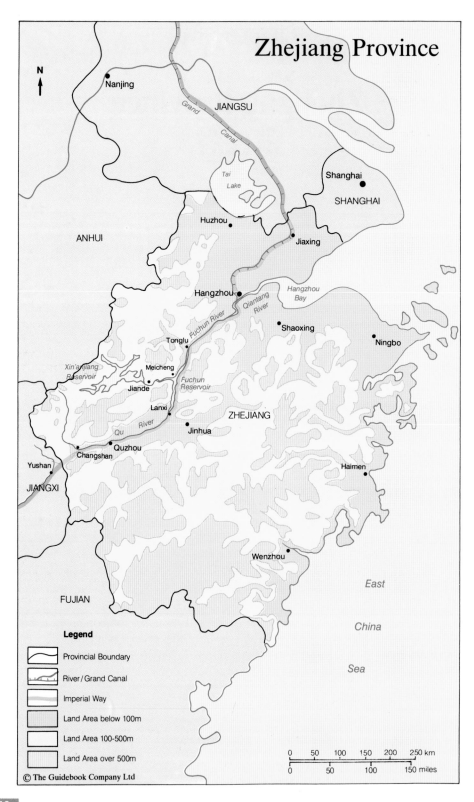

Zhejiang Province

N

Nanjing

JIANGSU

Grand Canal

Tai Lake

Shanghai

SHANGHAI

ANHUI

Huzhou

Jiaxing

Hangzhou

Qiantang River

Hangzhou Bay

Fuchun River

Shaoxing

Ningbo

Tonglu

Xin'anjiang Reservoir

Meicheng

Jiande

Fuchun Reservoir

Lanxi

ZHEJIANG

Qu River

Jinhua

Quzhou

Changshan

Yushan

Haimen

JIANGXI

Wenzhou

East

China

Sea

FUJIAN

**Legend**

Provincial Boundary

River / Grand Canal

Imperial Way

Land Area below 100m

Land Area 100-500m

Land Area over 500m

© The Guidebook Company Ltd

| 0 | 50 | 100 | 150 | 200 | 250 km |
| 0 | | 50 | | 100 | 150 miles |

# Towards the End of the Grand Canal

The canal continued to be of a width between sixty and a hundred yards, and its banks generally faced with stone, through the whole length of the rich and beautiful country, about ninety miles in length, which lies between [Suzhou] and [Hangzhou]. *(Staunton)*

The country seems to be one continued village on both sides as far as we can see, wonderfully beautiful and rich. Many mulberry trees are planted round the houses, but most of them have been stripped of their leaves. We are now in silk country... *(Macartney)*

10th November 1793. This morning the air was extremely cold and piercing. *(Anderson)*

9th November 1995.

A weak sun dangles in a low, white mist that hangs over the farmland. Its soft light glistens on a heavy frost that coats the rice lying cut but ungathered in the fields. On a level with the road, neat islands of land bursting with mulberry bushes and chrysanthemum plants stand amongst rice paddies, sunk like dry lakes, a metre or so below—this to facilitate flooding during the planting and growing season.

This area of northern Zhejiang, to the south of Tai Lake, around the town of Tongxiang 桐鄉, is famous for its chrysanthemum flowers, which are often used to add a delicate, almost peppermint flavour to Chinese green tea. Dinner plate-sized pads of the compressed flowers stand drying outside many houses. Here and there, amid tidy brick villages, long, tent-shaped bamboo barns covered with a thick reed thatch stand beside empty ponds. They are used for hatching and rearing ducks.

# Hangzhou 杭州

The main road to Hangzhou from the north-east, a wide, newly laid concrete road, is also the main highway from Shanghai. Consequently it is busy, very busy. A constant thundering stream of huge trucks, buses, cars, tractors and anything else on wheels, it seems, is heading in both directions. The road, parts of it still being completed, has already been outgrown.

The dust and traffic fumes hang over the fields of sugar cane that are to be found all over this area of Zhejiang. Periodically, long lines of hawkers sit at the roadside. In front of them bundles of the crop stand in stooks. Occasionally a truck or a car stops and after haggling, the driver finally tosses an armful into the vehicle. Cut into convenient half-metre lengths, travellers gnaw off pieces as they drive. Sucked of all their juice, mouthfuls of chewed fibre are spat from the windows—a hazard for the unsuspecting cyclist.

Mountains begin to rise from the skyline to meet an orange sun setting in a clear, crimson sky as the road descends towards the city. Through suburbs, past cooling towers, between factories with red-and-white-striped chimneys, beneath their large silver pipes that snake overhead and along railway sidings, the road plunges into the city towards towers topped with neon that glow in the twilight. The lights of the city begin to spread across the waters of the lake.

The next morning the lake has disappeared into a milky haze. It is absolutely still. There is no horizon. A few boats carrying tourists float silently across a nothingness. Behind

*A sign of the general growing affluence amongst the population of China, department stores like this one in Hangzhou stock a wide range of modern consumer goods, from karaoke machines to motor cycles.*

them the mountains, washed of all colour and detail, emerge out of the mist like flimsy grey silhouettes.

Hangzhou stands on the north bank of the Qiantang River surrounded by vast expanses of rice paddies, mulberry gardens, bamboo forests, fish ponds and tea plantations, which grow in its fertile delta. The city has a history spanning some 2,200 years. It was an ancient capital as long ago as the ninth century when, during the Five Dynasties period it was the capital of the state of Wuyue. Since then, over the ages, it has been the capital of no less than fourteen kings or emperors. In the tenth century the king of Wuyue, Qian Miao (AD 907–960), built a city wall with a circumference of seventy kilometres. Two centuries later the Southern Song dynasty extended this to 100 kilometres.

...the city hath a hundred miles of compass. And there are in it twelve thousand bridges of stone, for the most part so lofty that a great fleet could pass beneath them. And though the bridges be so high the approaches are so well contrived that carts and horses do cross them. *(Polo)*

There is much conjecture amongst scholars about the accuracy of many of Marco Polo's accounts; the Venetian is frequently prone to hyperbole. A few even question whether he visited China at all. Here it is suggested that he may well have confused miles with the Chinese measurement of li, which is equivalent to approximately half a kilometre. But in this instance we have the usually more reliable narrative of Friar Odoric to substantiate it.

I made diligent inquiry regarding the city, ... and all agreed ... that it had a circuit of one hundred miles. *(Odoric)*

The friar, too, mentions the incredible number of bridges, claiming there are 'more than twelve thousand'.

It had been the invasion of the Nuzhen armies that forced the imperial court of the Jin to evacuate their capital at Kaifeng 開封 and escape south to Hangzhou where they established the Southern Song dynasty. During this period Hangzhou came to prominence as a cultural centre pre-eminent in the development of painting, poetry and calligraphy.

By the time Hangzhou was visited by Marco Polo towards the end of the thirteenth century, and later by Friar Odoric and his contemporary Ibn Batuta early in the next century, it was already flourishing and had grown into a splendid city to rival Beijing in every respect.

This city is the greatest I have ever seen on the surface of the earth. It is three days' journey in length... The city is divided into six towns... each of which has a separate enclosure, whilst one great wall surrounds the whole.

In the first city was posted the garrison of the city, with its commandant... The next day we entered the second city by a gate called the Jews' Gate. This town was inhabited by Jews, by Christians, and by those Turks who worship the sun; they are very numerous... The third day we made our entrance into the third city, and this is occupied by the Mahomedans. It is a fine town, with the bazaars arranged as in Musulman countries, and with mosques and muezzins... *(Batuta)*

Here, amongst his own, Batuta clearly felt at home and was entertained royally. He writes more about the layout and sheer size and population of Hangzhou and gives us some insight into the city's luxurious and decadent lifestyle at the time. It is worth quoting from him at length.

The Musulmans in this city are very numerous... and every day and every night I was present at some new entertainment. The splendour of their banquets never flagged, and every day they took me about the city on horseback for my diversion. One day... we went into the fourth city, where the seat of the government is... This fourth town is intended solely for the dwellings of the emperor's officers and slaves; it is the finest of all the six towns, and is traversed by three streams of water. One of these is a canal from the Great River[1], and by it the supplies of food and of stones for burning are brought in small boats; there are also pleasure boats to be had upon it. The citadel is in the middle of the town; it is of immense extent, and in the centre of it is the palace of the government... We were [guests of an Amir] for three days, and one day he sent his son to escort us in a trip on the canal... Crowds of people in boats were gathered on the canal. The sails were of all bright colours, the people carried parasols of silk, and the boats themselves were gorgeously painted. They skirmished with one another, and pelted each other with oranges and lemons. In the evening we went back to pass the night at the Amir's palace, where the musicians came again and sang very fine songs.

The next day we entered the gate of the fifth city, which is the biggest of all the six, and is inhabited by the Chinese. It has splendid bazaars ...

...we proceeded to enter the sixth... This is inhabited only by seamen, fishermen, caulkers, carpenters... All of them are the emperor's slaves; no other class live with them, and their numbers are very great. The town of which we speak is situated on the banks of the Great River ... *(Batuta)*

Gongchen Bridge 拱宸橋 , built in the fifteenth century, was the gateway to the city on the Grand Canal and still exists today. It has a twenty-five-metre-high arch, which was high enough to allow the passage of the large grain barges loaded with up to three hundred tons of grain. Further south stands Wulinmen 武林門 , formerly an important wharf at the southern terminus of the 1,794-kilometre Grand Canal, which still acts as a port today, providing services for huge amounts of freight and large numbers of passengers that travel on the canal. In 1984 the construction of a seven-kilometre-long extension to the canal was begun which

*Gongchen Bridge in the north of Hangzhou is one of the few surviving classic three-arched bridges on the Grand Canal.*

[1] It is safe to assume that by the 'Great River' he is in fact referring to the Grand Canal. He later writes of this river extending from Hangzhou to Beijing.

now links it to the Qiantang River. Through a network of canals that lies to the south of the river it is possible for barges to reach the coastal port of Ningbo.

After sailing a great part of the day through a forest of mulberry trees, planted with much regularity, we arrived at the city of [Hangzhou], the capital of the province of [Zhejiang]. Here that branch of the grand canal which communicated with the [Yangtze River] terminates in a large commodious bason, at this time crowded with shipping. From this bason a number of smaller canals, passing through arches turned in the walls and intersecting the city in every direction, are finally united in a lake beyond the western wall called the [Xi Hu or West Lake]. *(Barrow)*

At the end of the eighteenth century, Hangzhou was still a major trading port for goods that passed between the northern and southern provinces. Merchandise could arrive by sea or via the rivers of Zhejiang and Fujian 福建 provinces. At this time there was no longer any direct connection between the Qiantang River and the Grand Canal, so everything had to be offloaded at the estuary and transferred to the wharf at Wulinmen and vice-versa.

[Hangzhou] is situated between the bason of the grand canal, and the river [Qiantang], which falls into the sea at the distance of little more than sixty miles to the eastward. The tide when full increases the width of this river to about four miles opposite the city. At low water there is a fine level strand near two miles broad, which extends towards the sea as far as the eye can reach. By this river, [Hangzhou] receives and exports great quantities of merchandize to and from the southern provinces. The goods are shipped and unshipped by means of waggons with four wheels to each, placed in a line, and forming a convenient pier, which is easily lengthened or shortened, by increasing or diminishing the number of waggons, according to the distance of the vessels from the shore. *(Staunton)*

Staunton writes too, about how it was difficult to pass along the narrow streets of the city because of 'the vast concourse of people... each individual going about his own concerns.' The absence of women on the streets and in the shops is explained by vast numbers of them being employed in the manufacture of flowered and embroidered satins and silk. Most of the men, he continues, were gaily dressed and appeared to be in comfortable circumstances.
Some idea of the extent and variety of trade in the city is given here by Barrow.

In the city of [Hangzhou], being particularly famed for its silk trade, we were not surprised to meet with extensive shops and warehouses; in point of size and the stock contained within them they might be said to vie with the best in London. In some of these were not fewer than ten or twelve persons serving behind the counter; but in passing through the whole city not a single woman was visible, either within doors or without. The crowd of people composed of the other sex appeared to be little inferior to that in the great streets of [Beijing]. Here, though mostly narrow they had in other respects much the advantage of those in the capital, being paved with broad flagstones, resembling the Merceria of Venice or courts of the Strand. They appeared to be kept extremely neat and clean. In every shop were exposed to view silks of different manufactures, furs, dyed cottons and nankins, a great variety of English broad-cloths, chiefly however blue and scarlet, used for winter cloaks, for chair covers and for carpets. The rest of the houses in the public streets through which we passed, consisted of butchers and bakers' shops, fishmongers, dealers in rice and other grain, ivory-cutters, dealers in laquered ware, tea-houses, cook-shops and coffin makers; the last of which is a trade of no small note in China. *(Barrow)*

VIEW of the TOWER of the THUNDERING WIND

London

**Plate No. 12** *"The lake was full of fish* [and] *in most places shallow... Vast crowds of pleasure boats were sailing on it. The parties consisted entirely of men: the women in this part of the country not appearing on such occasions. The lake formed a beautiful sheet of water, about three or four miles in diameter, and surrounded to the north, east, and south, by an amphitheatre of picturesque mountains. The margin of the lake... was ornamented with houses and gardens of mandarines, as well as a palace belonging to the Emperor,*

the *LAKE SEE-HOO*, *taken from the VALE of TOMBS.*

*J. Landseer & J. Shirt sculpt.*

*J. Nixon del.*

together with temples, monasteries. Upon the summit also were erected pagodas,
one of which attracted particular attention. It was situated on the verge of a bold peninsula that juts
into the lake, and was called the temple of the Thundering Winds. Four stories were yet standing,
but the top was in ruins. Grass, shrubs, and mosses were growing upon them.
The arches and mouldings were of red, the upright walls of yellow, stone. It is confidently asserted
to have been erected in the time of Confucius, upwards of two thousand years ago." (Staunton)

# SERICULTURE

Silk has been an important product of the region for a long time. Its low-lying, fertile land is ideal for growing good quality mulberry, essential for the rearing of silkworms, and the network of canals is an inexpensive and efficient means of transporting the cocoons to the spinning mills.

Historians agree that the Chinese were the first people to manufacture silk. As early as 2640 BC Confucius recorded that silk was first reeled from a cocoon. In fact silk production was already well established and highly developed by the time of Confucius: fragments of fabric found in excavations in Zhejiang Province have been carbon dated at 3000 BC.

From its very beginning sericulture, the raising of the silkworm and the manufacture of their fibres into silk fabric, was shrouded in secrecy. For the next 3,000 years China held a monopoly on silk production. There were periods in China's history when silk was so widely available that it was cheaper than any other textile. And because of its high tensile strength its uses were not just confined to making fine clothes, but used for such things as bowstrings and fishing lines.

It was during the third century BC that the famous silk routes came into being. The routes, over which the textile was transported by traders to the West, began at what is now Xi'an in Shaanxi Province and proceeded over mountains and through deserts to Antioch and Tyre (present-day Antakya in Turkey and Sout in Lebanon respectively). From there it travelled by sea to Europe and Egypt. At about the same time silks also arrived in Japan.

The history of silk is filled with colourful stories. One concerns the Byzantine Emperor Justinian who sent two monks to China in AD 552 with the mission of bringing back the secret of silk. When the monks returned to Byzantium, they brought

*Silk moth cocoons bob in baths of steaming water as their gossamer-like threads are spun and reeled. Although an average cocoon can unravel more than one kilometre of filament, it still takes over 100 of them to make a tie.*

with them some eggs of the silk moth that they had smuggled out in hollow walking sticks. Parts of Japan are said to have been raising silkworms as early as AD 300 when the Japanese learned the secret of sericulture from four Chinese girls they had kidnapped. Whether or not these stories are true, they give us some insight into silk's romantic and mystical past.

The silkworms are actually the larvae or caterpillars of the silk moth. There are many varieties of moth that produce silk cocoons in the wild but one in particular, *Bombyx mori*, is reared commercially. When they emerge from the egg at the beginning of their life the caterpillars are a mere three millimetres long. Being very delicate they require the utmost care and are placed on bamboo trays and given the best mulberry leaves on which to feed. The caterpillars are voracious eaters and during this thirty-day stage they must shed their skin four times to accommodate their remarkable growth. When fully grown they are eight to ten centimetres long and have multiplied their weight an astonishing 10,000 times.

It is at this stage that the caterpillar ceases to eat and begins the three-day process of spinning its valuable cocoon. With rhythmic movements of its head in a figure of eight pattern it lays between twenty to thirty concentric layers of silk thread, building its cocoon from the outside in. The caterpillar produces the silk filament through a minute hole in its lower lip called a spinneret. This is connected to two canals of the silk glands from which an almost invisible filament is merged with a glutinous substance to form a semi-liquid silk that hardens on contact with the air.

Once secure inside its finished cocoon the caterpillar then begins what must be one of nature's most amazing feats—the metamorphosis of caterpillar into moth. This whole complex transformation process takes only eight days. The mature insect will break out of its chrysalis and eject a brown fluid to soften the fibres of the cocoon, allowing it to push its way through and emerge as an adult moth. The insect will inflate its wings by pumping fluid into their veins. Once the wings have dried, the moths are ready to be mated and almost immediately afterwards the female moths will lay between 300 and 500 eggs. Then the whole cycle will begin once more.

Only the caterpillars spinning the largest and heaviest cocoons are selected and allowed to fulfil their life cycle. The other cocoons are sent to spinning mills and used for making silk, where they are subjected to steam or hot air to kill the chrysalis inside. If all the moths were allowed to emerge from their cocoons then the filaments would be broken into many short pieces.

Now ready for reeling, the cocoons are first cooked in a bath of hot water near boiling point to soften the gum holding the fibres together. Next, mechanical brushes beat the cocoon to loosen the floss, which is the mass of short fibres on the outside. This is the process of purging where the floss is removed and the end of the continuous filament forming the cocoon is picked out.

The reeler will assemble the filaments of between four to eight cocoons depending on the thickness of thread required. This thread is fed over a series of pulleys, while being lightly twisted to ensure good cohesion between the filaments. This raw silk is taken up on a reel and is then ready to be wound onto skeins and packaged into bales. A single three-gram cocoon can yield a filament up to 1,200 metres long. It takes approximately 110 cocoons to make a tie and 630 to make a blouse.

Only about half the silk of a cocoon is fit to be reeled. The rest is made into spun silk which requires more twisting than reeled silk to hold in all the fibres. As twisting decreases the lustre, spun silk appears less lustrous than reeled silk and so is less expensive. Silk can easily absorb dyes giving it a whole range of deep, lustrous colours. This coupled with a natural pearly sheen gives silk fabric its luxurious and sensuous appearance. Because of these special qualities silk has remained much coveted and sought after through the ages.

K.B.

Hangzhou's famous West Lake lies snuggled against the city surrounded on its other three sides by forest-covered mountains. Visited by emperors and kings, it was also a favourite haunt of writers, scholars and poets. They built many pavilions, pagodas, gardens and palaces on the lakeside. The Tang dynasty poet, Bai Juyi and Su Shi, a famous writer of the Song dynasty, both held the office of governor of the city. They enhanced West Lake by each building a causeway that bears their name. Lined by graceful willow trees and with several arched bridges, they are still there today, a favourite place for residents and visitors alike to sit and relax and enjoy the cooling breeze off the lake during the hot summer months.

*North of Gushan Temple, west of the Jia Pavilion,*
*Cloud mists hug the newly brimming banks.*
*Here and there first orioles contend in sunny trees;*
*To which households do new swallows wing, bearing their spring mud?*

*Riotous flowers more and more dazzle the eyes;*
*The short grass barely covers the horses' hooves.*
*I most love walking on and on, east of the lake,*
*Where green willows shade the white sand banks.*
By Tang dynasty poet Bai Juyi (772–846).

The natural and artificial beauties of this lake far exceeded any thing we had hitherto had an opportunity of seeing in China. The mountains surrounding it were lofty and broken into a variety of forms that were highly picturesque; and the vallies were richly cloathed with trees of different kinds...

The lake that extended from the walls of the city to the feet of the mountains, and threw its numerous arms into the wooded vallies, was the seat of pleasure, as well as of profit, to the inhabitants of [Hangzhou]. These amusements, however, of floating upon barges in the lake are principally confined to one sex. Few women, except those of loose character, join in the parties of men. (*Barrow*)

Nowadays the 'women of loose character' are not to be found on the water but appear instead on the promenade as the sun sets over the lake. Beneath a row of magnificent old camphor trees, the garishly dressed women, in twos and threes, proposition single men seated along the lakeside.

*(Opposite) Towards the end of May many farmers in this region are busy harvesting their crops of wheat or rape seed. Although wheat is a major crop in the north of China, a significant quantity is grown in Zhejiang Province.*

By day the promenade is filled with Chinese tourists from all parts of the country. They represent the newly affluent section of society—those now able to afford not just the cost of travelling but also the time to do so. Men talk into mobile phones as they stroll with their wives wearing the latest fashion and their single child, dressed as though off to a party. Young girls in frilly pink dresses look like bridesmaids at a wedding. As the city's traffic burbles past, punctuated by squealing brakes and blaring horns, the tourists stop occasionally to pose for the obligatory photographs by the famous lake. A woman bawls at them over a loudspeaker, encouraging them to take a boat ride to the islands in the middle of the lake for only sixteen yuan (almost US$2). Some of the larger boats look like floating railway carriages. Others, long skiffs with seats for four people either side of a small table under a blue canvas awning, are paddled skilfully by young men with a single paddle. In another corner of the lake the water is littered by a number of battered 'tunnel of love' paddle boats advertising Coca-Cola. In the shade of a small pavilion a group of old people gather to play their traditional instruments and sing their favourite arias from Chinese operas.

Nowadays in Hangzhou the people eat Kentucky Fried Chicken and drink cans of Budweiser beer; there are western-style shops selling French croissants and American yoghurt. Still, the vast majority of restaurants serve a variety of Chinese food, but there are signs that the average diner can now afford to be more discerning, or at least more extravagant than before. It is quite common to see plates piled on the table, overlapping each other—more food than can possibly be eaten, and indeed, much is often left untouched.

## HANGZHOU TO MEICHENG　杭州 - 梅城

Tea, like beer in England, is sold in public houses in every town, and along public roads, and the banks of rivers and canals. ...nor is it unusual for the burdened and wearied traveller to lay down his load, refresh himself with one cup of warm tea, and then pursue his journey. *(Staunton)*

...and, after having poured boiling water upon it, [they] cover it up: when it has remained in this state for a few minutes, they drink it without sugar, an article which the Chinese never mix with their tea. *(Anderson)*

South of Hangzhou the road winds through hills terraced with tea plantations and through small towns whose houses display the wealth now being made by individuals from their crop. Larger, white-tiled buildings of four or five storeys sport huge aerials on their flat roofs, like scale models of the Eiffel Tower. Round a bend, a lake at the end of a valley shimmering in the afternoon sunshine, turns out to be acres of polythene-covered greenhouses planted with strawberries. Although winter is fast approaching, in their artificial environment the plants display their delicate white flowers.

Ten kilometres upstream from the town of Tonglu 桐廬, between steep-sided mountains, the river is dammed to form, together with a tributary, the long, sinuous T-shaped Fuchun 富春 reservoir. Traffic, almost non-existent, is limited to small fishing boats and ferries.

Nowadays a railway line linking Hangzhou with Nanchang 南昌, the capital of Jiangxi Province to the west, takes care of the majority of freight. Many of the roads between these two provincial capitals, especially in Jiangxi, are atrocious. Some even appear never to have had a metalled surface, instead comprising of large angular pieces of stone. A few sections are only now being widened and re-laid.

A chain of granite mountains begins at [Hangzhou], with a direction to the southward. The gates and pavement of the city are formed of granite taken from thence. *(Staunton)*

[The river banks] were not deficient in beautiful views and picturesque scenery. The general surface of the country was mountainous and romantic, but well cultivated in all such places as would admit the labours of the husbandman. One city only occurred in the course of seven days; but we passed numerous villages situated in the valleys and the glens between the ridges of mountains; and fishermen's huts were constantly in view. There was here no want of trees, among which the most common were the tallow tree and the camphor, cedars, firs and the tall and majestic arbor vitae. *(Barrow)*

After many weeks of travelling through a flat, almost featureless landscape and confined for the most part to their barges, the members of the Macartney expedition were understandably excited about the variety of scenery now on offer. The sight of the mountains began to prompt memories of home. They had been away now more than a year and it was to be nearly another year before most of them would see Britain again.

The country is beautiful and romantic somewhat resembling the scenes on the river Conway between Lanroost and the sea. *(Macartney)*

*A view over the town of Tonglu 桐廬 beside the Fuchun River, a continuation of the Qiantang River at Hangzhou, and now the focus of our route south. The Imperial Way followed natural rivers through the mountainous landscape of northern Zhejiang and Jiangxi provinces.*

Staunton also mentions how the wider valleys alongside the river were often cultivated with sugar cane, which at that time of year was almost ripe and grew to about eight feet high. He compares this cane, by then about a year old, with that of the West Indies with which he was familiar, suggesting that the Chinese cane probably contained more juice. The plantations in China belonged to individuals and being relatively small they could not afford the expense of each having their own sugar mills.

The business of extracting the juice of the cane, and of boiling it into sugar is... a separate undertaking... The boilers of sugar travel about the country, with a small apparatus sufficient for their purpose... It is not a matter of great difficulty to travel with this apparatus, as there are few plantations of which some part is not accessible by water-carriage. A few bamboo poles and mats, are deemed sufficient for a temporary building... *(Staunton)*

Close to the town of Meicheng 梅城 the hillsides are for the first time covered with orange groves. The slopes, thickly planted with short, squat trees now speckled with brightly coloured fruit, as though decorated with thousands of tiny light bulbs. Alongside the road, pickers gather their baskets piled high with mandarins to be taken by truck to the wholesaler in the nearby town. There are at least three different kinds to be seen growing in this area of Zhejiang along with, sometimes, pomelos.

In the neighbourhood of the canes were likewise several groves of orange trees. Of the fruit of that tree was a great variety in size and colour. Some smaller than the Portugal orange, and some as large as any produced in the West Indies; but the sweetest and richest was a deep red orange, preferred to every other... *(Staunton)*

Several villages in this area are situated on low hills beside the river. The houses tightly clustered on different levels above a patchwork of paddies, give a three-dimensional effect in sharp contrast to those seen on the flat plains in the provinces to the north. New houses are beginning to sprout amongst their older counterparts. With white-washed or tiled exteriors, they often boast first-floor balconies. Outside in the concrete courtyard, under a warm sun in a hazy blue sky, crops are spread out to dry.

Here and there roads are lined with plane trees, now in autumn foliage. In places they arch across the road in a riot of shimmering gold, their leaves backlit by the sun. High mountains layered into the distance disappear like huge shadows into the haze. Occasionally, on hillsides that would have seemed too steep for cultivation, narrow strips have been ploughed vertically for a considerable distance up. There is no evidence of terracing.

In the centre of one village stands a majestic ginkgo tree. Beneath its multitude of small, lemon-yellow, fan-shaped leaves, children run home from school, their red neckerchiefs the only concession to a uniform. The paddy-fields have all been harvested of their rice and in many cases the stubble is being ploughed back in and winter vegetables planted. Rice straw stands around the trunks of trees in tall circular stacks.

The environs of the river still continued to be mountainous and full of picturesque beauty, heightened by the fancy and singular genius of the inhabitants, both as to cultivation and ornament. *(Anderson)*

*The ginkgo or maiden-hair tree is seldom seen growing wild outside cultivated parks and gardens. This deciduous tree, whose leaves turn a brilliant yellow in the autumn, is one of the oldest species of trees surviving from prehistoric times.*

## MEICHENG

The great secret of Meicheng, a small town in central Zhejiang, is that it is the unacknowledged snack capital of China. The town is peppered with good things to nibble, and breakfast is particularly fine. It is unlikely you will go there by chance as it is far from any conceivable beaten track but food is surely justification enough for a pilgrimage to a small riparian settlement in a beautiful part of China. We had not intended to stop there but Kevin—who was responsible for all navigation and so proficient is he we hardly ever got lost—decided that the two pagodas marking each side of the Fuchun river warranted exploration. It was an inspired decision and we took a detour.

We turned off the main road and fell amongst dense orange groves. The full evening light was warm, giving the fruit a rich luminosity. Riding on a band of bright black tarmac beside the soft rippling silver river I was aware we were heading to a place with some magic. The gently undulating road crossed the orchards and descended into town, passing a couple of small factories. One (smelling of yeast) was, I learnt later, Meicheng's renowned beer factory and major employer. The fringes of town were stacked with low concrete buildings. Our road was packed with people selling sugar cane and oranges to passengers waiting for buses which stopped randomly in the middle of the road. This caused a human surge followed by a wild struggle as everyone tried to squeeze on board. From there the road narrowed leading to a small square. An old market street heralded by a ornate stone gate led off to the right and a busy thoroughfare full of snack sellers to the left. Hanging above their heads were orange plastic bags bearing the imprint of 'The Pet Shop, Pollockshiels, Glasgow G4'.

We had arrived during Meicheng's rush-hour and the crossroads was a hubbub of bicycle bells and squeaking brakes. I asked a young man standing on the corner which was the best hotel in town. He replied that there was only one and led us directly to it.

The Meicheng Guest-house is a gem. Run by the local government (on the now passé principle of not making a profit) it is a thoroughbred relic of the nanny state. Like all Chinese guest-houses of this ilk the grand theme is 'spartan utility'. A large concrete entrance hall with a high wooden counter enclosing one corner greeted us. Two women were sitting behind the counter totally hidden from view. Our arrival put them into a state of giggling confusion and provoked a hurried scuffling for the right kind of forms. Other foreigners had stayed in the hotel, I was told, but they had all been overseas Chinese businessmen. We were the first tourists. Whilst waiting I examined the seven feet square hand-painted map of local 'scenic spots' above their heads. Chief amongst these was an ancient monastery which the kindly ladies told me was being restored. The two pagodas astride the river were also clearly marked.

Once the confusion over forms had subsided our 'reception' continued. Yes, we could leave the bikes in our rooms; no, there was no hot water until eight, and it did not last for long so could they suggest that we ran our baths immediately. Two businessmen from Hangzhou checking in behind us were clutching white plastic bags bearing the unmistakable blue logo of 'Boots' (a high street chemist in the

*The twin pagodas of Meicheng sit on opposite sides of the Fuchun River,
now a reservoir, and are known in Chinese as Shuang Ta Ling Yun* 雙 塔 凌 云 *,
or 'pair of towers rising to the clouds'. Meicheng's historic town wall, dating back to Tang dynasty,
was shaped like half a plum blossom—hence the town's name.*

United Kingdom). Like so many things, most of the world's plastic bags are made in China. Aware that foreign-looking articles are considered desirable the factories that produce them run off extras for the domestic market. How nonsensical it is to find something as prosaic as a UK supermarket bag transposed to an other-worldly town in the middle of China, and moreover being used, quite nonchalantly, by people so far removed from the diurnal rhythm of life in the western world. I suppose this is symbolic of our shrinking globe.

My room was spacious, with a desk in front of the window—a winning touch anytime, anywhere. For fifty yuan (US$6) a night I was treated to a choice of two hard single beds with plastic flip-flops waiting neatly at one end, a bean-bag pillow, a thick cotton wool quilt in a white cover with a large scarlet diamond stamped in its centre, and a coarse green carpet. Two thermoses with cork stoppers sat beside a turquoise plastic telephone on a low table between two deep, squeaky PVC armchairs. And most important of all: from the desk, a view. A twenty-feet tall 'rock' with water trickling from the top was the focal point of a threadbare garden. From my second floor redoubt I was level with its summit. The branches of tall thinning ginkgo trees criss-crossed my window like rats' tails, reaching up into the grey wintry evening. The ground was a washed-out yellow, littered with fallen leaves. A stream of people passed through the garden, making their way to the government offices behind the hotel.

That night I explored town: an expedition that netted a haul of good food. My first discovery—an eatery selling fried maize cakes—was the most compelling. I sat down and ate two. These ten-centimetre round patties made of ground maize flour, filled with sliced vegetables and beancurd, are unique to Meicheng, not found even in neighbouring towns. Tianjin, some 1,000 kilometres to the north, is the only other place where I encountered ground maize being consumed by humans. Maize is a common crop in China but is used largely as animal food, and is eaten on the cob by people only at harvest time. During this season you will pass mile upon mile of gravelled yellow-maize spread out on roads to dry in the autumn sun. Whilst savouring my tasty discovery I was vetted by a twenty-year-old girl who worked in the clothes shop next door. Wearing long knee socks, dangly earrings and a thick brown duffel-coat over her short skirt she looked very chic. She was also pretty, with hair elaborately tucked up onto her head. Her stock was on the trendy side of smart; it felt like a chic 'magasin' in a French ski resort—an unexpected and falsely bright lair of unrealizable consumerism which, on a cold night, leaves you wondering who would bother to spend so much money on such clothes in a place where there is little call for fancy dressing.

Other ingestibles that excited me included tangerines (freshly plucked with deep green leaves and twigs), crispy paper-thin savoury bread, knuckles of flaky pastry filled with fried pork, fresh tortellini, and sweet sugary biscuits. I went to bed on that cold wintry night feeling that China can be bountiful. It is only a question of being in the right place (but there probably are not many of them). I even managed to transpose some Christmas excitement into wintry Meicheng, such was my headful of satisfaction.

Meicheng had other treats too. The famous pagodas were no disappointment. That on the north bank sits at the top of a low hill beneath the pine-clad Wulong (Black Dragon) Mountain, and has a commanding view over the river and across to its neighbour on the south side. The southern pagoda is part of a whitewashed temple complex surrounded by low trees and scrub. We crossed the Fuchun River on a rusty ferry and then rode along the bank above a couple of rice fields to some rough-hewn steps that marked the start of the climb up to the temple. The gateway at the top was open; we stepped over the raised stone threshold and into a courtyard

*May is a back-breaking time for farmers—at the same time as the wheat is being gathered in, the paddy fields are being prepared and planted out with rice. In the background, beyond the impressive camphor tree, a pailou—or commemorative arch—can be seen.*

where a group of six brightly dressed men and women were absorbed in a noisy game of cards. They smiled widely at us but did not interrupt their game. A path led through an archway up the hillside to the pagoda. From its summit a fine view opened out over the river, wooded green hills and low fields—a just recompense for eight flights of stairs.

There was fun in the evening as well. A keen young blade in a blue corduroy jacket escorted me to the town's dance parlour. His uncle ran the restaurant at which we had eaten supper; when I had confessed to a fondness for boogieing he announced an unshakable determination to show me what Meicheng could offer. We walked up two flights of stairs and entered a sea of swirling dancers. Disco globes were hanging from the ceiling and the room was very dark. People danced beautifully. They waltzed and stepped and spun round the floor. Mostly they seemed not to have particular partners but to dance with anyone, the ladies waiting to be asked, but their body language displayed little intimacy. I sensed constrained embarrassment, formality and tension. A few flirted, but only a few. High-backed cubicles with tables and benches lined one wall; people sat and drank beer and cola, mainly the latter.

A man taller than me asked for a dance (not many people in China see over my head as I am five-feet-ten. I explained I could not waltz but would have a go if he did not mind leading. He did not and we tried. His hair, straight and lank, hung down to his shoulders. He was clearly something of a free-thinker. He told me he worked in the beer factory, had lived here all his life, was bored and wanted to move but probably would not be able to. Throughout our slow measured dance, as I tried hard not to land on his feet, he shook. He seemed dangerously highly-strung, a round peg that clearly did not fit into Meicheng's uniformly square holes.

The disc jockey changed tempo: it was time for Disco. My friend in the blue corduroy jacket told me I would have to lead the way and everyone gathered round me in a circle to watch. I faced the crowd self-consciously, eyes to the ceiling, a fixed grin on my face. My keen companion was eager to establish that I was his responsibility and anyone interested in finding out anything about me had to apply through him. He stood opposite me, wiggling. Two women, both in their late twenties and married, on a girls' night out, rescued me. I came to believe that this night out together was not a rare treat but how they passed most evenings. One was wearing a cream turtle neck under a voluminous A-line pinafore—she looked very smart and it hung magnificently when she pirouetted and swirled; the other had a shocking perm that pushed wide curls over her head like the lip of a jug. They accepted several dances from dainty-footed young men who spun them round the floor with finesse. After eagerly questioning me about my marital status and how I came to be among them they launched into a heartfelt warning about the dangerous underground elements of Meicheng. I had to be exceptionally careful of the 'bad men'. I could sense their noddings in the direction of my harmless long-haired swain. What would these two make of downtown Beijing? My attempts to leave solicited a screeching 'No! You cannot walk home alone. It is far too dangerous'. I defied them and set off under the stars, but they followed, kindly escorting me to my door.

A.R.

*Cattle pick over piles of rubbish on the banks of the
Qu River in the town of Longyou in eastern Zhejiang Province.*

# MEICHENG TO CHANGSHAN 梅城 - 常山

The river is... very unequal in its depth; in some places not less than ten or twelve feet, and in others so shallow that we were often suddenly stopped in our progress. It is quite wonderful to see the strength and expertness of the Chinese boatmen, who by main bodily might often dragged or lifted, over sands and gravel almost dry, the yachts we travelled in, some of which were heavy-laden and seventy feet in length by twelve feet in the beam. *(Macartney)*

After seven days of tedious navigation, if dragging... over a pebbly bottom on which the boats were constantly aground and against a rapid stream, could be so called, we came to its source near the city of [Changshan]. *(Barrow)*

[At Changshan], the river ceased entirely to be navigable. This river takes its rise in a range of mountains which surround that town on several sides... generally through a hilly and little frequented country; and it has no communication with any considerable road, river, or canal, until it reaches [Hangzhou]. Fewer vessels of any kind are seen upon it, than in any other part of the empire where the Embassy had passed by water... *(Staunton)*

It is worth noting that at the time of year Staunton travelled on this river (mid-November) the water level had dropped considerably. Taking into account the amount of trade at Hangzhou and the fact that not an inconsiderable volume of merchandise passed in both directions between there and Guangzhou and, remembering that piracy was widespread along the coast, it is fair to assume that more water traffic would have been observed during the summer when water levels were higher.

At the city of [Changshan] we had a neck of land to cross in order to join the barges that were prepared on another river falling towards the westward, by which a connexion was formed with the usual route from [Beijing] to [Guangzhou]. *(Barrow)*

# Chapter Six

# Jiangxi Province
# 江西省

Jiangxi, covering some 166,600 square kilometres, is the only landlocked province on our route. The hills and mountains that cover more than three-quarters of its total land area mostly lie in the south and around its periphery. They slope gradually towards the alluvial plain surrounding Poyang Lake.

The largest freshwater lake in China, Poyang Lake hangs like an enormous pendant from a loop in the Yangtze River which forms part of the province's northern boundary. The river systems of Jiangxi spread southwards like a giant fan from the lake. The Gan River 贛江, the longest river in Jiangxi, flows from south to north along almost the entire length of the province. With its huge watershed covering 82,000 square kilometres it provides half of the water flowing into Poyang Lake. Given its volume it also provides much of the region's power through several hydroelectric dams along its length.

With its vast areas of water in the north, fishing is a major industry here with many commercial fishing and hatchery centres set up along the Yangtze and in the lakeland areas.

Most areas in Jiangxi grow two crops of rice per year, some as many as three. It also includes one of the major tea-producing areas in China in the northern hill country. Timber and bamboo forests are concentrated along the borders of the province and among the mountainous areas in the upper reaches of the rivers. The products, used largely for construction, are sold mainly outside the province.

Being landlocked, railways provide the province with its all-important transport links with the coastal provinces of Zhejiang and Fujian. The new 'Imperial Way,' the Beijing–Kowloon railway, passes through the province and through the cities of Juijiang, Nanchang, Ji'an and Ganzhou (*see* Epilogue, page 221).

## YUSHAN TO YANSHAN 玉山 - 鉛山

Beyond Changshan, where we left the river in Zhejiang Province, a short land route crosses a range of hills forming a watershed and begins its descent towards the Xin River 信江 and the town of Yushan in neighbouring Jiangxi. Macartney had clearly enjoyed the respite from the confines of his boat and the opportunity to observe the countryside and methods of agriculture at close hand.

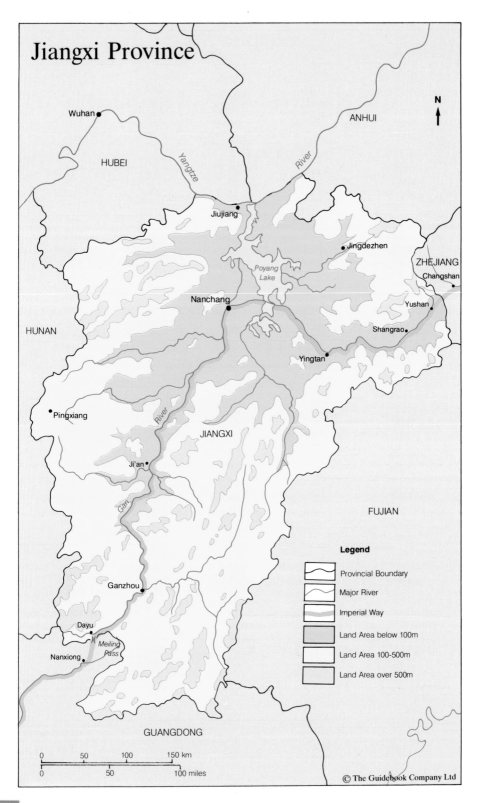

# Jiangxi Province

N

Wuhan

ANHUI

HUBEI

*Yangtze* *River*

Jiujiang

Jingdezhen

ZHEJIANG

*Poyang Lake*

Changshan

Nanchang

Yushan

HUNAN

Shangrao

Yingtan

*River*

Pingxiang

JIANGXI

Ji'an

FUJIAN

*Gan*

**Legend**

Provincial Boundary

Major River

Imperial Way

Land Area below 100m

Land Area 100-500m

Land Area over 500m

Ganzhou

Dayu

*Meiling Pass*

Nanxiong

GUANGDONG

| 0 | 50 | 100 | 150 km |
| 0 | 50 | | 100 miles |

© The Guidebook Company Ltd

...the weather was uncommonly pleasant... We found this short transition from the water to the land very agreeable, and were highly delighted with the face of the country we passed through. It is much diversified by hills of a moderate size... I did not see a spot in the whole way that was not cultivated with infinite industry and compelled to produce every grain and vegetable of which it was capable. The soil is naturally indifferent, which renders the farmer wonderfully active in his endeavours to fertilize it; the care with which everything convertible into manure is preserved would appear ridiculous elsewhere, but is here fully justified by the effect. Wherever the sides of the hills admit of it they are wrought into terraces, graduated with different crops and watered by the chain pump. The ponds and reservoirs are a public concern and great justice is observed in the distribution of their contents. The plough is the simplest in the world, has but one handle, is drawn by a single buffalo and managed by a single person, without any assistance. The husbandry is singularly neat, not a weed to be seen, everything is sown in drills, and there are never less than two crops in the year and often there are three. *(Macartney)*

Having finished this land journey of about twenty-four miles in the course of the day, we lodged at [Yushan], a small city of mean appearance and the following day embarked on flat-bottomed barges, remarkably long and narrow... but two complete days of heavy rain obliged us to remain quietly at anchor. *(Barrow)*

Once across the border, the hills are soon left behind as they shrink and disappear out of sight below the horizon. The road descends into a landscape that opens out into a fertile plain of rice paddies interrupted by a few orange groves, a little cotton and maize and an occasional plot of vegetables. The weather is cold, grey and misty. The rice harvest has long been gathered in. The fields, brown and bare, now wear their winter crew cut of dry, spiky stubble.

A couple of elderly women sit huddled together, chatting, at the edge of one field. One of them holds a buffalo on a tether while it chews on the grass beside the paddy. The other sits knitting as her animal grazes a short distance away. All over the south of China, especially in poorer areas, water buffalo are commonly used for ploughing. When not working they are often seen feeding on the grass between the paddy fields. It is generally the old folk or children that watch over them as they graze.

Standing away from the road beyond some rice paddies are three huge, circular piles of bricks, about seven or eight metres high and belled out slightly towards the top, like giant earthenware pots. They are brick kilns. The red clay-like earth found in this region is ideal for brick-making; hence these makeshift kilns are to be found dotted all over the lowlands.

About half a dozen men are digging the earth out of the hillside. They carry it in yoked baskets and tip it into a mixing machine that splutters and coughs out puffs of exhaust. Thoroughly churned into a smooth, sticky mixture the soil is extruded in a continuous, rectangular sausage of uniform red-brown clay. It is then cut off in measured lengths and pushed onto rollers, where a set of cheese wires cleanly slices it into a dozen bricks. Beside the kilns are row upon row of these freshly made bricks. Still with the damp, dark-red colour of unfired bricks, they are covered with reed matting to dry for a couple of days before firing.

Circled on the outside with previously made bricks held in place with wire bands, the new bricks are then stacked into a huge pot-shape. As the pile grows the bricks are carried, suspended from yokes, up a rickety wooden ladder. Inside the bricks are interspersed with straw and coal dust. When finished the kiln is lit using oil and finally earth is spread on the

*(Right and below)*
*The red sandstone peaks of Longhu Shan,*
*near the town of Yingtan. These oddly shaped peaks*
*reminded Staunton of the Chinese paintings he had seen*
*with seemingly fantastic peaks and crags.*

top to help contain the heat. Firing takes two days in this makeshift kiln. In the dark gloom of late afternoon the glow of the red-hot bricks inside is clearly visible between small gaps in bricks on the outside. Beside this the previous kiln, now cool, is being dismantled and the finished bricks are being stacked neatly nearby. This small but productive operation produces 2,000 bricks per hour and is entirely portable. The brick-making machinery can be easily transported to another site once this one has been exhausted of suitable earth.

We passed two brick kilns, with a small village around them, built for the accommodation of the workmen employed in the manufactory. We could form some judgement of the trade of the place by the large quantities of bricks formed in regular piles; both of those which were burned, and such as were ready for the kiln. *(Anderson)*

## Yanshan to Yingtan 鉛山 - 鷹潭

The road passes a stretch of the Xin River as it rounds a bend against a smooth sandstone cliff. Shallow but wide the water appears almost still. Under a grey sky, reflections of a curious dome-shaped rock and a man guiding a buffalo as they plough a field in preparation for its winter crop high on the opposite flood plain, are cast mirror-like on the water. Occasionally a slight breeze ripples the surface shattering the image.

The route continues through undulating countryside where cold air, thick haze and a dark, leaden sky deadens colours, reducing the world to one of bleak greyness. Dry, empty rice paddies fill valleys between rounded hummocks of red sandstone. The rock is weathered to blue-grey and streaked with rainwater that weeps from clumps of small trees and bushes and patches of grass that cling doggedly to the slopes. Not far to the south a collection of peaks of this red arenaceous rock stand like sentinels against the horizon. They are part of the Wuyi mountain range 武夷山 that forms the southern watershed of the Xin River—the route of the Imperial Way between Yushan and Poyang Lake.

About the city of [Shangrao] the weather was again wet, cold, and gloomy. The country had also a rude appearance. On each bank of the river were sometimes large masses of naked rock, of vast height, and resembling the rough scenes of nature which had been deemed to be exaggerated in Chinese drawings. The rock was a kind of dark red freestone, of which regular pieces were sometimes cut out for building, as from a quarry. *(Staunton)*

Weathering has produced some particularly unusual forms. Near the town of Yiyang 弋陽 is the bizarre collection of mountains known as Gui Feng 圭峰 , extolled through history by Chinese poets and writers. Or in the words of the tourist brochure, 'pouts from erery dynasty all lift their paiems on these nemarkble spectacle'. (sic)

Many of the other hills in the area have been all but quarried out of existence, hewn into large sandstone building blocks that are still used in the construction of many of the houses and buildings in the area.

Rain falls steadily. Trucks and buses hurtle noisily past, whipping up a fine spray in their wake. They sound their horns contemptuously at the Buddhist monk walking at the side of the road. Shaven-headed, dressed in grey robes with white stockings, oblivious to all around, he takes three strides, stops, and lowers himself on to his heavily-padded knees. Resting on his forearms, he bows his head to the ground whilst turning his palms towards the low grey clouds. Climbing wearily to his feet he takes another three paces, repeating the routine once more. And so he continues his damp, laborious progress.

Porcelain is made in China ... It is made by means of a certain earth got from the mountains ... 'Tis exported to India and elsewhere, passing from country to country till it reaches us in Morocco. 'Tis certainly the finest of all pottery-ware. *(Batuta)*

From the river were seen several excavations, made in extracting from the sides of the adjoining hills, the pe-tun-tse, useful in the manufactory of porcelain.

A village or unwalled town called [Jindezhen], was not very far distant from this part of the travellers' route, in which three thousand furnaces for baking porcelain, were said to be lighted at a time, which gave to the place, at night, the appearance of a town on fire. *(Staunton)*

Jingdezhen 景德鎮 in the north of Jiangxi has a long history of porcelain-making dating back over 2,000 years. It is probably the most famous centre for porcelain production in China. Jingdezhen porcelain, characterized as being 'bright as glass, thin as paper, white as jade and with the deep resonance of a bell,' was well-known to European traders at Guangzhou (Canton) and became prized by the aristocracy of Europe during the Ming and Qing dynasties.

# YINGTAN TO NANCHANG　鷹潭 – 南昌

Morning dawns clear. The sun is low in the sky and too weak to lessen the effects of the bitterly cold air. Past stubbled fields touched with frost the road crosses a bleak sandstone plateau. A solitary woman works in a field bundling rice straw. By lunch-time the sun had risen high enough to make the day pleasantly warm. Just outside the small town of Dongxiang 東鄉 on the road to Nanchang is a row of roadside restaurants typical of many in China. Trucks and other vehicles are parked on a mud and gravel forecourt. At the roadside stand several young ladies, many of them dressed in red, a colour often favoured by Chinese women. Coupled with their pale complexion and dark hair it can look outstanding. One in particular, in a long red dress with frills, holds a white parasol as she beckons to passing truck drivers inviting them to stop for lunch. Although the girls work as waitresses in the restaurants, in the words of George Staunton in reference to the ladies of Tai Lake, they are said 'to follow more than one profession'.

## BAO TA VILLAGE 寶塔村

The travellers, taking a course a little to the north-west, for the convenience of water-carriage, entered soon into that great extent of flat and swampy land, in the midst of which is the Poyang lake... For the distance of some miles... the face of the country is one wild and morassy waste, covered with reeds and rushes, and entirely inundated for a part of the year. Not a village is to be seen; nor any traces of habitation visible, except now and then a mean and solitary hut for the residence of a fisherman... These wretched beings subsist by fishing, and raising vegetables on hurdles of bamboo resting upon marshes, or floating upon the surface of the water. *(Staunton)*

It is scarcely possible for the imagination to form to itself an idea of a more desolate region than that which surrounds the Poyang lake. *(Barrow)*

On a day when a grey sky was closing down like the lid of a saucepan, Kevin and I cycled out of Nanchang to hunt for a pagoda. We rode for several hours into flat colourless lake country. Finding the tower was easy; there was little else rising out

*The end of November, not far from Nanchang, capital of Jiangxi Province.*
*In a flat, landscape of empty fields,*
*this village is typical of the area, with solid houses and decorative roofs.*

of the landscape. But it was enclosed by a high stone wall and the gate was locked. We had to settle with a short walk round the perimeter.

We turned back on to the road in search of lunch and soon reached a village full of squat solid houses. Muddy paths ran between the buildings—home to pigs and strutting chickens. A crowd of children latched on to us. They took us down to the edge of a large lake to see water buffalo paddling in the shallows. The inert water fused with a slate sky creating a blanket of grey; there was no light, every relief was flattened. I felt sealed within a two-dimensional world. The children were tumbling like foals along the banks, spinning like fish, ebullient and raucous, emitting peals of laughter as they scampered around. But their energy did not shake the gloom that numbed me. Contemplating existence in this place shrunk my heart. These lives seemed charmless and full of toil.

Rounding a corner back in the village I came face to face with two psychedelic bundles hanging from a shoulder-pole, borne by a stooped and wrinkled ancient. These were piles of incense sticks wrapped in crepe paper. He put them down and squatted on his haunches, breaking for a cigarette. I celebrated the colour, the pink— so warm and vivid against all this grey. An elderly woman and her scrawny husband were sitting, smoking, on the doorstep of their house. They watched whilst I tried to lift the load. It was too heavy for my unpractised shoulders and the bundles slumped to the ground. But the crowd that had been following at my heels laughed, and momentarily pushed back the greyness.

A woman called Jiang Hua invited us into her house to eat. She offered a bowl of bony cold fish together with rice which she had reheated in her wok. Thirty people were squeezed inside Jiang's concrete living room, pressing around us as we chewed.

'They can use chopsticks.... look!' they cried. A young girl pushed forward to present a bowl of carrots cooked with sesame and ginger. She said she had been home and taken it from her mother. I was grateful to her and for the colour and the freshness. The crowd closed in around her and watched.

I did not resent their curiosity (one expects it from people who have never seen anything like you before), and it was not hostile. But on this day I could not feign interest in the questions being directed at me—a litany that had not varied over 4,500 kilometres. My patience was finite. After three-and-a-half months of playing the monkey I was washed out. The start of the trip felt like a different lifetime. I couldn't believe I was still doing the same journey. The greyness of this village made me realise that I had come far enough. But because of the children this place was not a wasteland. They introduced colour to life, and they were also the manifestation of what life here was about: producing families, protecting families, celebrating family life and family traditions—a basic blue-print for existence. When Jiang Hua talked of her one son her eyes were bright. He was the purpose of her life.

A.R.

# NANCHANG 南昌

The metropolotan city of the Province of [Jiangxi] is [Nanchang]. It is not one of the largest or most flourishing cities, but it is known throughout the entire kingdom for the great number of the class of the literati who go out from here to take over government positions of dignity. In extent of territory it is about as large as [Guangzhou], but far inferior to it commercially. The people here are thrifty and accustomed to living on little... *(Ricci)*

We sailed near four whole days over the same kind of country and came, towards the evening of the last, to the city of [Nanchang], the capital of [Jiangxi], where we observed from four to five hundred of the revenue vessels lying at anchor. I took the advantage to go on board one of the revenue vessels and to measure the capacity of its hold. It was in length 115 feet, breadth 15 feet and depth 6 feet; the sides streight and the width nearly the same fore and aft; so that the burden might fairly be estimated at 250 tons. Independent, therefore, of the innumerable small craft, there were lying before this city 100,000 tons of shipping. *(Barrow)*

Temple of the Iron Shaft[1]. The size and the beauty of this temple are well worth beholding, and all around it there is an unbroken chain of public markets, where one can purchase almost anything he can think of. *(Ricci)*

...from the airborne pavilion stream vermilion colours... Sandbanks with cranes and islets with wild ducks wind about and intertwine; palatial halls of rare cassia and magnolia woods are ensconced among the hills. We opened the decorated portals and looked down at the carved eaves: mountains and plains spread out, entirely filling one's eyes, and the river and marshes offered a startling sight. Houses spread over the land, and bells rang forth from the noble mansions; boats shaped like blue peacocks and yellow dragons clogged the harbour. (Wang Po 王勃 )[2]

Nowadays it is a modern reconstruction of the Teng Wang Pavilion 滕王閣 which stands beside the Gan River. On a cold, gloomy overcast day, the five-storey-high building rises amongst a complex containing three or four smaller pavilions. Standing as it does on the wrong side of a modern four-lane highway, it appears somewhat lost and isolated from the city for which it has been a famous landmark for centuries. Today, virtually the only tourist attraction in this unattractive provincial capital, construction of further adjacent buildings is underway in an effort to extend the site and extract still more tourist dollars.

In the city itself many of the shops look exactly like those in any other average city in China. There is the usual myriad of small boutiques stocking the same type of clothes, modelled on the same type of mannequins or cardboard cut-out faces of famous stars.

A grey, three-storey concrete facade with square windows, all that remains of a building under demolition, stands like some relic from a war-time blitz. A handful of men are attacking it with sledgehammers. Behind, stands a tall apartment block—a garish, crimson and purple example of the kind of modern architecture that will likely replace it. Across the street, hawkers at a row of stalls outside a Buddhist temple are selling incense sticks and huge rolls of firecrackers that look like large red birthday cakes. Nearby calligraphers are painting slogans for Chinese New Year, still a couple of months away. Wearing a cloth cap and a pair of thick

---

1 Teng Wang Pavilion. 2 Written in AD 675 by Wang Po, seventh century Chinese traveller, writer and poet, as part of a preface to a collection of poems composed at a banquet to celebrate the renovation of the Teng Wang Pavilion. (Translated by Richard E. Strassberg). The tower has been restored at least twenty-eight times over the centuries.

spectacles, an old man with a steady hand that belies his age sits at a large wooden table. On a sheet of red paper, with skilful sweeps of a fat brush dipped in gold paint matching the row of fillings in his ready smile, he forms the character *fu* 福 meaning fortune or happiness that will adorn the door of somebody's home in the coming Year of the Rat. This character is made up of the symbols representing worship, mouth and field and reflects the importance of a good harvest to the well-being of the ancient Chinese—something that still holds true even today.

# NANCHANG TO JI'AN  南昌 – 吉安

... the yachts were now moving against the current of a rapid river which came from the south-west. *(Staunton)*

The river still continues wide, but in general very shallow. The shores are flat and sandy, and in the wet season the whole country must be under water to a vast extent. No trees or houses to be seen but on a few elevated spots. The weather cold, no sun. *(Macartney)*

South of Nanchang just outside the town of Fengcheng 丰城 the road runs alongside a huge levee about thirty metres high. Trucks heavily laden with sand are working to reinforce it against what must be a very real threat of flooding during the summer rainy season. The view from the top of the levee reveals the vast, flat flood plain of the lower reaches of the Gan River. Like an area of fen country, a patchwork of fields is cultivated as far as the river which is just visible in the hazy distance—the rich alluvial soil temporarily on loan from the river until the next time the water level rises.

For more than 300 kilometres the Gan River continues much like this, although the further south one travels the narrower the flood plain becomes. But it is always lush with winter vegetables. In many places during the dry season the river has shrunk to a narrow channel exposing banks of sand and gravel that have been washed down from the higher ground in the south. This makes the job of dredging the river an easy one. Everywhere one can see trucks driving down onto the sandbanks to be loaded with the fine alluvial soil to be used for building or agriculture.

# JI'AN TO YAOTOU  吉安 – 窑頭

This morning we approached the mountains and our course now lies among them, and generally close to the foot of them. There are some very pretty white pagodas of nine stories high, newly built on [small hills] near the banks. Stopped for a few hours at the town of [Ji'an]. *(Macartney)*

Approaching the town of Tai He 泰和 , roadside hawkers sell the white-feathered, black-skinned chickens for which this area is famous. The birds, with the distinctive tuft of white feathers on their head, sit on display on the tops of wicker baskets. Called *wuji* 乌雞 (literally, black chicken) their curious charcoal-coloured skin is only revealed once the birds have been plucked. Thought to be particularly nutritious by the elderly and possessing a delicate flavour with a soft texture, they are a special favourite in soups.

*ECONOMY of TIME and LABOR, exemplified in a CHINESE WATERMAN.*

**Plate No.13** *"The number of craft of all kinds on... the river... was immense; but they were all conducted without confusion. The watermen were uncommonly expert, and it was not unusual to see a large boat entirely managed by one man, who rowed, sailed, steered, and smoked his pipe at the same time. He held the sheet or strong rope belonging to the sail with one hand, he steered the boat with the other, and with his foot he pulled an oar, which he feathered at every stroke as neatly as could be done by the hand. A strong example of economy of time and labour."* (Staunton)

As the late afternoon sun finally breaks through the thick, grey clouds, the road out of Tai He crosses the large span of the concrete stretching over Gan River, and climbs steadily into the low hills visible through the haze. A simple, narrow tarmac road winds quietly through a countryside of undulating sandstone hills sparsely planted with young fir trees, and down into a bleak desert of stubbled paddies interrupted only by a few fields of vegetables. In a warm, soft evening light, small, tranquil villages stand amongst copses of trees often dominated by the majestic spread of a camphor tree.

...the large camphor tree, which grew at a little more distance from the river, was sometimes mixed with one of a still greater size, a species of the ficus, or Chinese yang-shoo [banyan tree], of which the branches spread horizontally to such an extent, that one tree may be almost sufficient to cover half an acre of land.

Our voyage today was through a country that afforded very beautiful scenery. The river is still shallow but very broad, spreading over a vast bed of small round pebbles. A forest of many miles in extent covered all the eastern bank. We passed a great many floats of timber, some of several hundred feet long. *(Macartney)*

A succession of timber yards covered the banks of the river, and a large quantity of timber was soaking in the water before them, which I understood to be in a state of preparation for building junks; a principal business of the place. It must, indeed, be a principal business of the country at large; for when the internal commerce of China is considered, and that almost the whole of it is carried on in these vessels, on the numerous rivers and canals which every where intersect, and form a communication through the greatest part of this extensive kingdom; the quantity of timber used, and the number of artificers employed, in the construction of them, must render any attempt at calculation an idle presumption in a person under such confined circumstances as myself. *(Anderson)*

## YAOTOU 窯頭

Yaotou is full of ancient camphor trees. Being a committed tree-hugger this place was inevitably going to leave a strong impression, and I find it is one village to which I am determined to return. Our road had taken us through a calming landscape of red earth and low green hills traced with small villages. There was no traffic and the surface was impeccable—a rare pleasure. Passing yellow earth farmhouses with dark-tiled roofs, wisps of sugar cane and pale green fields in the smoky quiet of late afternoon, we had one of the best rides ever. We had planned to go to Wan'an, the next major town on our route, but were so drawn by the beauty of this stretch that we were loath to lose any of it to darkness. We therefore opted to try for lodgings in the villages. Yaotou was the first place we came to.

The village is T-shaped: the down-stroke is a market street with cabbages, mirrors, red buckets, rush brooms, hair-dressers, bamboo plate scrubbers and a thousand other indispensable objects spilling all over it. If you turn right through this bustle you come to the door of the village's one hostel, an old tall building standing beside a huge camphor tree with a girth of several metres. It must have been there for

*Twenty-year-old Liu Chun-lan, whose name means 'spring orchid,' proudly holds her ten-week-old baby girl. Before they were married her husband Gao Ze-ren, five years her senior, was a soldier in the People's Liberation Army and was posted in Beijing. He now works in a factory in their small home town of Yaotou.*

*During the dry winter months the water level in the rivers drops significantly, sometimes leaving only a narrow channel still navigable. These people crossing the Gan River at Yaotou have had to walk most of the way. However, when the heavy summer rains fall it is not uncommon for the river to flood, rising above its banks.*

centuries: the village inn beside a great landmark, a travellers' lodging house from long ago.

A good-looking woman wearing blue leggings and a red turtle-neck stood up to greet us; she had been sitting on a low bamboo chair outside the door with three other women and a couple of children. Without hesitating she said she could accommodate us. We would pay 5 yuan (US$0.60) a night each.

We followed her into a dark room which took up the whole of the ground floor. It was sparsely furnished with six square tables, narrow wooden benches and a black and white television on a cupboard which attracted a crowd of villagers each evening. A door at the far end lead down a step into the kitchen. A young man emerged with a plate of boiled sweet potatoes and told me to take two. I was starving. Upstairs the floorboards, walls and roof were all wooden. A footstep at one end sent tremors across the whole creaking structure. The space was divided by dusty partitions into five small rooms; I was shown to one with two beds and a desk, all heavy with dirt. The door stuck in the frame. After three tugs at the nylon string handle (tacked on with a nail) it would jerk open causing all neighbouring partitions to shudder. There was no glass in the windows, only paper, and no 'bathroom facilities'. In fact, the toilets were outside the building, a communal dark hole, and there was nowhere at all to wash. I liked the accommodation; it had character.

Zhang Ping, our landlady, was refined, understated, at ease with everyone, yet somewhat incongruous to her surroundings. She did not fuss about our safety, which was surprising given the complete absence of security and comparative squalor of her lodgings. Maybe she enjoyed some kind of protection? In any case she was clearly a senior figure in the unwritten hierarchy of the village as no one passed her

*Constructed above the flood plain of the Gan River this levee protects the town of Yaotou.*
*The camphor tree growing by the levee is one of many around the town,*
*some are hundreds of years old and have grown to an enormous girth.*

without exchanging some friendly words. She was also a seat of maternal calm. Even I felt the tug of this. A small group of mothers and babies always hovered in range outside the inn door. Zhang would counsel and console, bringing even the most churlish children to heel. She ran the place with the help of two of her nieces. Only the youngest of her three children, a nine-year-old daughter, lived with her; the others worked in local towns. Her husband was nowhere to be seen and questions about him produced evasive answers. The feast prepared for us that night centred around a delicious river fish. Nieces, boyfriends, and a daughter joined us at a round table made ready with nine white bowls and nine pairs of chopsticks resting on the rim. The crowd that had gathered to examine us was shooed away and the door locked behind them. Zhang was determined there would be no intruders.

After supper we were taken to dance. We had received an invitation from the manager of the local foodstuffs factory to attend the evening session in his recreation room. About a dozen lads were sitting around the whitewashed walls on red plastic chairs beneath a rotating mirrored globe. There was a distinct shortage of women. My chief partner was an effeminate chap who leapt around athletically. The dancing was formal but stylish and many of the boys paired up. I knew none of the steps and was the focus of great mirth. Finally the 'disco' music was announced and I was told to lead. Scandinavian group 'Ace of Bass' was the only thing on the turntable that night. I explained that my moves were not choreographed but even so I was circled and imitated. Polite smiles failed to mask a general disappointment that my 'moves' were random and could not be memorised in sequence. Zhang Ping sat at the side with her niece eating tangerines. She danced with the manager but refused everyone else.

We walked back under bright winter stars, past a stagnant pond and scampering rats. Christmas was only a few weeks away and I could feel it. Back in my creaking dirt-laced room I relished the excitement of where I was. As I dropped off in greedy sleep, fully clothed and deep in cotton quilts, I listened to the old building sigh, muttering about the cold.

The next morning I ran into all my former dance partners squatting in the market street, passing the time of day. They said they weren't busy. Life in Yaotou was unpressured and if they didn't want to work, they didn't. Instead they took us to Yaotou's martial arts school. Inside a cavernous former cinema (now redundant), two fourteen-year-old boys were wrestling barefoot on the floorboards of a creaking wooden gallery. It heaved and shook each time one of them slammed to the ground. The school was run by a local man who had once competed professionally; he lived in a small room to one side of the gallery and his walls were adorned with photos of Bruce Lee and Jackie Chan. Kicks and punches echoed across the empty hall as the boys doggedly tried to bring each other to the ground. Their concentration made them trance-like, and hopefully lessened the pain of their thudding falls. The building's exterior was faded and peeling. A limp clutch of red stars on plaster work above the entrance was the only trace of the pride and pomp that had once been on display.

From Yaotou we rode to Wan'an. I was sad to leave. Zhang Ping was sitting outside her hostel under the camphor tree when we disappeared, surrounded by

*Mondays and Wednesdays are market days in Yaotou,*
*when the main street teems with people looking over the many stalls.*

her nieces, four women with babies and a small itinerant crowd of children, all wobbling within her orbit. Six hours later in my new hotel room I heard a knock at the door, and in she walked. Zhang had come by bus with a niece to see us. How kind, but what a riddle. Not for the first time I felt I was travelling with a brown paper bag over my head. The answers I wanted—about her role in the village, why she remained there, the source of her worldliness, the doings of her elusive husband—might have been apparent had I had a subtle understanding of how such communities worked, and been able to recognize the obvious signals. As it was I had no idea. She took us out to supper at a restaurant run by a friend of hers then climbed back on to her bus and disappeared.

A.R.

# WAN'AN TO GANZHOU 萬安－贛州

The river now becomes much narrower and deeper, being pent up between the mountains which shut it in so closely and approach so near to each other that till the moment we came to the opening we can scarcely imagine the possibility of a passage. To the left is the walled town of [Wan'an]. *(Macartney)*

In the town of Wan'an, beside what remains of the ancient city wall, a row of old wooden houses overlooks the river. A man stoops inside a makeshift shed, lengths of sturdy bamboo soak in a bath of hot water. Once softened, he is able to bend them slightly. Then, lashing five or six of these curved pieces together with wire, the thickest ends together at one end, he constructs a tapered raft about seven metres long. Fishermen use them, as they probably have done for centuries, for cormorant fishing. Standing with perfect balance they pole the rafts, half a dozen birds perched on the ends, as they glide across the wide, still river, like an anachronism beneath the massive Wan'an hydroelectric dam. Finished in 1992, the dam is one of several along the Gan River network.

After crossing the new dam the unmade road immediately begins to twist and climb steeply into forested mountains. Chinese characters painted in red on giant boulders at the roadside warn of the dangers of forest fires. The day is hot and sunny, the undergrowth tinder-dry in this season of little rain. Clusters of brown mud-brick cottages perch beside isolated valleys terraced with rice paddies. The smell of charcoal smoke from a cooking fire; the hollow clop of wood being cut; a cock crowing; the distant chatter of women and children echoing through the valley—these are the sights, sounds and smells that are typical of mountain villages throughout Asia, or even Africa.

High hills rise on each side of the river, planted and cultivated with trees and grain on terraces and embellished with small, neat villages perched on ledges of rock wherever the projection could sustain a superstructure. *(Macartney)*

---

*The Imperial Way follows the Gan River, towards its source in the mountains of southern Jiangxi. The river passes many small hamlets, tucked away amongst terraced valleys and hillsides. Steep and winding gravel tracks are their only communication with the next village.*

Cresting the highest point, some 800 metres above sea level, the surrounding mountains quickly disappear into thick haze that hangs in motionless air. Dropping down to the nearby village of Mianjin 棉津 the road passes a school, where children run on a playground of bare earth. A covered market area is deserted apart from two old men chatting in the shade. Beside it stands a row of small wooden stalls and a couple of noodle shops. Outside one shop a tray of oven-baked *shaobing* 燒餅 , long since gone cold, attracts a couple of bluebottles. Posters of Hong Kong pop stars plaster the walls of an empty hairdresser's. In a tailor's shop, two young girls work at a pair of sewing machines stitching pieces for a jacket. One of them, rising to fetch something from a hanger on the wall, wobbles awkwardly. Her feet are crippled, turned out through ninety-degrees they point in opposite directions. The treadle of her sewing machine has been adapted to make it possible for her to work.

At the village of Shaping 沙坪 there is more activity. It was market day and now, in the late afternoon, many stalls have already packed up. About ten young women are cycling out of the village, one behind the other along the dusty, rutted road. Each has a huge bundle tied to the back of her bicycle—clothes they have been trying to sell at the market. Making light of the hard going, they chat and laugh as they cycle home.

# Ganzhou 贛州

From this city the river is crossed on a bridge, made up of a number of boats lashed together, and this bridge is opened only once a day for boats to pass in each direction, after the required toll has been paid. After passing the city, you come to a place where a second river joins the one on which you are voyaging and increases its volume. *(Ricci)*

Ganzhou sits on a peculiar bulge of a peninsula, looking like the head of a Tang dynasty horse. It is formed by the confluence of two rivers and indeed, it is the names of these that have also combined to form the character representing Gan—the name of both the city and the arterial river that we have been following all the way from Poyang Lake in the north. Interestingly, the river flowing here from the east carries the name Gong Jiang 貢江 , which literally means tribute river.

As in Matteo Ricci's day there is still a pontoon bridge across the Gong River. It crosses about a kilometre north, or downstream, of the main road bridge. Used almost entirely by a steady trickle of bicycles, it is opened at certain times of the day to allow river traffic to pass.

A large part of the old city wall of this historic trading town still remains. It runs beside the rivers in the north and still looks as though it could fulfil the purpose for which it was originally built. This is where the oldest part of the settlement can be found. Inside the massive wall runs a street of trading houses displaying an architectural style usually associated with coastal ports that have a European influence. A long line of whitewashed, two- and three-storey, colonnaded buildings deal in all manner of goods. Rice, melon and sunflower seeds, groceries and dried seafood are displayed in open topped sacks—even plastic bags— much of which arrives by river. On the other side of the wall, there is activity along the wharf. Beside piles of timber and the rusty skeletal forms of a few idle derricks, various boats are unloading their cargoes of boxes and sacks.

---

*For the vast majority of China's population, washing machines remain a household appliance they can only aspire to. Here, beside the river in Ganzhou, as beside many rivers and streams across the country, women enact a daily ritual— the scrubbing and beating of laundry.*

*Built on a wide peninsula between the confluence of two rivers, Ganzhou is still a busy trading city.*
*For a long time it has had to rely only on water and road transport,*
*but the Beijing–Kowloon railway, opened in September 1996, now runs through the city.*

# Ganzhou to Meiling Pass 贛州－梅嶺關

We now observe vast plantations of sugar canes (ripe and fit for cutting) on the flats at each side above the river, which here sinks twenty feet below the surface of the country. The water is, however, easily raised to the level required by a wheel which the current gives motion to, [and made] chiefly of light bamboo. As this machine appeared to me equally simple and efficient I desired a model and a drawing to be made from it. *(Macartney)*

South through open, largely featureless country famous for its pomelos, the road briefly parallels the track of the new Beijing–Kowloon railway that passes through Ganzhou. On a telegraph wire beside a recently completed embankment of the line, perches a solitary rufous-backed shrike, surveying the empty paddy fields for likely insects. At the roadside, another bird, a majestic buzzard is suspended by a piece of string from the branch of a tree. With the cord around the base of its wings, it dangles as though hovering, its piercing eyes ever watchful. On the ground beneath it a second bird of prey, a kestrel, sits nervously in a basket, awaiting its fate. Both are for sale. Not to be eaten, as is so much of the rare and endangered wildlife in China but, according to the young man looking after them, sold instead as pets.

# Meiling Pass 梅嶺關

Mount Meiling stands between two rivers and marks the boundary lines of two provinces. It takes a whole day to cross it and the route over it is, perhaps, the most celebrated mountain pass in the whole kingdom. A tremendous amount of merchandise is brought here from many provinces to be carried over the mountain and sent south, and likewise, from the other side and over the mountain, to be sent in the opposite direction. Goods coming into [Guangzhou] from foreign kingdoms are transferred over this same pass into the interior of the realm. Travellers cross on horseback or in palanquins and the merchandise is transported on beasts of burden or by carriers, who seem to be innumerable, and the procession is constant all day long and every day. The result of this continual flow of traffic is that the two cities on the opposite sides of the mountain are veritable bee-hives of industry, and yet the order is such that great numbers of people, with no end of baggage, are despatched in a short space of time.

The mountain is common to the two provinces, which are separated by a tremendous gate built into the precipitous rocks. Formerly this mountain was impassable but science and labour opened a highway. The entire journey over it is made through rocky country covered with forests, but the stopping places, wayside inns, are so frequent that one can pass either day or night in them in security and in comfort. The military guards and the continuous stream of travellers are protection against robbers, and the road is never flooded, even by a torrential downpour. At the top of the mountain there is a fountain of good drinking water, and here also there is a magnificent temple, protected by a military guard. From this spot one is afforded a magnificent view of the two adjacent provinces. *(Ricci)*

The town of [Dayu], which the travellers had lately left, from their present situation seemed merely to be a heap of tiles, while the river that passed by it was like a shining line. *(Staunton)*

The road across the mountain was crowded with several thousand peasants, carrying large jars of oil to [Dayu], from whence it is sent by water to the more northern provinces of the empire. *(Staunton)*

*The Jesuit missionary Matteo Ricci wrote of Meiling, "...it is perhaps the most celebrated mountain pass in the whole kingdom." For centuries it was the only route across the mountain range separating Guangdong and Jiangxi provinces, and consequently thronged with porters and pack animals. Today it is a recently renovated, seldom visited tourist sight.*

Nearing the border with the southernmost province of Guangdong the mountains begin to take on the distinctive appearance of those characteristic of the landscape around Hong Kong—more angular in shape with steeply cleft valleys. Just beyond the town of Dayu 大余, which produces almost half the nation's tungsten ore, an inconspicuous stony track turns off the main road. It winds through a couple of villages before arriving at the foot of the Meiling mountains, part of the Dayu mountain range that here forms the border between Jiangxi and Guangdong provinces. A wide path paved with granite steps, worn smooth by countless feet, twists its way up to a pass nestled deep in a crevice high on the ridge. A magnificent view unfolds to the north, over hills, fields and villages to Dayu and beyond.

At the top a recently renovated stone archway stands astride the path. A short distance down the other side, beyond a beautiful old ginkgo tree in its autumn foliage of lemon-yellow, stands a small temple. Outside at a table sits an aged monk slowly sipping tea from a thimble cup. An old woman lights a fire on which to cook dinner. Smoke fills the air. Both are wrapped in several layers of clothing and warm hats against the sudden evening chill that descends as soon as the sun dips below the mountains.

A few kilometres to the west, lies the modern Meiling pass. As the sun sets on a cloudless autumn day, the tarmac road threads its way through a cutting blasted out of the granite rock. Above the horizon, a sky of intense purple deepens. In it a single bright pinpoint of light—the planet Jupiter—is clearly visible to the south-east. It dangles above the now darkened landscape that is Guangdong, as though a guiding star pointing the way towards the final stage of our journey.

# Chapter Seven

# Guangdong Province & Hong Kong
# 廣東省，香港

Guangdong is China's southernmost province. Its northern mountain ranges form the watershed between the Yangtze and Pearl River systems and were the reason the province lay cut off from the main body of China through much of early history. For a long time after the invasion of the region by Qin Shihuangdi in 221 BC, it was still regarded as one inhabited by outsiders and rebels.

Guangdong's trading history spans over 2,000 years and centres around its capital city, Guangzhou which lies at the heart of the Pearl River Delta. The city became the country's most important trading port and after the sixteenth century, with the coming of the European trading nations, it took on an increasing importance worldwide.

The delta, with its huge 11,000-square-kilometre network of rivers, is the most densely populated region of Guangdong and also the most productive. As with Jiangsu and northern Zhejiang provinces, the combination of low-lying fertile land and abundant water makes it ideal country for the production not only of rice but also of fish and silk. With its favourable climate for agriculture Guangdong is one of China's main rice producers.

In the far south, lying either side of the Pearl River estuary, are the Special Economic Zones of Shenzhen and Zhuhai that border on the territories of Hong Kong and Macao respectively. Along with Guangzhou they form an area of development and investment unrivalled in China, and possibly the world, today.

The population of the province seems to be in a constant state of flux. Many of the overseas Chinese who have migrated throughout the world, particularly to south-east Asia and North America, originate from Guangdong. Covering an area of 178,000 square kilometres, its population was approaching 67 million at end of 1994, but this figure is increasing rapidly as migrant workers flock to the region from across the country.

Sun Yat-sen 孫中山, known as the founder of the Republic of China, was born in 1866 in a coastal village south-west of Guangzhou. Observing the weakness of the Manchu government at the end of the Qing dynasty, and the threat of foreign powers, he gave up a career in medicine to pursue political reform. After sixteen years of struggle, he was inaugurated as president of the new republic on 1 January 1912. He died in Beijing in 1925.

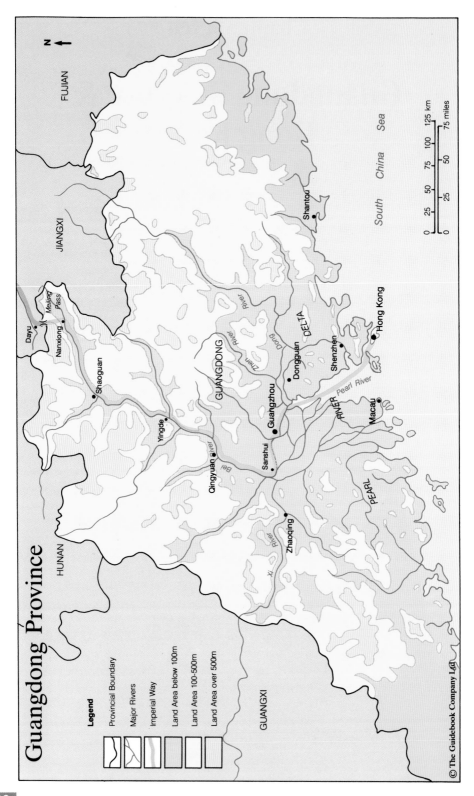

# Guangdong Province

**Legend**

Provincial Boundary
Major Rivers
Imperial Way
Land Area below 100m
Land Area 100-500m
Land Area over 500m

FUJIAN

JIANGXI

HUNAN

GUANGXI

GUANGDONG

South China Sea

Meiling Pass
Dayu
Nanxiong
Shaoguan
Yingde
Qingyuan
Bei River
Sanshui
Zhen River
River
Dong River
Guangzhou
Dongguan
Shenzhen
DELTA
Hong Kong
Pearl River
Macau
PEARL
RIVER
Zhaoqing
Xi River
Shantou

125 km
100
75
50
50
25
75 miles
50
25
0
0

# MEILING PASS TO NANXIONG 梅嶺關 – 南雄

We had no sooner passed the summit of the high mountain [Meiling] and entered the province of [Guangdong] than a very sensible difference was perceived in the conduct of the inhabitants. Hitherto the Embassy had met with the greatest respect and civility from all classes of the natives, but now even the peasantry ran out of their houses as we passed and bawled after us... opprobrious and contemptuous expressions, signifying foreign devils. It was obvious that the haughty and insolent manner in which all Europeans residing at, or trading to, the port of [Guangzhou] are treated, had extended itself to the northern frontier of the province, but it had not crossed the mountain [Meiling]; the natives of [Jiangxi] being a quiet, civil and inoffensive people. In [Guangdong] the farther we advanced, the more rude and insolent they became. *(Barrow)*

The whole distance from [Dayu] to [Nanxiong] is about thirty-three miles, and we performed the journey in nine hours... The horses on this road are remarkable small, but hardy and nimble. *(Macartney)*

# NANXIONG 南雄

The city of [Nanxiong] is very extensive and wonderfully populous. We were upwards of an hour in passing from our entrance at the first gate to our quarters, which were in a spacious public edifice with a large hall in the centre of it, where the provincial candidates for literary degrees (which alone qualify for civil offices in China) are examined and received. *(Macartney)*

The sun had set, when we arrived at the gates of the city of [Nanxiong]. It stands in a plain, surrounded on three sides by mountains; on the fourth and to the south, flows the river on which we were to continue our voyage. It is a place of some extent and considerable commerce. The streets, like those of almost all the towns we have seen in China, are very narrow, but they have the advantage of being well paved, and well kept in the material article of cleanliness. The houses are chiefly of wood, and their general height is two stories. Though elegance, either interior or exterior, is not the peculiar character of this place, some of the shops were gilt and varnished in a manner that might bring them within that denomination. At every door in the streets, after sun-set, a large paper lamp is hung up, and forms a very pretty illumination. These lamps display the name of the person who lives in the house, his trade, and the articles in which he traffics. The palaces of the mandarins are also ornamented with lamps, according to the dimensions of the building, or the rank of their inhabitants. *(Anderson)*

On arriving at [Nanxiong], the frontier city of the province, about eighteen miles from the pass upon the mountain, convenient but small covered barges, suited to the smallness of the river near its source, were found... *(Staunton)*

Progress has forgotten the town of Nanxiong. Two hundred years ago it was obviously an important commercial town, situated as it is on the southern side of the Meiling Pass. Nowadays the old pass is seldom visited, a half-forgotten tourist sight. Any goods travelling by road do so in the back of modern trucks, thundering through the town with little need to stop, as in times gone by when people or cargo had to be transferred between water and land. Much of today's freight travels by rail, but no railway passes through Nanxiong. The old

*Young people, even in the remotest village, make an effort to follow fashion.*
*With the practice of footbinding long since abolished, it seems ironic that this girl's elder sister*
*still squeezes her feet into tight shoes.*

Beijing–Guangzhou line crosses the provincial border far to the east, while the new Beijing–Kowloon railway follows a path to the west.

It is a chilly, frosty but clear morning. In the centre of town, the sun rises above the nondescript concrete buildings that surround the square, shedding a brittle early morning light on a curious stone sculpture—a brontosaurus. Rearing up on its haunches like some prehistoric equivalent of the Ferrari stallion, this primeval plant-eater with its long twisted neck, mouth open, looks incongruous standing amongst a display of yellow potted chrysanthemums.

A bridge crosses the Zhen River 湞江 which loops around the old town. This is where Macartney and his party would have boarded a fleet of small barges to continue their journey south. They no doubt saw the ancient seven-storey pagoda which still stands, aloof from its surroundings, set back from the river behind a cluster of ramshackle cottages that overlook the water. Balancing in his small boat a solitary fisherman gathers in his empty fishing net. The water level is low now. In some places more than half the shingle bed sits exposed; in other areas the water runs in a succession of gentle rapids.

Down river from the bridge a couple of small dredgers operate in the narrow channel, their conveyor belts scooping the gravel from below the water. A tractor and trailer waits on the bank. Beyond, the river runs past vegetable gardens and into open country. It is fringed by spectacular plumes of bamboo—the attractive *Arundinaria hindsii*, that is characteristic of southern coastal provinces of China.

## Nanxiong to Shaoguan 南雄 – 韶關

Nearby, in a small town, in the centre of a school compound, stands a porticoed hall. Apparently dating from the Qing dynasty, this was where the local civil service examinations used to be held. It was in such a place in Nanxiong that Lord Macartney and his men were barracked for the night. On its granite podium preserved in a coat of fresh, pink emulsion it now serves a very different purpose. Inside, a large mirror ball hangs from the centre of the ceiling beside some spotlights with coloured gels. Wall-lights sit behind trendy, heart-shaped, glass shades in red and green. A set of beefy-looking speakers stands in the corners. When it is not being used as a disco, a film projector and a screen that hangs on one wall mean it can double as a cinema.

It was probably in such a hall not far from here, without of course its modern accoutrements, that Hong Xiuquan 洪秀全 (1814–1864) failed his public service exams. A native of Guangdong Province, he represented a growing number of southern Chinese who were becoming resentful of their Manchu rulers. These northern officials, who held fifty per cent of the civil service positions despite being heavily outnumbered in terms of population by their southern counterparts, usually gained their posts by birthright rather than on the merits of passing examinations.

It was with mounting frustration amongst his obviously capable and ambitious peers that Hong Xiuquan led the Taiping Rebellion in 1851. Fighting for land reforms, the liberation

*Two centuries ago, Staunton wrote of passing five 'remarkable rocks' called the five horses' heads.*
*Now with the even more incongruous name of Wu Ma Gui Cao 五馬歸槽 ,*
*translated as 'Five Horses Returning to their Stables,'*
*these sandstone peaks are to be found to the east of Shaoguan.*

of women and preaching Christianity, he mustered tremendous support from the oppressed peasants. With a growing militia he scored a succession of victories against the Qing armies and by 1853 had secured the city of Nanjing. Following the great Yellow River flood of 1855 the government relief was scant, and much of the money that was made available was embezzled by corrupt officials. An overwhelming feeling of betrayal led to large numbers of peasants putting their weight behind the rebellion. Ironically, it was only a government alliance with the British, ever mindful of threats to their profitable trade, that meant this long and bitter struggle was eventually crushed in 1866 leaving, some estimates say, fifty million dead.

About midway between Nanxiong and Shaoguan lies the small town of Taiping 太平, now renamed Shixing 始興. It is in the villages around this area that one often sees large, solidly built fortress-like buildings. Usually square, constructed of grey granite blocks with a few tiny openings for windows and often turrets at the corners, they stand much taller than the surrounding houses.

Many of the hillsides here have long since been cleared of their timber, but in some areas attempts are being made to reforest them. In the valleys between, the lowlands are partitioned into rice paddies. Their crop has been harvested now and the fields will be left fallow over the winter until March when they are usually planted with either peanuts or tobacco, depending on the market price and farmers' preference. Then in June the land is flooded once more, ready for the rice-planting.

## BUS CRASH NEAR SHAOGUAN

The faces of the two people crouching at the side of the road had a mottled, inhuman pallor. Wet hair was plastered over their dazed eyes; wet clothes clung to their exhausted bodies. Their limbs were jumping uncontrollably. This was the look of salvaged life. The bus these two had been travelling in had plunged thirty feet down a steep bank into the Zhen River. It was designed to seat sixteen but as many as twenty-two people had been squeezed on to it with all their possessions. Only a few had managed to get free of the screaming cabin, flounder through the water and swim to the river's edge. The two beside the road had dragged their spent bodies up the steep bank, through brambles and undergrowth, muscles rigid with adrenalin and terror. At least sixteen others had drowned.

A crowd stood on the road looking down at the water. Oil traces were all that remained of the bus. A few had scrambled down to assist. Most had stopped their motorbikes to look, but only to look. I am unable to explain why so few attempted to help the survivors, why these people preferred to remain thirty feet above and watch. We rode on when maybe we should have stayed. Half a mile further on we saw a woman lying on her stomach beside the road, one arm stretched out, her head turned away from the river. Her shoes were missing and her face was grey and puffy. I imagined she had been fished out of the water, rolled up the bank and dumped beside the road. No one had covered her body. At that moment an ambulance came towards us, looking for survivors downstream. The two occupants pointed at us, grinning and waving. They drove straight past the dead woman, but turned round for a second look at us.

A.R.

# Shaoguan 韶關

We came to the city of [Shaoguan]; the suburbs of which extend to the water side, and where the houses are built in such a manner as to be in continual danger of falling on the heads of their inhabitants, and involving them in one common destruction. A wooden frame work resting sometimes upon a foundation of clay or stone, with a few slender uprights, are the only supports of those habitations that ranged along the shore; where frequent ruins manifested the folly as well as the frailty of such architecture. *(Anderson)*

The boats which ply from one part of the city to another are chiefly managed by females, who are generally young and neatly dressed, with an evident intent of attracting the attention of passengers. *(Staunton)*

Shaoguan lies on a peninsula shaped like an epiglottis dangling between the confluence of two rivers. Modern apartment blocks line the river banks. From a distance they look like a high city wall, defending its ranks of commercial office towers within. They form the heart of the largest city and economic centre in northern Guangdong Province.

This is how the Jesuit missionary, Matteo Ricci, who built a church and set up a mission here in the late sixteenth century, described Shaoguan:

The town... is situated between two navigable rivers, which come together at this point. The walled-in village, with its many dwellings, is built on the plain between the two rivers. Being so placed, the village proper can not expand, so they cross the river in both directions to enlarge the settlement. The west bank is more thickly populated, and there is a boat-bridge connecting it with the island settlement. There were about five thousand families in this town. The rich earth about is fertile in rice and fruit trees and there is an abundance of meat and fish and also good vegetables... *(Ricci)*

The Zhen River, flowing from the north-east beyond the town of Nanxiong, meets the Wu River 武江 which rises in Hunan Province to the north-west. Their confluence becomes the Bei or North River 北江 which runs from here south to Guangzhou and into the Pearl River Delta. But even here the river seems little used, apart from a few rafts of logs making their way down the Zhen River to the timber mills of Shaoguan.

Just as in Ricci's time the town spreads across the rivers to the east and west, only now in a much more dramatic way. It is continuing to develop apace. Few signs of the old city remain. Older residential areas are fast being replaced by gleaming white, twenty-storey apartment blocks reminiscent of those in Hong Kong. They house a growing population of over 2.8 million. New hospitals, fashionable department stores, banks and other commercial buildings line its roads. To the south along the North River, a grim industrial zone stretches beside a four-lane highway. Everything seems dusted with a grey grime.

Today's equivalent of the Imperial Way, the new Beijing–Kowloon railway runs through the town, which provides a transportation hub for Hunan, Guangdong and Jiangxi provinces, promising a continued increase in trade and development. As always progress has its price. Towards evening, as a handful of fishermen in flimsy craft cast their nets, the wind drops and a blanket of grey-brown smog settles over the whole town, suffocating the sun long before it reaches the horizon.

# SHAOGUAN TO SHAKOU 韶關 – 沙口

The influence of the extensive trade carried on by the English, was manifested some days before the yachts had reached the city of [Guangzhou]; for upon the river, as well as along its banks, it was not unusual to hear some English words attempted to be spoken by Chinese.

Many of the boats of burden which were sailing down the river were laden with goods destined to be sent to England. It was crowded, indeed, also in many places with vast rafts or floats of timber, mostly of the larch and camphor trees, on their passage towards the middle and northern province of the empire, which were too level and too well cultivated to produce much wood. The rafts bound together, extended sometimes above a hundred feet in length. Masts were erected in several parts of them, on which sails were set to waft them against the current whenever there was a favourable breeze. When otherwise, they were tracked by the people who lived upon them in cabins built for that purpose. Upon these rafts vegetables were often made to grow, and several domestic animals were reared. From the cabins children issued, almost like bees rushing from a hive. The people on board had likewise tackling to fish; and large nets were drawn up from them, as from the deck of a boat...
*(Staunton)*

South of Shaoguan, even the smallest towns take on an industrial appearance. A thick grey smog permanently fills the air; everything seems to have a coating of grey dust. At the side of the road the gutter is full of coal dust, the residue shaken from passing trucks supplying a chain of factories.

As if in an effort to escape the industry that lines the road, the North River takes a different route and heads south through the mountains, accompanied by the railway. So narrow and steep are some of the valleys that the track is seldom able to leave the river for long and runs virtually parallel to it for some 130 kilometres, passing through a number of tunnels, until just before the town of Qingyuan 清遠 , when it takes a shortcut to Guangzhou.

Large swathes of the hillsides are being logged although many of the trees look small and immature. The timber is carried on the back of old, battered, sky-blue trucks that bump and crash their way along the dusty road winding around hills overlooking the railway line and river. If the hills are not being used for forestry then they are being relentlessly blasted out of existence. At regular intervals throughout the day one can hear what sounds like the thunder of distant artillery barrages punctuating the air. The rock is then smashed in giant stone-crushing machines. Cement factories, too, are commonplace, belching thick plumes of smoke from batteries of chimneys.

We not only observed, but also heard the labours, of large bodies of people, who were employed in blowing up certain parts of the rocks, to obtain that stone with which the Chinese form their pavements ... *(Anderson)*

Many of the hills are cut down perpendicularly to the water's edge, in order to obtain from thence the immense masses of stone employed in pagodas, bridges, and for the platforms or foundations on which Chinese temples and palaces are erected. Quarries are frequently wrought at the sides of rivers, on account of the facility of transportation from thence. *(Staunton)*

But there are still some oases of natural beauty that have escaped man's destruction. Not far upriver from the small town of Shakou the valley widens somewhat. Below the level of the

*New apartment blocks like these line the riverside in Shaoguan, a sure sign that the route of the Imperial Way is approaching the prosperous Pearl River Delta region.*

*The Wu and the Zhen rivers join at the city of Shaoguan,*
*to form the North River, which flows south to the Pearl River Delta and Guangzhou.*

*Timber rafts are still to be seen on the Zhen River near Shaoguan,
although they were even more extensive 200 years ago—see Staunton's quote on page 202.*

road and railway line lies a flood plain of paddy fields bordered by a curtain of lush bamboo. Beyond this the river flows sluggishly past massive angular cliffs of granite on the opposite bank, rising almost sheer from the water. Through a deep cleft in the rock, the slanting rays of the late afternoon sun slice like swords through the haze.

A few barges slung with tyres, stutter and cough their way up river watched by an elderly man and his wife as they tend several water buffalo grazing on the bank.

The small country town of Shakou is dominated by a huge cement factory. In fact the road runs right through the middle of the vast compound, between massive concrete buildings that loom beside tall concrete chimneys. Everywhere and everyone is coated with a fine grey-brown dust. Many of the workers wear balaclava-like hoods and face masks. In the shadow of the factory sits the town itself. A large proportion of the population are employed by the factory or their business is somehow connected with it. It seems the one cannot survive without the other.

In the restaurant of a small hotel, a pretty girl in a bright red jumper serves dinner to two foreigners. She is seventeen, with full lips and large, delicately lashed eyes. The order taken, she re-enters the room alone, slides the door shut and sits at the circular table opposite them. These are the first foreigners she has ever met, yet she is neither nervous nor shy as is usual in such situations, but instead seems completely relaxed showing poise and maturity; and her questions are intelligent. At first she seems not to have understood when the strangers explain that they have ridden bicycles all the way from Beijing. When this fact finally sinks in she is completely overwhelmed. It is impossible for her to comprehend. In her whole life she has never been outside this dusty little town—not even to Shaoguan, a mere fifty kilometres to the north.

# SHAKOU TO YINGDE 沙口 – 英德

The river now flows between two rows of high, steep, green hills, broad, smooth and deep. On the side of one of these hills I observed a black patch of very considerable extent enclosed within a pale, and found upon a nearer approach that it was a great mass of coal emerging above the surface; and I understand that all this part of the country abounds with that substance... *(Macartney)*

Other hills consisted chiefly of mines of coal rising directly from the river and opening into day. They were worked by drawing a level from the river into the side of the mine, the contents of which are loaded immediately on barges from the mouth of an horizontal shaft. *(Staunton)*

The coals ... were immediately lowered from a pier into vessels that were ready to receive and transport them to the potteries of this province and of [Jiangxi]. *(Barrow)*

Coal is an important source of energy for Guangdong's power plants and especially for the iron and steel industries of Guangzhou and Shaoguan. The province is especially rich in mineral deposits and has considerable reserves of iron ore. Some of the largest in the country are to be found near the town of Yingde.

After a cloudy grey morning passing an endless string of quarries, stone-crushing plants and cement factories, the afternoon sees a watery sun trying to break through the suffocating haze that obscures all but the nearest hills and fields. Finally the road crosses a long bridge over the Bei or North River. A tatty, grey pagoda stands alone on the east bank opposite the old section of Yingde. On the wharf, a pair of rusty, green derricks stand idle as a procession of bare-chested labourers, their sinewy bodies dusted with a fine grey powder, look like ghosts in the half-light as they load bags of cement onto barges. Narrow streets and muddy alleys leading to the nearby market thread their way through an area of old two-storey houses looking Dickensian, dirty and humble.

Early in the morning the covered market area is a flurry of activity. By late afternoon it is deserted. Here fresh meat and fish is sold. Now only a curious mixture of dank and metallic smells linger. Outside, there is still plenty on offer. Two rows of stalls display a selection of vegetables and fruit—the usual wide variety of Chinese greens, carrots, potatoes, aubergines, cucumbers, winter melons, onions, peppers, garlic and ginger, bananas and apples, both imported and locally grown. Amongst these permanent stalls, men and women squat on pieces of polythene spread on the bare earth, hawking piles of small mandarin oranges they have grown themselves. The housewives jostle shoulder to shoulder, looking, smelling, selecting and bargaining.

The town itself, quiet and provincial, is unremarkable. It has fewer industrial buildings than most cities its size. The main road from Shaoguan passes far to the east, avoiding the narrow valley of the Bei River that it shares with the railway line. And because little of the freight now travels by barge, the town appears to have become a backwater. In some areas avenues of bauhinia trees covered with lilac flowers front rows of boxy buildings. One of these is the local middle school.

Playing cornets, cymbals and big bass drums, the school band practises after the end of the day's classes. As twilight approaches, they march around the perimeter of a large, dusty playground led by a young boy twirling a drum major's baton taller than himself. Most of the drummers are spry, elfin-like young girls. In the middle of the playground, around huge piles of brightly coloured school bags heaped beneath a couple of trees, some other girls are practising their fan dances. In groups of six they walk in circles, turning, squatting, stretching, while all the time their red paper fans flutter in a kaleidoscope of patterns.

## YINGDE TO QINGYUAN 英德 – 清遠

The road to Qingyuan continues to wind quietly through steeply cleft mountains, densely wooded with what looks like indigenous forest. Too steep for cultivation the trees have largely been left alone. The lush tropical valleys together with a decidedly warmer and more humid climate signal the approaching coastal plain. The river eases south paralleled by the railway line, which in some of the narrower valleys passes through a series of tunnels. On the water a steady stream of barges splutters in both directions.

## QINGYUAN 清 遠

We now passed the city of [Qingyuan], a place of great extent and commerce. It is surrounded by a wall, whose gates are flanked by strong towers, and which extends near three miles along the river... The suburbs had a mean appearance; and the houses projected over the water in the same insecure and alarming manner, as I have already described... The great number of junks which were here at anchor announced the commercial state of the city; and the succession of timber yards, all stored with great quantities of planks, and wood for every kind of construction, marked a principal article of its trade. *(Anderson)*

As it enters the huge, wide expanse of the Pearl River delta, the Bei River, now only sixty kilometres from Guangzhou, curls in a great loop to the west. On its north bank sprawls the prosperous city of Qingyuan. Across a one-kilometre-long bridge, on the opposite bank, completely masked by thick haze, stands another city. Modern, concrete-and-glass buildings housing banks, hotels and other international businesses tower above wide streets. There are no old buildings. This is the new Qingyuan—spacious, clean, and still expanding. Its pavements are strangely deserted, its roads empty of traffic. Some of them peter out into large, flat areas of orange earth, still bare, awaiting development.

## QINGYUAN TO GUANGZHOU 清遠 – 廣州

... the mountains abruptly ceased and we entered on a wide extended plain which, to the southward and on each side, was terminated only by the horizon. The country was now in a high state of tillage; the chief products were rice, sugar-canes and tobacco... *(Barrow)*

The weather was warm and pleasant, and the country in a fine state of cultivation; while the river increased in breadth, and admitted junks of a larger size than we had yet seen. As we proceeded, the

*An all too common sight in many parts of China, especially Guangdong Province—cement factory emissions belch uncontrolled into the atmosphere.*

country increased in beauty on both sides of the river, and soon became a continued chain of pretty villages, fruitful fields, and handsome houses. *(Anderson)*

It is in this area that the three main rivers of Guangdong Province, the Bei 北 , Dong 東 and Xi 西 (North, East and West), come together to meet the Pearl River and form a delta containing some of the most fertile land in China. This is reflected in the travellers' descriptions. Indeed, this would still have been true of most of the area until as recently as ten or fifteen years ago. Since then, and especially after the introduction of the late Deng Xiaoping's 鄧小平 economic reforms in the mid 1980s, industrial development in the delta has continued almost unchecked and at breathtaking speed.

Guangzhou, along with all the other towns of the delta, has burgeoned with the construction of industrial areas and the building of new housing to cope with the flood of migrant workers from the rural areas. New roads have been (and are still being) built to connect all these pieces together and the resulting jigsaw of development throughout their length has meant that the towns and cities now sprawl indistinguishably, one into another.

The White Cloud cement factory, on the outskirts of Guangzhou, is typical of this kind of development. It is apparently named after the nearby White Cloud Mountain, a scenic area just to the north of the city. But judging by the emissions that spew from its chimneys, one could be forgiven for thinking otherwise.

# THE THREAT TO FOOD PRODUCTION—
## AGRICULTURAL LAND VERSUS INDUSTRIAL DEVELOPMENT

Cycling through southern Guangdong Province, it quickly becomes apparent that much of what was once prime agricultural land has now become prime real estate ripe for development. The city of Guangzhou is spreading relentlessly, it seems, almost by the day across the fertile coastal plain of the Pearl River delta.

Small towns that once dotted the area around the port city have been hit by the rush for industrialization. Mushrooming, as they have in the past fifteen years or so since the introduction of Deng Xiaoping's 鄧小平 social and economic reforms, these satellite towns are beginning to merge with each other and become enveloped in what is now one of the largest and most densely populated industrial areas in southeast Asia. There seems little to stop the property developers' clamour for land, fuelled by the local governments' drive towards industrial development. But their ceaseless striving for prosperity is consuming some of the nation's most productive crop land. Land that was until recently growing two or even three crops of rice per year for centuries is disappearing in the space of little more than a decade.

This scenario is being mirrored around Shanghai. Not only is the municipality itself expanding westward, but as we have already seen, nearby cities like Suzhou are developing apace to meet it. The urbanization and industrialization is encroaching on the farm land in between, swallowing it up, planting in its place industrial parks and their inevitable allies—commercial buildings, offices, hotels, residential apartments and four-lane highways. China's housing stock has increased enormously under the recent reforms and is just as much responsible for consuming agricultural land.

It is a cruel coincidence that this is happening in areas with some of the most fertile land in the country. China depends heavily on southern Jiangsu and Guangdong provinces for their rice harvest; only about ten per cent of this vast country is suitable for cultivation. The crop land in China is almost all concentrated in a 1,000-kilometre stretch along the eastern and southern coasts. This area is substantially less than the corresponding farmland in the USA which has to support only a quarter of the population.

The rush for industrialization is taking priority over the production of food crops. With a population now of over 1.2 billion, growing at a rate of some 12 million annually (this despite the one child per family policy in urban areas since 1981), the loss of agricultural land to factories, offices and highways comes at a time when China needs to increase its grain yields.

As I write this, torrential rains have already caused flooding in large areas of Zhejiang, Jiangxi, Hunan and Guangxi provinces destroying the summer rice crop. An estimated five million people have been mobilized in an effort to prevent the Yangtze River from bursting its banks and causing an even greater natural disaster. Once the waters subside, farmers will struggle to rescue or replant any of their crop in time. Clearly this year's grain harvest will fall woefully short of that needed or planned for.

During the early 1990s China underwent a dramatic turn-around. From being a net exporter of grain, it is now the world's second largest importer. All this has prompted concern that China's European and American suppliers will be unable to meet future demand; and not only because of the country's population growth. Changes in recent years now mean that many of the people earn significantly more than before, and with these higher incomes comes a change in diet. More meat, poultry, eggs and dairy produce and more beer is being consumed. The production of all these is bringing about an even greater grain drain.

With widespread use of high-yield crops along with massive amounts of fertilizers and pesticides, some believe that China's agricultural land has reached full capacity. In some areas the problem has been exacerbated by a shortage of water. The farmers in the agricultural areas surrounding Beijing have traditionally had problems with the arid climate and low water table. The city has sunk more than sixty centimetres in the past forty years due to excessive use of underground water. In the spring of 1994 the farmers were banned from the reservoirs that they depend on for irrigation because the water was needed not only for the rapidly growing residential areas but also to satisfy the all-important demand of industry. Beijing is not alone; many other cities are facing a similar problem.

By a cruel irony of nature, while the southern provinces suffer from regular flooding the north is plagued by droughts. These have a devastating impact on agriculture, with more than 20 million hectares of farmland affected each year. In the years 1990 to 1994 droughts caused the loss of more than three and a half million tonnes of grain.

As in every other country, most of China's water is used in agriculture. But Chinese water is greatly underpriced. Very much like the California farmers in the USA, Chinese farmers are paying less than one-tenth of the real cost on delivered water. There is no incentive for them to use the water efficiently and perhaps as much as sixty to seventy per cent of water is actually being wasted. So, by implementing more effective techniques for land irrigation, China has tremendous potential to improve the efficiency of water use, thus conserving supplies from rivers and underground aquifers.

Another factor standing in the way of increased productivity is the lack of incentives for farmers. They are forced to shoulder a burden of heavy taxation which, paradoxically, goes towards funding the huge cost of the industrialization that is helping to swallow their agricultural land. While the economic reforms have allowed many in the private sector to enjoy the benefits of free enterprise and the rise in incomes that it brings, agricultural incomes have failed to keep pace or, in some instances, have stagnated. There are even reports of land being left fallow because the level of taxation means there is little chance of making a profit if it is cultivated.

A further problem is that many rural workers are migrating to the urban areas in an effort to benefit from the increased opportunities and salaries being earned by their counterparts in the cities. So far the Chinese government has been unsuccessful with new policies to raise the farmers' incomes and stop them flooding into the cities. However, if China can solve the social problems of mass migration towards the cities, it would be left with smaller numbers remaining on the land.

These people would then be able to benefit from a greater share of the agricultural pie. Besides, with modern farm machinery such as rice harvesters already making an appearance in some areas the threat of large-scale unemployment on the land cannot be far off.

Instead of China looking to the rest of the world to support it with grain imports there are several ways by which it can make its demand more efficient. Encouraging the population to eat more fish and chicken, both excellent sources of protein, rather than pork or beef, would minimize grain feeding and maximize the number of people that could be fed from diminishing amounts of land. Additionally, planting high yield, high quality forage crops instead of grain for use as an alternative source of animal feed would also reduce the country's dependency on grain.

The problem of large cities being adjacent to the most fertile agricultural land is not unique to China. Every country in the world faces this problem as it grows and becomes industrialized. To what degree can yields be raised on the land that remains, especially given the fall in the rural population, is a question that needs to be answered.

If official figures are to be believed, then in 1995 China posted a record harvest—the third in the last five years—producing 21 million tonnes of grain more than the year before. Some experts point to the doomsday scenarios of the 1960s and how the world food supply has so far managed to keep up with the massive population growth. So the prospect for the future need not be so bleak. Nevertheless, it is obvious that in the years to come the conflict between China's urban growth and its demand for food will be one of the greatest dilemmas that this country has to face.

K.B.

# GUANGZHOU 廣 州

The first city to which I came in this country was called [Guangzhou], and 'tis a city as big as three Venices. It is one day's voyage from the sea, standing upon a certain river ... And this city hath shipping so great and vast in amount that to some it would seem well nigh incredible. Indeed all Italy hath not the amount of craft that this one city hath. The geese too are bigger and finer and cheaper than anywhere in the world. And as it is with the geese, so also with the ducks and fowls; they are so big that you would think them perfectly marvellous. Here too there be serpents bigger than anywhere else in the world, many of which are taken and eaten with great relish. *(Odoric)*

We arrived at [Guangzhou]... one of the greatest cities, and one of those that has the finest of bazaars. One of the largest of these is the porcelain bazaar, and from it china-ware is exported to the other cities of China, to India, and to Yemen. In one of the quarters of this great city is the city of the Mahomedans where they have their cathedral mosque, convent and bazaar. *(Batuta)*

By the time Macartney's embassy reached the delta it was already the middle of December 1793, and they had been travelling, largely confined to their barges, for almost two-and-a-half months. For a variety of reasons they had been obliged to press on without much opportunity for rest, recreation or sightseeing. The members of the party were by now becoming travel-weary. After all, they had been away from home for nearly a year and three months. This would have been a trial even given today's conditions of travel, but for them it must have been exhausting. And reading the various journals, it begins to show in their writings, except one—that of Aeneas Anderson, Macartney's valet. Far from becoming lacklustre, he seems to have been positively inspired as they approached the great city of Guangzhou, or Canton as it was known then to the Europeans. His had always been one of the less stilted accounts, and his vivid and jaunty descriptions of the city and its population as they appeared to him 200 years ago are quoted here.

# GUANGZHOU

## WEDNESDAY 18TH DECEMBER 1793.

...the suburbs of [this city], are built on each side of the river; which, for many miles, was covered with junks laden with merchandise, or preparing to receive it; and some of them were of very large dimensions. ...its trade must be immense, and its opulence in proportion.

The river continued to be covered with a crowd of junks; so that it was with some difficulty the fleet proceeded on its voyage...

In passing down this spacious river it is impossible to describe the magnificence of its navigation; for we saw, without exaggeration, several thousands of trading junks ... while the banks on either side were covered with houses, built very much in the style of European architecture.

Here we saw great numbers of boats, containing all kinds of provisions, fruits and merchandize, for sale. They rowed backwards and forwards, announcing, at the same time, their various commodities, with very violent vociferation, as is seen and heard among the owners of provision wherries on the Thames.

[Guangzhou] is situated on the south side of the river, to which it gives a name. It is surrounded by a wall, near thirty feet in height, built of stone, and defended in every direction, particularly towards the river, by very strong forts, mounted with heavy artillery, and garrisoned with numerous troops.

## STREETS & SHOPS

The streets of the city are, in general, from fifteen to twenty feet in breadth, and paved with broad stones. The houses seldom rise above one story, and are built of wood and brick. The shops have their fronts fancifully ornamented, with a balcony, that rises from the penthouse roof over the door, and is adorned with gilding and colours.

## WEARING OF FURS

The dress of the inhabitants does not differ from those which have been already described. It is, however, a very remarkable circumstance, that notwithstanding this city is so much to the southward of Pekin, the winter should be so severe as to induce the inhabitants to wear furs: and that such cloathing is not altogether considered as a matter of luxury, or confined to the higher order of the people, is evident from the great numbers of furrier's shops which I saw, and, as it appeared, stocked with large quantities of fur cloathing. It consisted of the skins of leopards, foxes, bears, and sheep. The skins were well dressed, made up in the form of jackets, and are worn with the rough side towards the skin.

## POPULATION

The number of inhabitants in this city is estimated at a million: and its large and extensive suburbs may, without exaggeration, be said to contain half that number. Indeed, if the persons are included, who navigate, and live on board, the very numerous junks and sampans, or fishing boats, with which the Canton river is covered, my calculation will be considerably exceeded.

## SIZE OF RIVER

This river, as it approaches the city, is equal in breadth to the Thames, in its widest part. It abounds also in various kinds of fine fish; but the water is very unwholesome for strangers, till it has stood long enough for a very considerable sediment to subside: the people, however, who live in the junks, use it, as I am informed, for every purpose, and without any inconvenience that I could learn.

## COMMERCIAL SUBURBS

Though this is the only port in the empire of China, where Europeans are suffered to trade, all commercial business is transacted in the suburbs, which are about a mile from the city. They are very extensive, and without any pretensions to grandeur or elegance. The streets are, in general, very narrow, and always thronged with people. The houses are of wood, consisting only of a ground floor and upper story. They all contain shops, and are fitted up within after the English manner, to which the inhabitants appear to have a decided partiality. Indeed, it was not uncommon to see their names written on the signs, in English characters... The porcelain warehouses which I saw here, are said, and I believe with great truth, to exceed any similar repositories in the world, for extent, grandeur, and stock in trade. The warehouses of the tea merchants are also filled with extensive ranges of chests, which contain an article, now become almost a necessary of life in our country, and of increasing use in every other part of Europe.

## EUROPEAN FACTORIES

The factories of the several European companies, who trade to this part of the eastern world, are formed in the style of that quarter of the globe to which they belong. The buildings are constructed of stone and brick, on a very substantial plan; they so far conform to the architectural designs of the country, which I believe to be the best, that they inclose large courts, where there are apartments for the supercargoes and writers, as well as for the captain and mates of ships, during the time they are loading their ships.

The several nations whose trading companies have factories here, are England, Holland, France, Sweden, Denmark, Portugal, Spain, and America. But the English, both from the extent of their buildings, and the number of their ships, appear to engross almost the whole of the China trade to themselves. *(Anderson)*

Monday 18th December 1995.

Beneath a leaden sky, the heavy overnight rain has eased to a light drizzle as the streets quickly begin to fill with commuters on bicycles, in buses and in cars. The all-pervading dust that collects even on city streets has turned to a grey mud, licked up by the wheels into a filthy spray. Everything appears in shades of grey. The only relief are the bright colours of the plastic cycling capes in reds, blues, and yellows; as though the inhabitants are stoically refusing to be demoralized by this grim city on a miserable and wet winter's day.

Down narrow streets, where the lights of shops selling televisions and refrigerators pierce the gloom; along wide streets and over modern concrete flyovers soaring above tightly-packed ageing buildings, the whole city becomes clogged with people going to work. A huge construction site looms behind billboards; a major thoroughfare is diverted left and right down side-streets; yet somehow the whole thing keeps moving—just.

The highway towards Shenzhen 深圳 is still busy, despite a newly opened expressway. Buses full of passengers, groan under mountains of baggage piled on the roof. Horns blare. Lorries destined for the border and the insatiable demand of Hong Kong are packed with pigs, nose to tail. Gears grate, engines rev and black fumes belch as they meet an incline. An enormous, hollow metallic bang—a tyre has exploded. The human occupants clamber out to investigate and begin the miserable, wet task of changing the wheel. Three tramp-like figures in wet, grubby clothing, slouch in flip-flops along the roadside. One of them wears a tatty straw hat, his only protection from the steady drizzle. Huckleberry Finn-like sodden bundles of possessions are thrown over their shoulders. Unable to afford even the bus fare, they too are heading towards Shenzhen—in search of work.

The scenery is now one of isolated pockets of green. Vegetables and banana trees sprouting amongst a sordid landscape of scarred hillsides, scrap metal dumps, telegraph wires, pylons, concrete, mud and dirt. China, it seems, has been buried.

South of the three-hundred-odd square kilometres of the Special Economic Zone of Shenzhen, across the Chinese border, lies the end of our route—the territory of Hong Kong.

# HONG KONG 香港

The south China coast in late December. Classical Chinese pavilions stand crimson in the warm sunshine, linked by winding galleries and decorative pebble-stone paths that pass through moon gates. Abruptly the peace is shattered; a jumbo-jet roars low overhead, and banking steeply it drops down behind apartment blocks to land at Hong Kong's Kai Tak 啟德 Airport.

This is the Kowloon Walled City Park, until 1994 a squalid slum area of closely-packed high-rises. Now it is a Chinese garden designed and built according to the traditional style of the famous gardens of Suzhou. The old Yamen 衙門 building stands in the middle of the park, preserved and restored as a reminder of the original Kowloon Walled City 九龍城寨 .

In the mid-nineteenth century, the Yamen was the administrative office and residence of the Commodore of Dapeng 大鵬, who commanded a military garrison of 150 soldiers— the very southernmost end of the Imperial Way. Communications travelled between the Commodore and his superior, the Governor-General of Guangdong and Guangxi provinces based in Guangzhou. From there messages were dispatched to Beijing, some, it is recorded, directly to the emperor. One such communication requested the imperial court to strengthen the region's defences and led, in 1847, to the construction of the defensive wall that gave rise to the name Walled City.

As far back as the Han dynasty, the region around Hong Kong was an important salt producer. The largest of the salt fields, close to what is now Kai Tak Airport, was guarded by a garrison under the supervision of an imperial commissioner. The industry continued to flourish for almost 2,000 years until the beginning of the Qing dynasty.

Pearl-fishing, one of the oldest local industries, was carried on in the waters all around Hong Kong, but particularly in what is now Tolo Harbour, then known as 'The Pearl Pool'. From about AD 900 various Chinese governments controlled and sometimes exploited the industry. This continued until the beginning of the Ming dynasty, when production was already in decline due to over-harvesting.

Rice was also an important product of the area, and remained so right up until the 1950s. Indeed, the land around Sha Tin 沙田 (literally, sand fields) in today's New Territories was renowned for growing some of the best rice in China. At times this was much in demand by the imperial court and consequently was delivered to the capital by means of the Imperial Way.

But in this pre-colonial period, perhaps Hong Kong's most notable commodity is one that was only produced relatively late in its history. The incense tree, first grown in southern Guangdong Province during the Tang dynasty, does not seem to have been introduced to Hong Kong until the beginning of the Ming dynasty. The soil on the hill slopes of the region is perfect for its cultivation. A particular species of the tree, commonly known as *Guan Xiang* 莞香 (*Aquilaria sinensis*), yielded a highly prized incense.

All the locally grown produce was collected by agents of the incense merchants and shipped in junks from Tsim Sha Tau 尖沙頭 (present day Tsim Sha Tsui) to a small bay named Heung Gong 香港 . It was then re-shipped in large sailing vessels to Guangzhou and

---

*"The country is rich and fertile, several lofty pagodas successively enlivened the distant parts"* — wrote Anderson about this part of the Pearl River Delta in 1793.
*Here at Dongguan, one such pagoda still stands doggedly whilst all around has changed.*

from there transported along the Imperial Way, via the Meiling Pass, and distributed throughout the Yangtze Basin. Cultivation and trade of the incense reached its height during the Ming dynasty, when the annual export amounted to 10,000 taels of silver.[1]

It was essentially a luxury commodity, used by wealthy people to give fragrance to their apparel, and for rituals of worship in temples on special occasions and was in great demand by the people of Guangdong, Jiangsu and Zhejiang provinces. It was a particular custom for the citizens of Suzhou to use this incense on the evening of the Mid-autumn Festival to worship the moon.

The modern name of Hong Kong originated from that of the small bay situated within what is now Aberdeen harbour. This is the site of the former village of Heung Gong Tsuen 香港村[2] which once acted as the sole export agent for the incense producers. Heung Gong in the local Cantonese dialect means 'fragrant harbour'—because of the incense. Later it became anglicized as Hong Kong.

Both the lucrative salt-making and incense-producing industries suffered a fatal blow at the beginning of the Qing dynasty when an imperial decree ordered the abandonment of the coastal strip. This was a futile bid by the government to stamp out the pirates that infested the coastal waters. Although the coastal areas were resettled they still suffered raids from the pirates and the industries were never able to recover fully.

A British naval party first raised a flag on Hong Kong Island on 26 January 1841. At that time they would have found a village population numbering less than 4,000, with a further 2,000 fishermen living on boats. The Kowloon Peninsula was later ceded to Britain at the Convention of Peking in 1860.

Finding a stable administration in place in Hong Kong, and an economic climate that was conducive to and positively encouraging trade, immigrants flooded into the territory from across the border. By the end of the nineteenth century the population had reached half a million, including 15,000 Europeans. Then in 1898 the New Territories (covering almost 1,000 square kilometres with over 200 islands) was leased for a period of ninety-nine years bringing its 600-odd villages and communities of farmers also under this protective umbrella.[3]

The beginning of the twentieth century brought the railway to the territory, as in China, and in 1906 the building of the government-owned Kowloon–Canton Railway (KCR) was begun. With the founding of the Republic of China in 1912, it was finally linked to Guangzhou. Divided from the rest of Hong Kong by the Kowloon hills the New Territories had existed in almost total isolation until this railway cut through its midst. But even then it brought little change and the area remained virtually timeless.

Because of a lack of a suitable means of transport and the often overwhelming humidity, most of the European inhabitants of Hong Kong had rarely sought to venture beyond the city. The opening of the new railway meant they could travel through the hinterland in relative comfort. In 1920 one woman traveller on the KCR wrote:

The Sha Tin valley was being harvested by women wielding sickles, while a small portion of the earlier ripening rice was being threshed by hand. A few buffalo and cows tended by children grazed at the foot of the railway embankments, while the roads where they paralleled the line were deserted but for the occasional drover with half a dozen animals or a swarm of ducks. On the water the odd sampan... could be seen, and in distant Tolo Harbour a junk or two was under sail.

*Looking north across the harbour from Hong Kong Island, the neon lights of Nathan Road can be seen stretching towards the Kowloon hills. Central Plaza, for now Hong Kong's tallest building, dominates the foreground.*

Alexander Grantham, a government cadet and later post-war governor of Hong Kong, was quite unlike the majority of Europeans. A fluent Cantonese speaker and enthusiastic explorer of the New Territories, he often would walk with his wife and in the 1930s he wrote:

> We passed through tiny villages where I would chat with the farmers. We followed ancient paths paved with heavy granite slabs, old as the hills themselves. We came on miniature temples far away from any habitation where travellers might rest or offer incense to one of the gods.

Ironically it was another European, Thomas Dealy, who leaves us with perhaps the most eloquent picture of how the traditional Chinese way of life had been preserved in the villages of the New Territories. Although written at the end of the nineteenth century, his poem highlights a lifestyle that continued little changed until the late 1950s.

> *Behind the sailing clouds, the falling sun*
> *Sends streams of light that patch the seas with blaze*
> *Of shifting dull red gold. A purple haze*
> *Enwraps the many distant isles. The dun*
> *Hills, clad with fragrant pine, have now begun*
> *To catch the sunset glow; athwart the rays,*
> *The burdened coolie down the hill-side ways*
> *Hies slowly home—his daily toil done.*[4]

This was in fact a way of life much like that observed by our travellers along the Imperial Way—one of paddy fields, water buffalo and farmers toiling from dawn to dusk. But, paradoxically, while their life continued virtually unaltered, protected and unexploited by government, across the border in China the rural life it mirrored was disintegrating in revolution and chaos.

Meanwhile, on the other side of the Kowloon hills that divided the New Territories from the Kowloon Peninsula and Hong Kong Island, urban development had been continuing apace. And it was this massive post-war modern economic growth and industrialization that would eventually sweep aside these centuries-old rural traditions. A cultural heritage that had been the backbone of the development of China for thousands of years.

---

1 A tael was considered equal in value to one ounce of silver.
2 The modern town of Aberdeen is now known in Cantonese as Heung Gong Tsai 香港仔 (Little Hong Kong).
3 It was this agreement that consequently led to Hong Kong having to be returned to China on 1 July 1997—Hong Kong Island and the Kowloon Peninsula being unable to survive alone without the New Territories.
4 Thomas Dealy was a master at Queen's College (attended at one time by Sun Yat-sen). This poem was published in the first edition of the college magazine in 1899.

# Epilogue
# The Modern Imperial Way

The appearance of the railways at the beginning of the 1900s signalled the decline of the water-based transport and communications routes through China. Towards the end of the Qing dynasty, modern railways and a modernization of road transport rendered these ancient arteries superfluous in many regions. The Imperial Way, as a means of communication between north and south, fell into disuse.

Many cities along the Imperial Way had been substantial trading centres, bustling with merchants and traders from all over China and indeed from south-east Asia, Central Asia, Arabia and the Mediterranean. Because the new roads and railways followed alternative, more direct routes, these previously important commercial hubs went into steep decline, some now no more than isolated backwaters.

Some of these areas have rich fertile soil and good agricultural potential, but with no efficient transport route by which to deliver their produce their development has stagnated. Other areas are rich in labour or other natural resources. Jiangxi Province in particular is potentially one of China's top mineral producers. Its transport linkage, however, is so inadequate that it has been unable to exploit or develop its resources fully, and so has remained one of the country's poorer provinces.

But even with modern forms of transport, China suffers greatly from its sheer size. The volumes of both people and freight are staggering, and insufficient or incomplete road and rail networks mean that transport is always overloaded or overcrowded—constantly running at saturation point with bottlenecks leading to serious congestion in many places.

To ease the chronic transport shortage the Chinese government, in their Eighth Five-Year Plan which spanned 1991 to the end of 1995, designated a brand new railway as its key project: the Beijing–Kowloon Railway It was the largest single investment in the history of China's railway. It was also to be its longest—a total of 2,536 kilometres—connecting Beijing in the north to Hong Kong on the south coast. Also known as the Jingjiu 京九 Railway, it is the modern-day equivalent of the old Yuan dynasty *yi dao* 驛道 or post road. Apparently the idea had first been suggested by Sun Yat-sen, when he pointed out the importance of a railway trunk line linking the north and south.

Costing around 40 billion yuan, it was scheduled to be completed within an astonishing three years, to be open in time to commemorate the return of Hong Kong to Chinese sovereignty on 1 July 1997. Engineers raced to meet the deadline. Some 210,000 workers were employed on the project (compare this with the 5.5 million peasants that slaved for six years to complete the original Grand Canal in the Sui dynasty). Crossing 1,045 bridges (totalling 152 kilometres), through 150 tunnels (totalling thirty-two kilometres) and passing 214 stations, it traverses the country's economic heartland: through Tianjin, Shandong, Henan, Anhui, Hubei, Jiangxi and Guangdong provinces.

The final section of track was put in place in November 1995, and the first train left the new Beijing West Railway Station on the forty-eight-hour journey to Shenzhen on 1 September 1996. Trains are not due to travel the additional twenty-one kilometres to Kowloon until the official hand-over of Hong Kong. And towards the end of 1997 it is also planned to shorten the journey time to thirty-eight hours.

In the next ten years a further 60 billion yuan has been allocated for infrastructure and

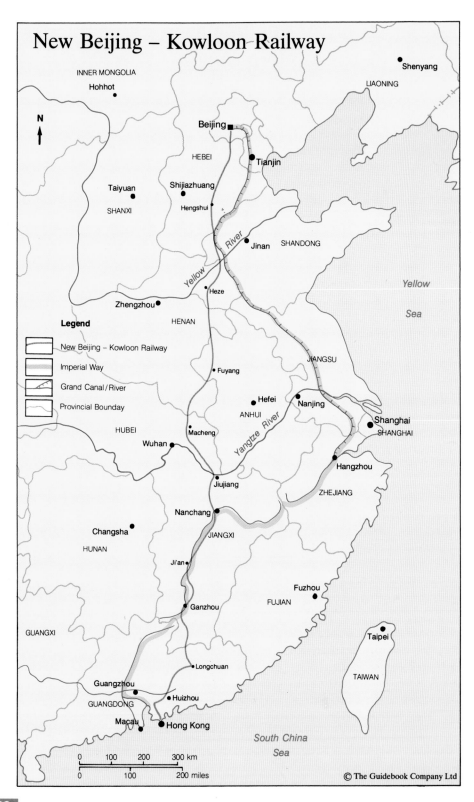

# New Beijing – Kowloon Railway

Shenyang

INNER MONGOLIA

LIAONING

Hohhot

N

Beijing

HEBEI

Tianjin

Taiyuan

Shijiazhuang

SHANXI

Hengshui

Jinan

SHANDONG

Yellow River

**Legend**

Heze

Yellow

Sea

Zhengzhou

HENAN

New Beijing – Kowloon Railway

Imperial Way

Fuyang

JIANGSU

Grand Canal / River

Provincial Boundary

Hefei

Nanjing

ANHUI

HUBEI

Macheng

Shanghai

SHANGHAI

Wuhan

Yangtze River

Hangzhou

Jiujiang

ZHEJIANG

Nanchang

Changsha

JIANGXI

HUNAN

Ji'an

Fuzhou

FUJIAN

Ganzhou

GUANGXI

Taipei

TAIWAN

Longchuan

Guangzhou

GUANGDONG

Huizhou

Macau

Hong Kong

South China

Sea

0    100    200    300 km

0         100       200 miles

© The Guidebook Company Ltd

development projects along the railway. This is on top of the money already spent on constructing the line itself. Cities along the route will be provided with improved access roads.

In regions accessible to the new railway there are some forty coalmines with a known reserve of 20 billion tonnes, and iron and petroleum with combined reserves of 500 million tonnes. Coal is by far the most important source of energy in China and although the railways are a very inefficient means of transporting it, there is little or no alternative in many areas.

In Hong Kong itself new railways are also planned. Connecting with the new line from Beijing, these will enable container traffic from all over China to be transported directly to the territory's container terminals—the busiest in the world. Plans are already afoot for a second container port with double the capacity. Some sixty-five per cent of cargo currently passing through Hong Kong is entrepôt trade with China.

But the canals are by no means finished. In Jiangsu and northern Zhejiang the Grand Canal is still very active with a constant stream of barges and barge-trains hauling coal, sand, gravel, bricks, cement and other building materials. In several places in this area the canal is being widened, the embankments improved and new wharves built.

Canals offer a cheap, reliable and environmentally sound alternative to the railways, especially for the transport of bulk raw materials such as coal. Huge barges ply between Xuzhou in northern Jiangsu to the Yangtze River, each carrying over 3,300 tonnes. Much of the coal comes from the north of China, from the provinces of Shanxi, Shaanxi and Inner Mongolia, arriving by rail before being transferred to barges. In 1995 some 24.5 million tonnes of coal were transported along the canal, a figure which is expected to increase significantly in the future.

In the past twenty or thirty years there has been talk of reviving the Grand Canal along its entire length from Beijing to Hangzhou. In the 1980s steps were taken to reopen the northern section passing through Shandong Province, but these eventually came to nothing, foundering on the perpetual problem of water supply in this region.

More recently other schemes, far more ambitious than merely reopening the Grand Canal, have been mooted. One is the Shoutian Canal, which would channel water from the Yellow River near Yinchuan 銀川 in the northern province of Ningxia 寧夏 via Baotou 包頭, Datong 大同 and Beijing all the way to Tianjin, a distance of 867 kilometres. If this were carried out then it could provide much needed water for irrigation to the arid northern provinces, as well as for the capital itself, that suffers the perennial problem of a shortage of water for drinking and irrigation. It would also provide the water necessary to reopen the northern section of the Grand Canal south of Tianjin and thus create an unbroken waterway on which to transport coal from its source in the north to energy-hungry Shanghai and the cities of southern Jiangsu Province.

Such a scheme has been estimated to cost 34.5 billion yuan, 5 billion yuan less than the new Jingjiu Railway, and said to give a greater long-term economic benefit. However, it is debatable whether the Yellow River would be able to supply such a constant volume of water. Through history the river's flow has been erratic at best, flooding one year and suffering a drought the next. In recent years there have been reports of the river running dry towards its mouth due to the heavy demand put on it from irrigation. It is questionable whether or not it can provide a continuous and reliable source of water.

A further scheme, equally enterprising but perhaps more realistic and feasible, would be to construct another new canal from Beijing, in a south-westerly direction, some 1,000 kilometres to the Danjiangkou 丹江口 Reservoir , on the border between Hubei and Henan provinces. This would then link to the Yangtze, via the Han River 漢水 , at the huge, industrial, central Chinese city of Wuhan 武漢 .

At present China's rail network carries around seventy-five per cent of the nation's freight. However, despite continued expansion and improvement of the network, experts predict that growth in demand will continue to outpace growth in supply, and at best it will be able to satisfy only about sixty per cent of overall demand for freight and passenger services.

For China to continue to maintain its economic growth it will need to exploit and develop as many forms of transport as possible, and the revitalization of its ancient canal system must surely play a crucial part in the country's future. The canals, the oldest first dug some 2,500 years ago, are perhaps destined for a new lease of life that their creators could not possibly have dreamt of.

# Biographical Summary

ANDERSON, AENEAS, valet to Lord Macartney during the 1792–1794 diplomatic mission. He kept a journal of the voyage which was published in 1795.

BARROW, JOHN (1764–1848), comptroller on the Macartney mission and tutor to Sir George Staunton's son Thomas, who accompanied them. Staunton's librarian in 1794, and secretary to Macartney in 1800. A founder of the Royal Society of Geography and author of *The Mutiny and the Piratical Seizure of H.M.S. Bounty (1831)*.

BATUTA, IBN, a Muslim scholar who left his home in Tangier in 1325, at the age of twenty-one, with the intention of making a pilgrimage to Mecca. He returned almost thirty years later at the beginning of 1355, having travelled some 120,000 kilometres—three times that of Marco Polo—through North Africa, the Middle East, Central, Southern and South-eastern Asia. He visited China around 1347.

CREE, EDWARD HODGES, Surgeon R.N. (1814–1901), served in the Royal Navy between 1837 and 1869. His service took him to many parts of the world including ten years in the Far East, where he saw action in the First Opium War of 1839–1842. His journals were later published along with sketches and water-colour paintings he made at the time.

MACARTNEY, LORD GEORGE (1737–1806), previously ambassador to the Russian court, secretary for Ireland, governor-general of British West Indies and governor of Madras. Between September 1792 to September 1794, he led a diplomatic embassy to the court of Emperor Qianlong in an effort to improve trading conditions with China. His journals and correspondence of the mission remained unpublished for many years. He was made an earl upon his return from China.

ODORIC of PORDENONE, (c.1286–1331), Franciscan priest born in the district of Pordenone in northern Italy. Between 1316 and 1330 he travelled from Venice via Persia and South India before arriving in China. He spent several years in the country.

POLO, MARCO (1254–1325), he left Venice in 1271 with his father and uncle at the age of fifteen and arrived at Kublai Khan's palace in 1275, to spend seventeen years in China. In 1296, a year after his return to Venice, he was taken prisoner by the Genoese, and it was during his three year imprisonment that he related the tales of his travels to a fellow prisoner. But it is his failure to mention such obvious details as the Great Wall of China and tea drinking, among other things, that have prompted modern scholars to question whether the Venetian ever travelled as far as China.

RASHIDUDDIN, born in Hamadan c. 1247, he was physician to the court of the Khans of Persia. Made Wazir of the Persian Empire in 1295. His Historical Encyclopaedia contains histories of the ancient nations of Tartary. Many of his facts are to be found in no other history. He was aided by information from Genghis Khan's envoy at Tabriz, himself a great Mongol prince, and who was said to have an unrivalled knowledge of such matters.

RICCI, MATTEO (1552–1610), born in Italy of minor nobility, he studied at the Jesuit College in Rome with an ambition to work in the Orient. At the age of twenty-five he left Europe never to return. He reached Macau in 1582, and the next year entered China. He spent the rest of his life working in the country as a missionary, the last nine years of which were in Beijing, where he died. During his time in China he mastered the language and literature of the country to such an extent (even compiling the first dictionary into a European language) that he won the unqualified respect of Chinese scholars, who came to regard him as an equal.

STAUNTON, SIR GEORGE LEONARD (1737–1801), had been Lord Macartney's deputy in the West Indies and later India, for which he was knighted. Accompanied him to China as deputy and minister plenipotentiary of the embassy. His detailed journals of the mission were published in 1797 in two volumes, accompanied by a folio volume containing maps and the sketches of William Alexander. They were translated into several languages and became a success throughout Europe.

# Bibliography

ANDERSON, AENEAS. *A Narrative of the British Embassy to China, in the years 1792,1793,and 1794.*
J. Debrett. London. 1795.

BALL, J. DYER. *Things Chinese, with an introduction by H. J. Lethbridge.*
Oxford University Press. Hong Kong. 1982.

BARROW, JOHN. *Travels in China containing descriptions, observations, and comparisons, made and collected in the course of a short residence at the imperial palace of yuen-min-yuen, and on a subsequent journey through the country from Pekin to Canton.*
T. Caldwell & W. Davies. London. 1804.

BREDON, JULIET. *Peking, with an introduction by H. J. Lethbridge.*
Oxford University Press. Hong Kong. 1982.

BUCHANAN, KEITH., FITZGERALD, CHARLES P., and RONAN, COLIN A. *China: The Land and the People.*
Crown Publishers Inc. New York. 1980.

CAMERON, NIGEL. *Barbarians and Mandarins, Thirteen centuries of western travellers in China.*
Oxford University Press, Hong Kong. 1989.

CHATER, SIR CATCHICK PAUL. *The Chater Collection, pictures relating to China, Hong Kong and Macao 1655-1860, with historical and descriptive letterpress by James Orange.*
Thornton Butterworth Ltd. London. 1924.

CHEN CHENG-SIANG. *China — Essays on Geography.*
Joint Publishing Co. Hong Kong. 1984.

COTTERELL, ARTHUR. *China: A History.*
Random House. London. 1990.

CRANMER-BYNG, J. L. (Edited with an introduction and notes by) *An Embassy to China. Being the journal kept by Lord Macartney during his embassy to the Emperor Ch'ien-lung 1793–1794.*
Longmans. London. 1962.

CREE, Dr. EDWARD H. *Naval Surgeon: The voyages of Dr. Edward H. Cree, Royal Navy, as related in His Private Journals, 1837–1856.*
E. P. Dutton. New York. 1982.

CRONIN, VINCENT. *The Wise Man from the West.*
Rupert Hart-Davis. London. 1955.

FAIRBANK, JOHN KING. *China: A New History.*
Harvard University Press. 1992.

FAIRBANK, JOHN KING and SSU-YU TENG. *Ch'ing Administration: Three Studies.*
Harvard University Press. 1961.

FITZGERALD, C. P. *China: A Short Cultural History.*
Westview Press. 1985.

GRAYLING, A.C. & WHITFIELD, SUSAN. *China: A Literary Companion.*
John Murray. 1994.

HOU, REN ZHI 侯仁之 . *Beijing Lishi Dituji* 北京歷史地圖集 .
Beijing Chubanshe 北京出版社 . 1988.

LO HSIANG-LIN. *Hong Kong and its External Communications before 1842.*
*The history of Hong Kong prior to British arrival.*
Institute of Chinese Culture, Hong Kong. 1963.

MACARTNEY, LORD GEORGE — see CRANMER-BYNG.

MORSE, HOSEA BALLOU. *The Trade and Administration of The Chinese Empire.*
Kelly and Walsh Ltd. Shanghai. 1908.

NEEDHAM, JOSEPH. *Science and Civilisation in China. Vol IV. Part III.*
Cambridge University Press. 1971.

PEYREFITTE, ALAIN. *The Collision of Two Civilisations: The British Expedition to China in 1792-4.*
Harvill. London. 1993.

POLO, MARCO. *The Book of Ser Marco Polo*
Translated by Henry Yule and Henri Cordier, 2 vols.
John Murray, London. 1975.

REISCHAUER, EDWIN O. *Ennin's Travels in T'ang China.*
Ronald Press Company, New York. 1955

RICCI, MATTEO. *China in the Sixteenth Century: The Journals of Matthew Ricci: 1583-1610.*
Translated by Louis J. Gallagher.
Random House, New York. 1953.

SPENCE, JONATHAN D. *The Search for Modern China.*
Century Hutchinson, London. 1990.


STAUNTON, SIR GEORGE LEONARD, (1757–1801). *An Authentic Account of an Embassy from the King of Gt. Britain (George III, 1738–1820) to the Emperor of China (Ch'ien-Lung, 1736–1796).*
G. Nicol. London. 1798.


STOKES, EDWARD. *Hong Kong's Wild Places: An Environmental Exploration.*
Oxford University Press. Hong Kong. 1995


STRASSBERG, RICHARD E. *Inscribed Landscapes: Travel Writing from Imperial China.*
University of Cailfornia Press. Los Angeles. 1994.


TWITCHETT, DENIS., AND LOEWE, MICHAEL. (Edited by). *The Cambridge History of China. Vol 1. The Ch'in and Han Empires (221 BC–AD 220).*
Cambridge University Press. 1986.


WU, SILAS H.L. *Communication and Imperial Control in China.*
Harvard University Press. 1970.


YULE, SIR HENRY. *Cathay and the Way Thither.* Translated and edited by Sir Henry Yule, revised by Henri Cordier. 4 Vols.
The Hakluyt Society, London. 1915.

# The Dynasties of China

| | | |
|---|---|---|
| Xia Dynasty<br>夏 朝 | 17 Sovereigns<br>Capital Luoyang | 2205–1766 BC |
| Shang Dynasty<br>商 朝 | 28 Sovereigns<br>Capital Luoyang, later Xi'an | 1766–1122 BC |

Zhou Dynasty
周 朝
37 Sovereigns
Capital Xi'an,
later Luoyang

| | |
|---|---|
| {Western Zhou Dynasty<br>{ 西 周 | 1122–771 BC |
| {Eastern Zhou Dynasty<br>{ 東 周 | 770–256 BC |
| {Spring and Autumn Period<br>{ 春 秋 | 770–476 BC |
| {Warring States<br>{ 戰 國 | 475–221 BC |

| | | |
|---|---|---|
| Qin Dynasty<br>秦 朝 | 4 Sovereigns<br>Capital Xi'an | 221–207 BC |

Han Dynasty
漢 朝

| | | |
|---|---|---|
| {Western Han<br>{ 西 漢 | 14 Sovereigns<br>Capital Xi'an | 206 BC–AD 25 |
| {Eastern Han<br>{ 東 朝 | 14 Sovereigns<br>Capital Luoyang | AD 25–220 |

Three Kingdoms
三 國

| | |
|---|---|
| {Wei<br>{ 魏 | 220–265 |
| {Shu Han<br>{ 蜀 漢 | 221–263 |
| {Wu<br>{ 吳 | 222–280 |

| | |
|---|---|
| Western Jin Dynasty<br>西 晉 朝 | 265–316 |
| Eastern Jin Dynasty<br>東 晉 朝 | 317–420 |

| | | | |
|---|---|---|---|
| Northern and Southern Dynasties 南北朝 | {Southern {Dynasties { 南 朝 | {Song { 宋 | 420–479 |
| | | {Qi { 齊 | 479–502 |
| | | {Liang { 梁 | 502–557 |
| | | {Chen { 陳 | 557–589 |
| | {Northern {Dynasties { 北 朝 | {Northern Wei { 北 魏 | 386–534 |
| | | {Eastern Wei { 東 魏 | 534–550 |
| | {Northern Qi { 北 齊 | | 550–577 |
| | {Western Wei { 西 魏 | | 535–556 |
| | {Northern Zhou { 北 周 | | 557–581 |

Sui Dynasty
隋 朝                                                   581–618

Tang Dynasty  20 Sovereigns                       618–907
唐 朝       Capital Xi'an

| | | |
|---|---|---|
| Five Dynasties 五 代 13 Sovereigns | {Later Liang { 後 梁 | 907–923 |
| | {Later Tang { 後 唐 | 923–936 |
| | {Later Jin { 後 晉 | 936–946 |
| | {Later Han { 後 漢 | 947–950 |
| | {Later Zhou { 後 周 | 951–960 |

| | | |
|---|---|---|
| Song Dynasty 宋 朝 18 Sovereigns Capitals Kaifeng, Nanjing & Hangzhou | {Northern Song Dynasty { 北 宋 | 960–1127 |
| | {Southern Song Dynasty { 南 宋 | 1127–1279 |

| | | |
|---|---|---|
| Liao Dynasty 遼朝 | 9 Sovereigns<br>Capital Beijing | 916–1125 |
| Jin Dynasty 金朝 | 10 Sovereigns<br>Capital Liaoyang, Beijing<br>& Kaifeng | 1125–1234 |
| Yuan Dynasty 元朝 | 10 Sovereigns<br>Capital Beijing | 1271–1368 |
| Ming Dynasty 明朝 | 16 Sovereigns<br>Capital Nanjing, then Beijing | 1368–1644 |
| Qing Dynasty 清朝 | 10 Sovereigns<br>Capital Beijing | 1644–1911 |
| Republic of China 中華民國 | | 1912–1949 |
| People's Republic of China 中華人民共和國 | | 1949–present day |

# Index